THE PEOPLE OF
DERRY CITY
1921

Extracted from the
Derry Almanac and Directory

By
Brian Mitchell

Copyright © 2016
Brian Mitchell

ISBN 978-0-8063-5800-0

CLEARFIELD

Introduction

Derry Almanac and Directory of 1921 names 8,288 heads of household in Derry city.

As the 1926 census for Northern Ireland was used for waste paper in World War II the first census that survives for city and county of Londonderry, since 1911, is that of 1937 and this will be available for inspection in the year 2038 (unless the 100 year closure rule is waived before then). This means that each annual edition of *Derry Almanac* is the closest surviving census document for Derry city in the period from 1912 to 1936.

From 1868 right through to 1949 inclusive each annual edition of the *Derry Almanac and Directory* contained a 'Street Directory' where heads of households were identified against their street address in Derry city. The recording of house numbers, against each householder, first appeared in the *Almanac* of 1897.

This list of inhabitants, in alphabetical order by surname, in Derry City in 1921 contains 5 fields:

Surname of Head of Household
First Name of Head of Household
Street Address
House Number
Page Number of the listing in *Derry Almanac*

Historical Background

1921 was a year of great turmoil in Ireland. In June 1920, a six day 'civil war' between Nationalist and Unionist supporters in Derry city had left 23 people dead and many wounded.

The **Irish War of Independence** (Anglo-Irish War) was a guerrilla campaign mounted by the Irish Republican Army against the British government and its forces in Ireland. It began on 21 January 1919, following the Irish Republic's declaration of independence. Both sides agreed to a truce on 11 July 1921, though violence continued between Republicans and Loyalists in Northern Ireland until June 1922.

The post-ceasefire talks led to the **Anglo-Irish Treaty**, signed in London on 6 December 1921, which ended British rule in most of Ireland and established the Irish Free State. However, six northern counties would remain within the United Kingdom as Northern Ireland; it was created as a distinct division of the United Kingdom under the Government of Ireland Act 1920. This Act was the legislative instrument that partitioned Ireland, though its provisions envisaged and attempted to provide for the eventual reunification of the island.

The **Irish Civil War**, 28 June 1922 to 24 May 1923, was a conflict that accompanied the establishment of the Irish Free State. The conflict was waged between two opposing groups of Irish nationalists: the forces of the Provisional Government that established the Free State on 6 December 1922, who supported the Anglo-Irish Treaty, and the Republican opposition, for whom the Treaty represented a betrayal of the Irish Republic. The war was won by the Free State forces.

The People of DERRY CITY, 1921:
Extracted from the *Derry Almanac and Directory*

Surname	First Name	Street	House Number	Page Number
Abraham	Samuel	Cuthbert Street	31	171
Acheson	Joseph	Beechwood Avenue	47	128
Acheson	George	Clarendon Street	15	134
Acheson	Mrs	Alexandra Terrace	6	154
Adair	William & Son	Bishop Street	28	130
Adair	John	Clarendon Street	6	134
Adair	Hugh	Deanery Street	30	136
Adair	William	Governor Road	32	144
Adair	W. J.	Meadowbank Avenue	9	152
Adair	George	Mountjoy Terrace	1	153
Adair	John	Ebrington Terrace	2	173
Adair	Mrs	Florence Street	31	173
Adair	James R.	Simpson's Brae	1	177
Adams	John	Lorne Terrace	49	125
Adams	T.B.	Bishop Street	Secretary	130
Adams	Mrs	Fountain Place	3	141
Adams	John	Francis Street	45	143
Adams	T. B.	Lawrence Hill		148
Adams	Albert J.	Marlborough Villas	5	151
Adams	George	Queen Street	18	157
Adams	Andrew	Victoria Street	2	163
Adams	Mrs	Ernest Street		167
Adams	Mrs	Alfred Street	18	168
Adams	John	Duke Street	34	172
Adams	Mrs	Ebrington Street	11	173
Adams	David	Gortfoyle Place	3	174
Aherne	David	Clooney Terrace	16	171
Aickin	W. G.	Rock Buildings		160
Aiken	R. J.	Clarence Avenue	19	134
Aiken	Joseph	St. Columb's Terrace	101	148
Aiken	R. J.	Shipquay Street		159
Aitkin	James	Harding Street	9	145
Alenay	Michael	Thomas Street	5	162
Alexander	James	Bishop Street	90	130
Alexander	J.	Castle Street	9	133
Alexander	James	Miller Street	6	152
Alexander	Samuel	Princes Street	14	156
Alexander	William	New Row	5	160
Alexander	John	Barnewall Place	17	169
Alexander	James	Barnewall Place	20	169
Alexander	Mrs	Deanfield		171
Alexander	Thomas	Dervock Place	2	171
Alexander	P. M.	Spencer Road	70	177
Alexander	Mrs	Hawkin Street	3	146
Alexander Motor Co.		Great James Street	45	144
Alford	Mrs	Fountain Hill	100	174

Surname	First Name	Street	House Number	Page Number
Algeo	Mrs	Clarence Avenue	8	134
Algeo	David	West-End Park	12	165
Allen	William	George Street	11	143
Allen	John	Glasgow Terrace	23	144
Allen	Mrs	Hollywell Street	12	147
Allen	James	Kennedy Street	10	148
Allen	David & Sons	Richmond Street	5	158
Allen	James	Victoria Street	17	163
Allen	William	Victoria Street	10	163
Allen	W. J.	West-End Terrace	1	165
Allen	Mrs	Derry View Terrace	2	171
Allen	Mrs	Dungiven Road	21	172
Allen	James	Spencer Road	21	177
Allen	Archibald	Violet Street Upper	2	179
Allender	Mrs	Aubrey Street	4	128
Allender	Mrs	Fountain Place	10	141
Allison	William	Argyle Street	55	127
Allison	Robert	Edenmore Street	16	138
Allison	Robert	Marlborough Terrace	4	152
Allison	Joseph	Society Street		159
Allison	Miss	Rosemount Avenue	Parkview	168
Allison	Joseph	Clooney Terrace	29	170
Alton	P. G.	Strand Road	23	160
Anderson	R N & Co	Abercorn Road		125
Anderson	Robert	Albert Street	20	126
Anderson	Joseph	Barrack Street	12	128
Anderson	Robert	Bennett Street Lower	20	129
Anderson	William	Bennett Street Lower	34	129
Anderson	Stewart	Bennett Street Lower	49	129
Anderson	George	Carlisle Road	10	133
Anderson	T.	Castle Street		133
Anderson	David	Charlotte Place	3	134
Anderson	Lewis	Collon Terrace	13	135
Anderson	Frank	Ewing Street	1	139
Anderson	Robert G.	Fountain Street	97	140
Anderson	James	Gordon Terrace	9	144
Anderson	James	Governor Road	2C	144
Anderson	James (factory)	Great James Street		144
Anderson	Mrs	Long Tower	13	150
Anderson	A. E.	Marlborough Street	28	151
Anderson	Charles	Nailor's Row	8	153
Anderson	William	Nassau Street Upper	29	153
Anderson	Samuel	Nassau Street Upper	2	153
Anderson	David	Nassau Street Upper	16	153
Anderson	Patrick	Nelson Street	11	153
Anderson	William	Park Avenue	17	156
Anderson	A. E.	Queen's Quay		157
Anderson	James	Aberfoyle Terrace	23	160
Anderson	Harry	Walker's Place	33	163
Anderson	John	William Street	62	165

Surname	First Name	Street	House Number	Page Number
Anderson	Robert	Windmill Terrace	31	166
Anderson	Robert	Mount Street	2	167
Anderson	George	Clooney Terrace	3	170
Anderson	Sir R. N.	Deanfield	Deanfield House	171
Anderson	William J.	Duke Street	6	172
Anderson	William J.	Duke Street	10	172
Anderson	William J.	Duke Street	10A	172
Anderson	Alexander	Limavady Road	Silverton	175
Anderson	Thomas	Limavady Road	Arnside	175
Anderson	Charles	Spencer Road	105	177
Anderson	W. J.	Spencer Road	109	177
Andrews	James	Abercorn Place	1	126
Andrews	Samuel	Charlotte Place	5	134
Andrews	Lieutenant H. J.	Clarendon Street	30	134
Andrews	Rev. J. S.	Lawrence Hill		148
Andrews	James	Templemore Park		162
Arbuckle	David	Abercorn Road	32	125
Arbuckle	Hugh	Abercorn Place	9	126
Arbuckle	John	Beechwood Avenue	29	128
Arbuckle	Alexander	Bridge Street	9	131
Arbuckle	John	Ivy Terrace	7	147
Arbuckle	Ernest	Northland Terrace	8	155
Archibald	Thomas	Brandywell Road	7	131
Archibald	David	Fountain Place	1	141
Archibald	L. B.	Water Street		164
Archibald	William	York Street	24	179
Armour	Thomas	Chamberlain Street	10	134
Armour	Thomas	Windmill Terrace	3	166
Armour	James	Wapping Lane	15	163
Armour	John	Wapping Lane	17	163
Armour & Co.		Sugarhouse Lane		162
Armstrong	Mrs	Academy Terrace	5	126
Armstrong	G. E.	Clarence Avenue	18	134
Armstrong	John	Clarence Place	1	134
Armstrong	Richard	Clarendon Street	16	134
Armstrong	William	De Burgh Square	11	136
Armstrong	William	Howard Street	16	147
Armstrong	F.W.	Marlborough Villas	2	151
Armstrong	William	Miller Street	38	152
Armstrong	John	Mountjoy Terrace	4	153
Armstrong	Robert	Richmond Crescent	1	157
Armstrong	William	Alfred Street	1	168
Armstrong	George	Herbert Street	7	174
Armstrong	Mrs	King Street	58	175
Armstrong & Crowe		Sackville Street	1	158
Arnold	Mrs S.	Dungiven Road	28	173
Arthur	John	Edenmore Street	9	138
Arthur	W. J.	Long Tower	1, 3	150

Surname	First Name	Street	House Number	Page Number
Arthur	Hugh	Marlborough Street	37	151
Arthur	W. J.	Westland Avenue	19	165
Ashe	Mrs	Francis Street	7	143
Ashton	Howard	Wellington Street	5	164
Atcheson	Miss	Princes Terrace	7	156
Atcheson	George	Wesley Street	1	168
Atkinson	Frederick	Foyle Road	37	142
Austin	A	Carlisle Road	13	132
Austin	John	Clarence Avenue	15	134
Austin	A. E. S.	Clarendon Street	17	134
Austin	Miss	Clarendon Street	47	134
Austin	William & Co.	Foyle Street		141
Austin	George	Derry View	5	171
Austin	James	May Street	7	175
Austin	Hugh	Strabane Old Road	36	178
Austin	George	Victoria Park	Hillmount	178
Austin & Co.		Diamond		137
Austin & Co.		Ferryquay Street		140
Austin's Medical Hall		Diamond		137
Austin's Medical Hall		Ferryquay Street		140
Ayton	Hugh	Bond's Place	12	170
Babington	Hume	Deanfield	Thorncliffe	171
Bagnell	George	Spencer Road	86	177
Bailey	Miss	Clarendon Street	46	135
Bailey	Miss K.	Marlborough Street	23	151
Bailey	Thomas	Barnewall Place	5	169
Bailey	Thomas	Clooney Terrace	1	170
Bailey	William	Emerson Street	13	173
Bailey	Thomas	Spencer Road	25	177
Bailey & Parke		Market Buildings		161
Baird	Mrs	Brandywell Avenue	6	131
Baird	W. J.	Fountain Street	9	140
Baird	Andrew	Glasgow Street	1	143
Baird	Henry	Governor Road	12	144
Baird	John	Linenhall Street	9	149
Baird	Thomas	Mary Street	14	152
Baird	Matthew	Princes Street	31	156
Baird	W. D.	Caw	Ballyowen	170
Baird	Thomas	Cuthbert Street	14	171
Baker	Charles	Bellevue Avenue	11	129
Baker	Edward	Foyle Road	56	142
Baldrick	William	Corbett Street	2	135
Baldrick	George	Rossville Street	47	158
Baldrick	David	Cottage Row	2	168
Baldrick	Martha	Duddy's Row	2	171
Baldrick	Mrs	Glendermott Road	36	174
Baldrick	J & Co	Foyle Street	3	141

Surname	First Name	Street	House Number	Page Number
Baldrick	J. & Co.	Commercial Buildings		141
Baldrick & Co.		Bishop Street	2	130
Baldrick & Co.		Diamond		137
Ball	Archibald	Howard Street	12	147
Ball	Charles	Moore Street	11	152
Ballantine	William	Marlborough Street	48	151
Ballantine	W. G. S.	Princes Quay		157
Ballantine	J & J	Queen's Quay		157
Ballantine	M. & J.	Bond's Hill		169
Ballantine	William A.	Glendermott Road	The Workhouse	174
Ballantine	M. & J.	Mill Street		176
Ballantine	Sarah	Spencer Road	87	177
Ballantyne	William R.	Ebrington Terrace	12	173
Ballard	R. M.	Bond's Hill	19	169
Ballard	Albert	Bond's Street	10	170
Ballintine	Mrs	Clarendon Terrace	2	134
Ballintine	J. J. Ltd	Bluebellhill Terrace		149
Ballintine	Miss	Stewart's Terrace	4	160
Ballintine	J. & J. Ltd	Strand Road	26	161
Ballintine	J. & J. Ltd	Strand Road		161
Ballintine	J. & J. Ltd	Strand Road	84	161
Bannon	Edward	Lecky Road	17	148
Bannon	Sergeant	Mount Street	9	167
Barber	Joseph	Sackville Street	5	158
Barbour	Mrs	College Terrace	3	135
Barbour	Samuel	Northland Road		154
Barclay	H.	Northland Road	gate lodge	155
Barlow	Constable M.	Stewart's Terrace	19	160
Barnes	Mrs	Clarence Place	6	134
Barnett	William	Bennett Street Lower	43	129
Barnett	David	Blee's Lane		131
Barnett	Robert	Spencer Road	17	177
Barnhill	J J S	Edenballymore	Creggan	137
Barnhill	William	Ebrington Street	15	173
Barnhill	J. J. S.	Foyle Street		141
Barr	Sarah	Ann Street	11	126
Barr	William	Aubrey Street	9	128
Barr	Mrs	Alexander Cottages	2	133
Barr	Hugh	Cedar Street		133
Barr	Mrs	Chamberlain Street	7	134
Barr	Mrs	Creggan Terrace	4	135
Barr	James	Elmwood Terrace	2	138
Barr	Daniel	Elmwood Terrace	43	138
Barr	Joseph	Fahan Street	111	139
Barr	Catherine	Fahan Street	108	139
Barr	Andrew	Glasgow Terrace	30	144
Barr	Mrs	Great James Street	63	145
Barr	Thomas	Gresham's Row	4	145

Surname	First Name	Street	House Number	Page Number
Barr	Mrs	Harvey Street	1	146
Barr	Mrs	Hawthorn Terrace	3	146
Barr	John	Lecky Road	23	148
Barr	William E.	Marlborough Terrace	14	152
Barr	John	Mountjoy Street	4	153
Barr	Mrs A.	Nailor's Row	42, 43, 44	153
Barr	Neil	Tyrconnell Street	10	163
Barr	Joseph	Waterloo Street	4	164
Barr	Mrs	Creggan Road	135	166
Barr	Mrs	Bentley Street	4	169
Barr	William	Fountain Hill	3	173
Barr	Robert	King Street	5	175
Barr	Hamilton	King Street	16	175
Barr	Henry	Pine Street	13	176
Barr	James	Simpson's Brae	19	177
Barr	Mrs	Spencer Road	137	177
Barr	James	Spencer Road	108	177
Barr	William	Brandywell Avenue	17	131
Barr	James	Bridge Street	34	132
Barr	Neal	Cable Street	11	132
Barr	William	Carlisle Road	19	132
Barr	James	Rossville Street	57, 59	158
Barr & McClements		Carlisle Road	2	133
Barr & McClements		Fountain Street	1, 3, 5	140
Barrett	Mary	Abbey Street	45	125
Barrett	John	Bishop Street	225	130
Barrett	Hugh	Carrigans Lane	5	133
Barrett	Robret	Fountain Street	109	140
Barrett	James	Philips Street	13	156
Barrie	H. T. Ltd	Foyle Street	22	142
Barton	James	Bishop Street	201	130
Barton	Peter	Bishop Street	268	131
Barton	Bertram	Shipquay Street	8	159
Bass	R. T.	Diamond		137
Bates	W. S.	West-End Park	7	165
Battisti Bros. Co.		Ferryquay Street		140
Baxter	James	Abercorn Road	51	125
Baxter	Mrs	Clarence Avenue	17	134
Baxter	David	George Street	14	143
Baxter	William	Harding Street	12	145
Baxter	David	York Street		179
Bayer	Charles & Co	Foyle Road	Star Factory	142
Bayne	David	West-End Park	13	165
Beattie	William	Beechwood Avenue	7	128
Beattie	William	Fountain Street	39	140
Beattie	R. J.	Meadowbank Avenue	35	152
Beatty	Joseph	Abercorn Road	24	125

Surname	First Name	Street	House Number	Page Number
Beatty	William	De Burgh Square	7	136
Beatty	Mrs	Marlborough Avenue	24	152
Beatty	Samuel	Nicholson Square	13	154
Beatty	Alfred	Creggan Road	81	166
Beatty	Hugh	Bond's Place	4	170
Beatty	Alexander	Clooney Terrace	55	171
Begley	Daniel	Fahan Street	125	139
Begley	Mrs	Ferguson Street	46	140
Begley	John	Howard Street	11	147
Begley	Mrs	Lecky Road	116	149
Begley	William	Northland Avenue	22	155
Begley	Francis	Kerr's Terrace	21	166
Begley	Mrs	Distillery Brae Upper	1	171
Begley	John	Duddy's Row	1	171
Begley	Nellie	Meehan's Row	10	176
Begley	John	Union Street	21	178
Begley	Patrick	Union Street	29	178
Begley	John	Violet Street Upper	23	179
Behan	Thomas	New Market Street	1	154
Bell	Miss J	Abercorn Place	5	126
Bell	Samuel	Collon Terrace	1	135
Bell	John	Creggan Street	27	135
Bell	Hugh	Creggan Street	27	135
Bell	John	Dark Lane	20	136
Bell	Wesley	Demesne Terrace	2	137
Bell	Mrs	Duncreggan Road	Meadowbank	137
Bell	Norman	Philips Street	41	156
Bell	Laurence	Union Street	21	163
Bell	Mrs	Westland Avenue	11	164
Bell	Robert	Cuthbert Street	24	171
Bell	Joseph	Fountain Hill	94	174
Bell	Samuel	Beechwood Avenue	23	128
Bell	A. & Sons	Ferryquay Street		140
Bell	Hugh	Foyle Road	28	142
Bell	Samuel	Glasgow Street	5	144
Bell	Miss	Grove Place	8	145
Bell	Lizzie	Henry Street	10	146
Bellew	Mrs	Northland Villas	1	127
Bennett	Robert	Fountain Place	7	141
Bennett	William	Governor Road	14	144
Bennett	John	Hawkin Street	26	146
Bennett	Sergeant T.	Benvarden Avenue	17	169
Benson	Joseph	Garden City	11	136
Best	John	Argyle Street	70	127
Best	John	Argyle Terrace	34	127
Best	John	Nicholson Terrace	2	154
Best	David	Sackville Street	19	158
Best	Sarah	Florence Street	6	167
Bibble & Simmons		London Street	3	150

Surname	First Name	Street	House Number	Page Number
Bible	Mrs	Templemore Park		162
Bigger	Mrs	Abercorn Road		125
Bigger	Mrs	Foyle Road	Riverview	142
Biggers Ltd		Foyle Street		141
Bigger's Ltd		Sugarhouse Lane		162
Bingham	Samuel	College Terrace	7	135
Binks	John T.	Mill Street		176
Birney	Alexander	Argyle Street	56	127
Birney	Mrs	Edenmore Street	24	138
Birney	John	Orchard Row	36	155
Black	John	Albert Street	7	126
Black	Joseph	Ferguson Street	38	140
Black	R. J. & co.	Foyle Street		142
Black	Robert L.	Hawkin Street	42	146
Black	R. J. & Co.	Lorne Street		150
Black	James	Northland Avenue	1	155
Black	J. H. M.	Aberfoyle Terrace	17	160
Black	Alex & Co.	Strand Road	10	161
Black	Robert	Wellington Street	20	164
Black	William A.	Chapel Road	12	170
Black	Robert	Ebrington Street	3	173
Black	Mrs	Ebrington Street Lower	3	173
Black	Joseph	Emerson Street	16	173
Black	Andrew	Limavady Road	gate lodge	175
Black	William	Moore Street	10	176
Black	John	Moore Street	28	176
Black	Joseph	Meehan's Row	12	176
Black	Mrs	Mountain View		176
Black	William	Strabane Old Road	27	177
Blacklay	James	Marlborough Street	13	151
Blackmore	George	Mount Street	14	168
Blain	Fred W	Barry Street	8	128
Blair	Robert	Bennett Street Lower	29	129
Blair	Samuel & Co	Butcher Street	18	132
Blair	Thomas	Clarendon Street	36	135
Blair	Mrs	London Street	16	150
Blair	Robert	Northland Road		154
Blair	Samuel & Co.	Strand Road	21	160
Blair	Robert senior	Benvarden Avenue	21	169
Blair	Robert junior	Benvarden Avenue	41	169
Blair	James	Glendermott Road	7	174
Blair	James	Moore Street	23	176
Blair	Mrs	Spencer Road	35	177
Blair	William J	Abercorn Terrace	3	126
Blee	John	Bishop Street	205	130
Blee	Joseph	Bishop Street	223	130
Blogh	Elias	Abercorn Road	38	125
Bloomfield	E. R.	Clooney Terrace	36	170
Boal	Miss	Lorne Terrace	47	125

Surname	First Name	Street	House Number	Page Number
Boddie	C. L.	Bishop Street	Surveyor	130
Boggs	John	Fountain Street	37	140
Boggs	Mrs	Harvey Street	6	146
Boggs	John	Hawkin Street		146
Boggs	John	Melrose Terrace	10	175
Bogle	Samuel	Carlisle Road	38	133
Bogle	James	Fountain Street	102	141
Bogle	William	Princes Street	7	156
Bogle	William junior	Princes Terrace	3	156
Bolton	James	Fairman Place	26	140
Bolton	Samuel	Kennedy Street	19	148
Bonar	Bridget	Creggan Road	28	167
Bonar	Speakman	Violet Street Upper	4	179
Bond	Mrs	Artillery Street	1	127
Bond	Oliver	Castle Street		133
Bond	Mrs	Harding Street	21	145
Bond	James H.	Harding Street	23	145
Bond	Thomas	Marlborough Avenue	25	152
Bond	John	Mountjoy Street	3	152
Bond	Thomas A.	Alexandra Terrace	5	154
Bond	Mrs	Benvarden Avenue	39	169
Bond	John	Irish Street		174
Bond	James	Violet Street Lower	53	178
Bond	T. A. & Co.	Castle Street		133
Bond's Hotel		Carlisle Road	45, 47	132
Bones	James	Spencer Road	15	177
Bonner	James	Bellevue Avenue	4	129
Bonner	Margaret	Bishop Street	294	131
Bonner	William	Brook Street Avenue	19	132
Bonner	Owen	Fahan Street	19	139
Bonner	Owen	Fahan Street	20	139
Bonner	Owen	Fahan Street	30	139
Bonner	Michael	Foyle Road	69	142
Bonner	Margaret	Foyle Road	123	142
Bonner	Mary Jane	Gallagher's Square	2	143
Bonner	James	Meadowbank Avenue	25	152
Bonner	William	Moore Street	5	152
Bonner	James	Nailor's Row	7	153
Bonner	William	Nelson Street	28	154
Bonner	Mary	Townsend Street	1	162
Bonner	Edward	Wellington Street	72	164
Bonner	John	Creggan Road	145	166
Bonner	Bridget	North Street	1	168
Bonner	Thomas	Clooney Terrace	49	171
Bonner	William	Cross Street	16	171
Bonner	Robert	Duddy's Row	8	172
Bonner	Patrick	Union Street	27	178
Booth	Robert	Fairman Place	5	139
Borland	Moses	Great James Street	17	144
Borland	William	Great James Street	49	144

Surname	First Name	Street	House Number	Page Number
Borland	M. & Co	Great James Street		145
Bothwell	Matthew	Windmill Terrace	28	166
Bovaird	William	Marlborough Terrace	2	152
Bovaird	James	Nassau Street Lower	30	153
Bovaird	W. & Co.	William Street	24	165
Bowdler	Winifred	Duke Street	80	172
Boyce	Hugh	Cross Street	9	171
Boyd	Alexander	Albert Street	32	126
Boyd	Mrs	Asylum Road	13	127
Boyd	John	Bishop Street	65	129
Boyd	Mrs	Carlisle Road	33	132
Boyd	Mills	Elmwood Terrace	27	138
Boyd	Hugh	George Street	13	143
Boyd	Thomas	George Street	15	143
Boyd	J. J.	Governor Road	2A	144
Boyd	Charles	Hawkin Street	17	146
Boyd	Hugh	John Street	25	147
Boyd	Samuel	Kennedy Street	11	148
Boyd	John	Major's Row	7	151
Boyd	Robert	Marlborough Avenue	23	152
Boyd	William	Marlborough Avenue	2	152
Boyd	James	Market Street		152
Boyd	John	Mary Street	8	152
Boyd	William	Meadowbank Avenue	13	152
Boyd	William	Meadowbank Avenue	21	152
Boyd	Mrs	Mountjoy Street	5	152
Boyd	James	Nassau Street Lower	12	153
Boyd	Rebecca	Nelson Street	42	154
Boyd	John	Wapping Lane	1	163
Boyd	William	Rosemount Avenue		168
Boyd	Joseph	Alfred Street	30	168
Boyd	Henry	Chapel Road	63	170
Boyd	John	Dungiven Road	Rossdowney	173
Boyd	Alex	Fountain Hill	96	174
Boyd	James	Pine Street	27	176
Boyd	John	Spencer Road	41	177
Boyd	Mrs	Violet Street Upper	5	179
Boyd's Hotel		Carlisle Road	49	132
Boylan	Richard J.	Castle Street	1	133
Boylan	R. J.	Shipquay Street		159
Boyle	Michael	Argyle Street	25	127
Boyle	Mrs Mary	Asylum Road	10	127
Boyle	Cornelius	Beechwood Street	6	129
Boyle	M R	Bishop Street	27	129
Boyle	William	Bishop Street	237	130
Boyle	Mary	Bishop Street	253	130
Boyle	Miss M. C.	Clarendon Street	1	134
Boyle	John	Corbett Street	3	135
Boyle	Mrs	Deanery Street	7	136
Boyle	Hugh	Edenmore Street	26	138

Surname	First Name	Street	House Number	Page Number
Boyle	Mrs	Edenmore Street	32	138
Boyle	John	Elmwood Street	6	138
Boyle	Denis	Guildhall Street		145
Boyle	Miss	Hawkin Street	2	146
Boyle	Mrs	Kildarra Terrace	3	146
Boyle	John	Hollywell Street	7	147
Boyle	Mrs	Lecky Road	5	148
Boyle	John	Bluebellhill Terrace	166	149
Boyle	Condy	Marlborough Terrace	20	152
Boyle	Miss	Mountjoy Street	6	153
Boyle	Miss	Sloan's Terrace	19	159
Boyle	Magnus	Rock Buildings		160
Boyle	Jane	St. Columb's Street	1	161
Boyle	John	St. Columb's Wells	64	162
Boyle	Daniel	Wellington Street	23	164
Boyle	William	Wellington Street	70	164
Boyle	Mrs	William Street	65	165
Boyle	Thomas	Creggan Road	48	167
Boyle	Patrick	Donegal Street	32	167
Boyle	John	Epworth Street	17	167
Boyle	John	Alfred Street	24	168
Boyle	Mrs	Benvarden Avenue	5	169
Boyle	William	Cross Street	14	171
Boyle	Mrs	Duke Street	9	172
Boyle	Patrick	Fountain Hill	106	174
Boyle	Daniel	Glendermott Road	34	174
Boyle	Patrick	King Street	34	175
Boyle	Mary	Hamilton Street	1A	145
Boyton	Captain G. G.	Culmore Road	Cosy	136
Boyton	R. A. S.	Culmore Road	Cosy	136
Boyton	R. & G.	Commercial Buildings		141
Bradford	Miss	Beechwood Avenue	9	128
Bradley	William	Albert Street	18	126
Bradley	Fanny	Ann Street	13	127
Bradley	John	Argyle Terrace	3	127
Bradley	Mrs	Bennett Street Upper	23	129
Bradley	William	Bishop Street	37	129
Bradley	Miss	Bishop Street	165	130
Bradley	Daniel	Bishop Street	169	130
Bradley	Mrs	Bishop Street	64	130
Bradley	William	Bishop Street	190	131
Bradley	Hugh	Bridge Street	59	132
Bradley	Mrs	Bridge Street	70	132
Bradley	Robert	Cedar Street	6	133
Bradley	John	Cedar Street	12	133
Bradley	Charles	Deanery Street	2	136
Bradley	Michael	Eden Place	11	138
Bradley	Mary	Eden Place	14	138
Bradley	Joseph	Elmwood Road		138

Surname	First Name	Street	House Number	Page Number
Bradley	William	Commercial Buildings		141
Bradley	John	Frederick Street	15	143
Bradley	Mrs	Glasgow Terrace	26	144
Bradley	William	Governor Road	6	144
Bradley	James	Governor Road	18	144
Bradley	Edward	Hamilton Street	22	145
Bradley	Patrick	Hamilton Street	24	145
Bradley	Cassie	Harvey Street	9	146
Bradley	William	Howard Street	15	147
Bradley	Daniel	John Street		147
Bradley	John	Lecky Road	245	149
Bradley	John	Lecky Road	247	149
Bradley	Patrick	Lecky Road	264	149
Bradley	Miss C.	Little James Street		150
Bradley	Patrick	Long Tower	78	150
Bradley	Edward	Lower Road	9	151
Bradley	William J.	Miller Street	21	152
Bradley	Daniel	Nassau Street Lower	23	153
Bradley	Francis	Nassau Street Upper	31	153
Bradley	James	Nassau Street Upper	39	153
Bradley	James	Philips Street	9	156
Bradley	Con	Rossville Street	1, 3	158
Bradley	Joseph	Stanley's Walk	37, 38	160
Bradley	Mrs	Stanley's Walk	42	160
Bradley	Alexander	St. Columb's Street	7	161
Bradley	Denis	St. Columb's Street	2	161
Bradley	Daniel	St. Columb's Street	6	161
Bradley	Michael	Sugarhouse Lane	3	162
Bradley	Daniel	Union Street	17	163
Bradley	James	Wellington Street	3	164
Bradley	Con	Wellington Street	75	164
Bradley	Charles	Wellington Street	62	164
Bradley	Con	William Street	49	165
Bradley	Con	William Street	46	165
Bradley	Mrs	Creggan Road	73	166
Bradley	Hugh	Epworth Street	1	167
Bradley	Robert	Osborne Street	8	168
Bradley	Sam	Barnewall Place	22	169
Bradley	Denis	Bond's Hill	1	169
Bradley	Miss	Chapel Road	44	170
Bradley	James	Clifton Street	2	170
Bradley	James	Distillery Lane Upper	10	171
Bradley	Joseph	Fountain Hill	39	173
Bradley	Patrick	Margaret Street	10	175
Bradley	Neil	Mountain View		176
Bradley	Mrs	Riverview Terrace	4	176
Bradley	Daniel	Riverview Terrace	9	176
Bradley	Mrs	Simpson's Brae	3	177
Bradley	William J.	Spencer Road	127	177

Surname	First Name	Street	House Number	Page Number
Bradley	H.	Spencer Road	yard	177
Bradley	John	Spencer Road	60	177
Bradley	Denis	Spencer Road	62	177
Brady	James	Bennett Street Upper	11	129
Brady	William	Bishop Street	53	129
Brady	Miss Frances	Fahan Street	2	139
Brady	Edward	Great James Street	79	145
Brady	Edward	Nailor's Row	21	153
Brady	Sergeant P.	Park Avenue	18	156
Brady	Hugh	Rossville Street	8	158
Brady	William	Waterloo Street	5A	163
Brady	Hugh	Waterloo Street	5	163
Brady	Hugh	Waterloo Street	45	164
Brady	William	Waterloo Street	6	164
Brady	Joseph	Waterloo Street	12	164
Braide	George	Bellevue Avenue	14	129
Brandon	Francis	Hogg's Folly	5	146
Brandon	Hugh B. & Co.	Shipquay Street		159
Brannigan	Thomas	Francis Street	21	143
Bratton	James	Dungiven Road	87	173
Breason	James	York Street	23	179
Breen	James	William Street	84	166
Brennan	Mrs	Bellevue Avenue	27	129
Brennan	William	Alma Terrace	38	142
Brennan	Mrs	Foyle Road	105	142
Brennan	James	Kildarra Terrace	6	146
Brennan	John	Kildarra Terrace	10	146
Brennan	John	Long Tower	67	150
Brennan	Mrs	St. Columb's Wells	6	162
Brennan	Hugh	West-End Terrace	3	165
Brennon	Sergeant P.	Marlborough Avenue	10	152
Breslin	Arthur	Bishop Street	39	129
Breslin	Mrs	Bishop Street	38	130
Breslin	Charles	Cable Street	5	132
Breslin	James	Castle Gate		133
Breslin	Patrick	Clarendon Street	40	135
Breslin	John	Deanery Street	35	136
Breslin	Mary A.	Deanery Street	4	136
Breslin	William	Fahan Street	74	139
Breslin	Patrick	Foyle Street	37	141
Breslin	Thomas	Mitchelburne Terrace	89	142
Breslin	James	High Street	12	146
Breslin	John	Hollywell Row	79	148
Breslin	John	Bluebellhill Terrace	192	149
Breslin	Mrs	Rossville Street	78, 80	158
Breslin	John	St. Columb's Wells	34	162
Breslin	Thomas	St. Columb's Wells	94	162
Breslin	James	Thomas Street	4	162
Breslin	James	Waterloo Street	26	164
Breslin	William	Westland Avenue	35	165

Surname	First Name	Street	House Number	Page Number
Breslin	James	Cuthbert Street	15	171
Breslin	Robert	Cuthbert Street	6	171
Breslin	Mrs	Gortfoyle Place	9	174
Breslin Bros		Sackville Street	17	158
Brewster	Frederick	Clarence Avenue	16	134
Brewster Ltd		Little James Street	4, 5, 6, 7	150
Brogan	Patrick	Lecky Road		148
Brogan	Patrick	Lecky Road		148
Brogan	Pat	Stanley's Walk	22	160
Brogan	Mrs	St. Patrick Street	6	162
Brogan	(store)	Union Street	3	163
Brogan	Edward	Creggan Road	119	166
Brolly	Mrs	Alma Place	4	126
Brolly	Mrs	John Street		147
Brolly	Robert	Glendermott Road	21	174
Brolly	Hugh	Margaret Street	14	175
Brolly	Miss	Riverview Terrace	10	176
Brolly	Patrick	Strabane Old Road	5	177
Brothers	Robert	Distillery Brae Upper	3	171
Brown	Alexander	Abercorn Road	2	125
Brown	Mrs	Alexandra Place	27	126
Brown	William	Alma Place	1	126
Brown	Robert	Argyle Terrace	12	127
Brown	Catherine	Barry Street	39	128
Brown	Patrick	Beechwood Street	23	129
Brown	Stanley	Bellevue Avenue	13	129
Brown	Samuel	Bishop Street	181	130
Brown	Andrew	Blucher Street	23	131
Brown	Andrew	Brandywell Road	20	131
Brown	James	Fountain Street	67	140
Brown	John	Fountain Street	99	140
Brown	Robert	Fountain Street	46	141
Brown	James	Fountain Place	32	141
Brown	Alex & Sons	Foyle Street		141
Brown	Robert	Fulton Place	6	143
Brown	Patrick	Fulton Place	18	143
Brown	James	Glasgow Terrace	33	144
Brown	William	Bluebellhill Terrace	150	149
Brown	David	London Street	5	150
Brown	Robert	Long Tower	28	150
Brown	Joseph	Long Tower	50	150
Brown	Samuel	Marlborough Avenue	14	152
Brown	Arthur	Miller Street	4	152
Brown	John	Mountjoy Street	23	152
Brown	Daniel	Nassau Street Upper	27	153
Brown	William	Orchard Row	4	155
Brown	James	Philips Street	5	156
Brown	Patrick	Quarry Street	12	157
Brown	Thomas	Queen Street		157
Brown	Thomas	Shipquay Place		159

Surname	First Name	Street	House Number	Page Number
Brown	Mrs	Sloan's Terrace	13	159
Brown	Samuel	Stewart's Terrace	9	160
Brown	James	New Row	6	160
Brown	Edward	Strand Road	24	161
Brown	John	Strand Road	82	161
Brown	John	St. Columb's Wells	71	161
Brown	Mrs	St. Columb's Wells	73	161
Brown	George	St. Columb's Wells	98	162
Brown	John	Waterloo Street	49	164
Brown	James	William Street	74	166
Brown	John	William Street	88	166
Brown	John	Ashfield Terrace	29	166
Brown	Mrs	Creggan Road	157	166
Brown	Mrs	Rosemount Avenue	5	168
Brown	Patrick	Bentley Street	3	169
Brown	Mrs	Carlin Street	10	170
Brown	Henry	Dervock Street	1	171
Brown	Joseph	Dervock Street	3	171
Brown	David	Derry View	4	171
Brown	Alex	Spencer Road	28	177
Brown	Mrs	Strabane Old Road	64	178
Brown	Robert J.	Violet Street Upper	11	179
Brown	James	Creggan Terrace	14	135
Brown	Matthew	De Burgh Square	4	136
Brown	W J	Edenballymore	Creggan	137
Brown	John	Edenmore Street	10	138
Brown	William S.	Fairman Place	4	139
Brown	William	Ferguson Street	4	140
Brown	Bella	Howard Place	2	147
Brown	Andrew	Moore Street	12	176
Brown & Co.		Ferryquay Street		140
Browne	Mrs	Victoria Terrace	11	127
Browne	William	Cedar Street	10	133
Browne	S.	Foyle Street		141
Browne	William	Hawthorn Terrace	2	146
Browne	Dr. David J.	Pump Street	28	157
Browne	William J.	Stanley's Walk	16	160
Browne	William J.	Clooney Terrace	15	170
Browne	John	Emerson Street	25	173
Brownell	Jervis	Melrose Terrace	17	175
Brownlow	James & Co.	Carlisle Road	5	132
Brownlow	James	Clarendon Street	55	134
Bruce	John	Bennett Street Upper	7	129
Bruce	Mrs	Crawford Square	17	135
Bruce	Mrs	Foyle Road	113	142
Bryan	Mrs	Ivy Terrace	12	147
Bryars	John	Henry Street	18	146
Bryce & Weston		Clarendon Street		134
Bryce & Weston		Carlisle Chambers		172
Bryson	Patrick	Bishop Street	79	129

Surname	First Name	Street	House Number	Page Number
Bryson	Michael	Bishop Street	167	130
Bryson	Patrick	Cable Street	3	132
Bryson	James	Fairman Place	23	139
Bryson	Samuel	Foyle Street		142
Bryson	Patrick	Henrietta Street		146
Bryson	James	Nelson Street	12	154
Bryson	Charles	St. Columb's Wells	46	162
Bryson	George	Cottage Row	4	168
Bryson	Samuel	Bond's Hill	21	169
Bryson	Hy.	St. Mary's Terrace	33	170
Bryson	William	Clooney Terrace	51	171
Bryson	William	Duke Street	60	172
Buchanan	William	Alexandra Place	5	126
Buchanan	David	Aubrey Street	10	128
Buchanan	Samuel	Garden City	1	136
Buchanan	William	Garden City	3	136
Buchanan	J. E.	Diamond		137
Buchanan	Alex	Lawrence Hill		148
Buchanan	James	Linenhall Street	11	149
Buchanan	Robert	Miller Street	42	152
Buchanan	John	Mountjoy Street	19	152
Buchanan	William	Northland Road	Alt-an-Aros	155
Buchanan	R. E.	Shipquay Street	6	159
Buchanan	R. E.	Templemore Park		162
Buchanan	Mrs	Windmill Terrace	14	166
Buchanan	William	Alfred Street	44	168
Buchanan	Joseph	Glendermott Road	26	174
Buchanan	John	Maple Street	3	175
Buchanan	Robert	Pine Street	4	176
Buchanan	John	Grafton Terrace	4	144
Buchanan Bros		Foyle Street		142
Buck R R & Sons		Bishop Street	23	129
Buckingham	William	Marlborough Street	42	151
Bullock	William	Garden City	15	136
Bunn	A. E.	Mountjoy Terrace	6	153
Burke	Leslie	Argyle Terrace	23	127
Burke	James	Aubrey Street	18	128
Burke	Robert	Barrack Street	11	128
Burke	Thomas	Clarendon Street		134
Burke	Mrs	Dark Lane	13	136
Burke	Patrick	Donegal Place	22	137
Burke	Mary	Fulton Place	19	143
Burke	John J.	Henry Street	11	146
Burke	James	Long Tower	20	150
Burke	Alex	Stanley's Walk	26	160
Burke	Samuel	Stewart's Terrace	17	160
Burke	Mrs	Sugarhouse Lane	13	162
Burke	James	Waterloo Street	17	163
Burke	Mrs	Waterloo Street	47	164

Surname	First Name	Street	House Number	Page Number
Burke	James	Bond's Street	20	170
Burke	Houston	Cuthbert Street	20	171
Burke	James	Derry View	2	171
Burke	Patrick	Dungiven Road	2	173
Burke	James	Margaret Street	21	175
Burke	John	Margaret Street	25	175
Burke	John J.	Spencer Road	32	177
Burke	William	Violet Street Lower	23	178
Burnett	James	Nassau Street Lower	33	153
Burns	William	Academy Terrace	1	126
Burns	E.	Culmore Road	Shantallow	136
Burns	William & Co.	Alma Terrace		142
Burns	James	Lecky Road	105	148
Burns	Mary Ann	St. Columb's Wells	116	162
Burns	Miss	Union Street	20	163
Burns	E.	Waterloo Place		164
Burns	G. & J.	Water Street		164
Burns	Joseph	Mill Street	29	176
Burns	G & J. Ltd	Princes Quay		157
Burns	George	Sackville Street	8	158
Burns	James	Chapel Road	31	170
Burns M. & H.		Commercial Buildings		141
Burnside	Alexander	Argyle Street	53	127
Burnside	Joseph	Argyle Terrace	35	127
Burnside	Walter	Barry Street	16	128
Burnside	Walter	Edenmore Street	20	138
Burnside	John	Northland Avenue	13	155
Burnside	William	Park Avenue	4	156
Burnside	William	Florence Street	10	167
Burnside	William	Lewis Street	31	167
Burnside	Charles	Barnewall Place	24	169
Burnside	Mrs	Bond's Street	26	170
Burton	William A	Beechwood Avenue	21	128
Butcher	Joseph	Alma Place	15	126
Butcher	Charles	Elmwood Road	2	138
Butler	William	Argyle Street	12	127
Butler	James	Argyle Terrace	9	127
Butler	Richard	Glasgow Street	4	143
Butler	Francis	Glasgow Terrace	11	144
Butler	Richard	Glasgow Terrace	15	144
Butler	Stephen	Harding Street	17	145
Butler	Mary Ann	Long Tower	5	150
Butler	Mrs	St. Columb's Wells	57	161
Butler	Mrs	Donegal Street	18	167
Byrne	A	Butcher Street	8, 10	132
Byrne	James	Walker's Place	25	163
Cabena	Lloyd	Abercorn Road	4	125
Cabena	William J.	London Street	7	150
Cabena	William J.	London Street		150

Surname	First Name	Street	House Number	Page Number
Cadden	James	Alexandra Place	29	126
Cadden	Francis	Mountjoy Street	24	153
Cafolla	A.	Spencer Road	1, 3	177
Cafolla & Sons		Duke Street	43	172
Cairnes	Samuel	Spencer Road	7	177
Cairns	J. C.	Marlborough Villas	1	151
Cairns	Mrs	Walker's Place	38	163
Cairns	Joseph	Wellington Street	14	164
Cairns	H.	Artisan Street	15	166
Cairns	William	Creggan Road	20	167
Cairns	James	Carlin Street	1	170
Cairns	Miss	Riverview Terrace	8	176
Cake	Captain S. F.	Harding Street	20	145
Calderwood	Mary	Laburnum Terrace	12	148
Caldwell	Joseph	Carrigans Lane	4	133
Caldwell	Douglas	Collon Terrace	9	135
Caldwell	William	De Burgh Terrace	11	137
Caldwell	Mrs	Demesne Terrace	13	137
Caldwell	S. E.	Diamond		137
Caldwell	George	Ewing Street	28	139
Caldwell	William	Ferguson Street	28	140
Caldwell	Joseph	Henrietta Street	12	146
Caldwell	David	Alexandra Terrace	2	154
Caldwell	Samuel	Princes Street	19	156
Caldwell	William	Shipquay Street	23	158
Caldwell	S. E.	Shipquay Street	2	159
Caldwell	John	Benvarden Avenue	40	169
Caldwell	Mrs	Dungiven Road	13	172
Caldwell	Henry	Emerson Street	8	173
Caldwell	Miss	Glendermott Road	90	174
Caldwell	John	King Street	14	175
Caldwell	Mrs C. S.	May Street	3	175
Caldwell	Miss M. J.	Spencer Road	66	177
Caldwell	James	Union Street	1	178
Caldwell	S. B.	Victoria Road	5	178
Caldwell & Robinson		Castle Street	11	133
Callaghan	Timothy	Argyle Terrace	36	127
Callaghan	Sergeant H	Beechwood Avenue	16	128
Callaghan	Miss	Bennett Street Upper	6	129
Callaghan	Patrick	Lecky Road	41	148
Callaghan	Rose Ann	Lecky Road	20	149
Callaghan	T.	Northland Avenue	24	155
Callaghan	Patrick	Rossville Street	74, 76	158
Callaghan	Rose Ann	Wellington Street	2	164
Callen	James	Strabane Old Road	24	178
Callon	Joseph	Bond's Hill	6	169
Callon	Matthew	Derry View Terrace	8	171
Campbell	Alexander	Albert Street	17	126
Campbell	Joseph	Argyle Street	13	127

Surname	First Name	Street	House Number	Page Number
Campbell	John	Argyle Street	60	127
Campbell	Samuel	Aubrey Street	2	128
Campbell	Mrs	Bennett Street Lower	30	129
Campbell	William	Bishop Street	78	130
Campbell	William	Cottage Row	3	131
Campbell	William	Millar's Close		132
Campbell	William	Clarence Place	2	134
Campbell	A. C.	Clarendon Street	73	134
Campbell	Miss	Clarendon Street	38	135
Campbell	Mrs	Culmore Road	Ballynatrua	136
Campbell	Isabella	Deanery Street	24	136
Campbell	Henry	De Burgh Terrace	2	136
Campbell	Miss M. A.	Diamond		137
Campbell	Patrick	Elmwood Terrace	31	138
Campbell	Patrick	Ewing Street	34	139
Campbell	Mrs	Fahan Street	109	139
Campbell	John	Fahan Street	139	139
Campbell	James	Mitchelburne Terrace	98	142
Campbell	Mrs	Frederick Street	3	143
Campbell	Mrs	Glasgow Street	2	143
Campbell	Ellen	Glasgow Street	3	143
Campbell	Joseph	Grafton Terrace	5	144
Campbell	Mrs	Great James Street	72	145
Campbell	James	High Street	14	146
Campbell	Alexander	Howard Place	5	147
Campbell	Mrs	St. Columb's Terrace	85	148
Campbell	James	Little Diamond	3	150
Campbell	William H.	London Street	8	150
Campbell	Patrick	Lower Road	7	151
Campbell	Mrs	Lower Road		151
Campbell	Miss	Dixon's Close	3	151
Campbell	Hugh	Nelson Street	54	154
Campbell	William	Nicholson Square	3	154
Campbell	Alex	Northland Avenue	12	155
Campbell	Miss	Orchard Street	21	155
Campbell	Miss	Orchard Street	16	155
Campbell	William	Templemore Terrace	1	156
Campbell	Mrs	Philips Street	7	156
Campbell	Joseph	Philips Street	31	156
Campbell	Andrew	Philips Street	28	156
Campbell	John	Pitt Street	4	156
Campbell	James	Princes Street	29	156
Campbell	Mrs	Rossville Street	70	158
Campbell	Patrick	Sugarhouse Lane	15	162
Campbell	William	Thomas Street	3	162
Campbell	Joseph	Thomas Street	29	162
Campbell	Andrew	Thomas Street	8	162
Campbell	James	Tyrconnell Street	18	163
Campbell	Robert	Victoria Street	8	163
Campbell	Agnes	Waterloo Street	55	164

Surname	First Name	Street	House Number	Page Number
Campbell	Joseph	Wellington Street	16	164
Campbell	George	Wellington Street	18	164
Campbell	Letitia	Wellington Street	50	164
Campbell	Mrs	William Street	103	165
Campbell	Mary	William Street	30	165
Campbell	John	William Street	64	165
Campbell	Constable Edward	Mount Street	3	167
Campbell	Mrs	Rosemount Terrace	9	168
Campbell	Miss	Rosemount Terrace	14	168
Campbell	William	Wesley Street	6	168
Campbell	Thomas	Benvarden Avenue	42	169
Campbell	Joseph	Bond's Street	3	169
Campbell	James	Bond's Street	21	169
Campbell	Mrs	Bond's Place	9	170
Campbell	William	Clifton Street	1	170
Campbell	William	Duddy's Row	7	172
Campbell	A. P.	Carlisle Chambers		172
Campbell	Mrs	Duke Street	20	172
Campbell	John	Fountain Hill	71	174
Campbell	James	Gortfoyle Place	7	174
Campbell	Thomas	Maple Street	4	175
Campbell	Miss M.	Melrose Terrace	3	175
Campbell	W. J.	Melrose Terrace	12	175
Campbell	William J.	Riverview Terrace	6	176
Campbell	William	Tamneymore		178
Campbell	John	Violet Street Lower	30	178
Campbell	Mrs	York Street	8	179
Campbell & Patton		Carlisle Road	42	133
Campbell Bros		Princes Quay		157
Campell	D. C.	Templemore Park		162
Canavan	Mrs	Dungiven Road	77	173
Candy	James	Mill Street		176
Canney	James	Distillery Lane Upper	12	171
Canning	Michael	Ann Street	23	127
Canning	James	Ann Street	2	127
Canning	Patrick	Beechwood Street	13	129
Canning	Mrs	Bennett Street Lower	33	129
Canning	Robert	Bishop Street	187	130
Canning	Bernard	Bishop Street	44	130
Canning	Mrs	Deanery Street	21	136
Canning	John	Fahan Street	101	139
Canning	Alfred	Foyle Road	50	142
Canning	William	Hollywell Street	13	147
Canning	Mrs	Laburnum Terrace	9	148
Canning	Mary	Bluebellhill Terrace	156	149
Canning	William	Bluebellhill Terrace	174	149
Canning	Mrs	Miller Street	26	152
Canning	John	Nassau Street Lower	35	153

Surname	First Name	Street	House Number	Page Number
Canning	Henry	Nassau Street Upper	12	153
Canning	Thomas	Northland Road	gate lodge	155
Canning	Samuel	Orchard Row	7	155
Canning	James	Quarry Street	16	157
Canning	William	Sloan's Terrace	29	159
Canning	James	Strand Road	40	161
Canning	Dan	St. Columb's Wells	4	162
Canning	William	Walker's Place	28	163
Canning	John	Waterloo Street	42	164
Canning	John	William Street	80	166
Canning	Samuel	Lewis Street	28	167
Canning	Michael	Osborne Street	4	168
Canning	James	Barnewall Place	9	169
Canning	John	Benvarden Avenue	43	169
Canning	Hugh	Benvarden Avenue	28	169
Canning	John	Bond's Street	5	169
Canning	John	Bond's Street	45	169
Canning	Alex	Cuthbert Street	7	171
Canning	John	Derry View Terrace	3	171
Canning	William	Duke Street	51	172
Canning	Mrs	Emerson Street	5	173
Canning	Hugh	Glendermott Road	6	174
Canning	Charles	Glendermott Road	16	174
Canning	Mrs	Union Street	22	178
Cannon	Neal	Creggan Road	20	167
Canny	John	Hamilton Street	9	145
Canny	Michael	Nailor's Row	47	153
Canny	James	Thomas Street	28	162
Carabine	Bernard	Gortfoyle Place	6	174
Carbine	Joseph	Cable Street	15	132
Carey	Mrs	Fountain Street	94	141
Carey	Thomas	Hogg's Folly	12	146
Carey	Mrs	Long Tower	26	150
Carey	David	Stable Lane	2	159
Carey	Samuel	North Street	39	168
Carey	Michael	Cross Street	17	171
Cargill	Robert	Aubrey Street	12	128
Cargill	Thomas	Kennedy Place	10	147
Cargill	Thomas	Linenhall Street		149
Cargill	Mary Ann	Waterloo Street	53	164
Cargill	James	Cuthbert Street	18	171
Cargill	George	Moore Street	16	176
Carlin	John	Adam Street	2	126
Carlin	James	Bishop Street	33	129
Carlin	Andrew	Sunbeam Terrace	17	130
Carlin	Mrs	Bishop Street	154	131
Carlin	Daniel	Brandywell Road	6	131
Carlin	Kate	Brandywell Avenue	18	131
Carlin	Hugh	Creggan Street	Lodge	135
Carlin	Mrs	Elmwood Terrace	23	138

Surname	First Name	Street	House Number	Page Number
Carlin	Mrs	Elmwood Street	12	138
Carlin	Maggie	Fahan Street	15	139
Carlin	Daniel	Fahan Street	24	139
Carlin	James	Fulton Place	22	143
Carlin	James	Joseph Street	11	147
Carlin	William	Lecky Road	55	148
Carlin	Mrs	Foster's Terrace	153	148
Carlin	Michael	Lecky Road	265	149
Carlin	James	Lecky Road	68	149
Carlin	John	Bluebellhill Terrace	146	149
Carlin	James	Long Tower	2	150
Carlin	Patrick	Marlborough Terrace	7	152
Carlin	Mrs	Miller Street	2	152
Carlin	Manasses	Nailor's Row	6	153
Carlin	Manasses	Nailor's Row	18	153
Carlin	William	Friel's Terrace	1	153
Carlin	W. J.	Nelson Street	33	154
Carlin	A.	Princes Quay		157
Carlin	Michael	Sloan's Terrace	11	159
Carlin	Thomas	Sloan's Terrace	26	159
Carlin	Thomas	St. Columb's Wells	61	161
Carlin	Mary J.	St. Columb's Wells	92	162
Carlin	Michael	Thomas Street	6	162
Carlin	Anthony	Tyrconnell Street	16	163
Carlin	A.	Water Street		164
Carlin	Michael	Chapel Road	53	170
Carlin	Mrs	Cross Street	11	171
Carlin	Frank	Cross Street	29	171
Carlin	John	Dungiven Road	7	172
Carlin	Neal	Fountain Hill	13	173
Carlin	Hugh	Fountain Hill	23	173
Carlin	William	Margaret Street	18	175
Carlin	Mrs	Meehan's Row	6	176
Carlin	Mrs	Strabane Old Road	11	177
Carmichael	W. H.	De Burgh Terrace	Victoria Villa	137
Carmichael	R.	Water Street		164
Carmichael	Matthew	William Street	99	165
Carnwath	John	Ebrington Street Lower	2	173
Carr	Joseph	Bennett Street Upper	3	129
Carr	Albert E.	Garden City	9	136
Carr	Michael	Deanery Street	18	136
Carr	Annie	William Street	53½	165
Carr	John	Violet Street Lower	55	178
Carr	Annie	Corbett Street	8	135
Carr	John	Glasgow Street	6	144
Carr	G. N.	Hawkin Street	29	146
Carr	Hugh	Cross Street	32	171
Carrigan	William	Chapel Road	57	170

Surname	First Name	Street	House Number	Page Number
Carroll	James	High Street	5	146
Carroll	Paul J.	King Street	48	175
Carruthers	David	Argyle Street	17	127
Carruthers	William	Collon Terrace	3	135
Carruthers	Samuel	Ewing Street	32	139
Carruthers	William	George Street	9	143
Carruthers	John	Harding Street	27	145
Carruthers	Robert	Harding Street	29	145
Carruthers	James	Creggan Road	123	166
Carruthers	Miss	Lewis Street	20	167
Carson	William	Barrack Street	13	128
Carson	Patrick	Miller Street	40	152
Carson	William	Nicholson Square	19	154
Carson	James	Park Avenue	26	156
Carson	James	Glendermott Road	23	174
Cartan	James	Stanley's Walk	43	160
Carther	Arthur	Deanery Street	52	136
Cartin	Patrick	Bishop Street	120	130
Carton	James	Cable Street	7	132
Carton	Michael	Corbett Street	4	135
Carton	Mrs	Lower Road	37	151
Carton	Peter	Orchard Row	34	155
Carton	J.J.	Prince Arthur Street		156
Carton	J. J.	Rossville Street	2	158
Carton	James	Clooney Terrace	12	171
Carton	Patrick	Cross Street	20	171
Carton	John	Ebrington Terrace	15	173
Cary	E. G.	Crawford Square	3	135
Case	Lieutenant-Colonel	Crawford Square	23	135
Casey	Patrick	Fulton Place	12	143
Casey	Hugh	Laburnum Terrace	1	148
Casey	Daniel	Marlborough Avenue	26	152
Casey	Mrs	Marlborough Terrace	17	152
Casey	Patrick	Nelson Street	65	154
Casey	Thomas	Palace Street	3	155
Casey	James	St. Columb's Wells	53	161
Casey	Hugh	St. Columb's Wells	55	161
Cassidy	John	Argyle Terrace	25	127
Cassidy	Miss	Bellevue Avenue	29	129
Cassidy	Miss J. W.	Carlisle Road	28	133
Cassidy	James	Chamberlain Street	32	134
Cassidy	William	Collon Terrace	7	135
Cassidy	Margaret	Deanery Street	14	136
Cassidy	Mrs	Donegal Place	6	137
Cassidy	Mrs	Elmwood Terrace	10	138
Cassidy	James	Fahan Street	128	139
Cassidy	John	Gordon Place	2	144
Cassidy	Michael	Harvey Street	13	146
Cassidy	Mrs	Hawkin Street	28	146

Surname	First Name	Street	House Number	Page Number
Cassidy	John	Ivy Terrace	18	147
Cassidy	William	Ivy Terrace	36	147
Cassidy	Hugh	Nassau Street Lower	8	153
Cassidy	John	Nassau Street Lower	28	153
Cassidy	Hugh	Nassau Street Upper	9	153
Cassidy	Denis	Rossville Street	53	158
Cassidy	Francis	Stanley's Walk	21	160
Cassidy	Patrick	Stewart's Terrace	6	160
Cassidy	Patrick	Wellington Street	39	164
Cassidy	John	Wellington Street	45	164
Cassidy	Mrs	William Street	12	165
Cassidy	Thomas	Chapel Road	41	170
Cassidy	Joseph	Spencer Road	114	177
Cassidy	Robert	Violet Street Lower	14	178
Cassidy & Smith		William Street	58	165
Casson	John J.	Ewing Street	36	139
Casson	William	Meehan's Row	17	176
Cassone & Son		Carlisle Road	26	133
Cassoni	Augusto	Rock Buildings		160
Cathcart	Charles	Cottage Row	30	168
Catterson	Patrick	Lecky Road	26	149
Catterson	Constable	William Street	61	165
Cattley	Herbert	Bishop Street	26	130
Cattley	Herbert	London Street	1	150
Cauley	Joseph	Dervock Place	4	171
Caulfield	Peter	Fahan Street	49	139
Caulfield	James	Fahan Street	26	139
Caulfield	Owen	Long Tower	23	150
Caulfield	Maurice	St. Columb's Street	3	161
Caulfield	Mary	Walker's Place	37	163
Cavanagh	James	Alexandra Place	17	126
Cavanagh	Patrick	Harvey Street	4	146
Cavanagh	Patrick	Lecky Road	70	149
Cavanagh	Patrick	Nassau Street Lower	40	153
Cavanagh	Eliza	Chapel Road	48	170
Cavanagh	James	Pine Street	14	176
Chadwick	W. H.	Shipquay Street	21	159
Chadwick	W. H.	Westland Avenue	5	164
Chadwick	Mrs	Westland Avenue	23	165
Chambers	William U	Beechwood Avenue	31	128
Chambers	Matthew	Bishop Street	48	130
Chambers	James	Carlisle Road	3	132
Chambers	James	Carrigans Lane	8	133
Chambers	Mrs	Clarence Avenue	20	134
Chambers	John	Grafton Street	5	144
Chambers	Thomas	Kennedy Street	3	148
Chambers	Joseph	Marlborough Street	24	151
Chambers	Joseph	New Market Street		154
Chambers	William & Son	Pump Street	19	156

Surname	First Name	Street	House Number	Page Number
Chambers	Thomas	Pump Street	6	156
Chambers	Miss	Wesley Street	14	168
Chambers & Craig	T. & R. N.	Shipquay Street	33	159
Chapman	Sergeant	Stewart's Terrace	2	160
Cherry	Thomas	Chapel Road	14	170
Cheshire	John	Clooney Terrace	46	171
Chillingworth	Rev D H	Sunbeam Terrace	2	130
Chinneck	G. P.	Crawford Square	1	135
Christy	John	Bellevue Avenue	22	129
Christy	John Ltd	Foyle Street		142
Christy	John Ltd	Abercorn Quay		157
Christy	William	Clooney Terrace	47	171
Clandillon	Seamus	East Wall		137
Clare	J. J.	Bishop Street	Warder	130
Clarke	Henry	Alexandra Place	12	126
Clarke	Joseph	New Street	9	133
Clarke	Samuel	Custom House Street		136
Clarke	George	De Burgh Terrace	13	137
Clarke	Robert	Fahan Street	46	139
Clarke	Thomas	Francis Street	1	143
Clarke	Miss	Major's Row	1	151
Clarke	James R.	Marlborough Street	21	151
Clarke	Mrs	Union Street	7	163
Clarke	Francis	Wellington Street	73A	164
Clarke	John	Benvarden Avenue	59	169
Clarke	Constable	Benvarden Avenue	12	169
Clarke	Robert	Cuthbert Street	4	171
Clarke	James	Duke Street	10	172
Clarke	Miss	Primrose Street	19	176
Clarke	William J.	Primrose Street	8	176
Clarke	John	Violet Street Lower	28	178
Cleary	William	Mary Street	12	152
Clendinning	J. R.	Hawkin Street	38	146
Clendinning	Constable A. E.	Mount Street	7	167
Clifford	Hugh	Bridge Street	7½	131
Clifford	James	Millar's Close		132
Clifford	James	Fahan Street	148	139
Clifford	John	Foyle Road	31	142
Clifford	James	Mitchelburne Terrace	91	142
Clifford	Henry	Foyle Road		143
Clifford	Patrick	Glasgow Terrace	24	144
Clifford	Henry	Joseph Street	3	147
Clifford	Patrick	Joseph Street	6	147
Clifford	Elizabeth	Sugarhouse Lane	19	162
Clifford	Maggie	Thomas Street	11	162
Clifford	Mrs	Wesley Street	15	168
Clinton	Grace	Waterloo Street	41	164
Cloran	Michael	Laburnum Terrace	17	148
Cochrane	Mrs	Barrack Street	3	128

Surname	First Name	Street	House Number	Page Number
Cochrane	Edward	Ferguson Street	49	140
Cochrane	James	McLaughlin's Close	2	140
Cochrane	S.	Bond's Hill		169
Cochrane	Samuel	Melrose Terrace	18	175
Coghlan	Mrs	Abercorn Road	30	125
Coghlan	John	Creggan Road	3	166
Cogley	Mark	Waterloo Street	7	163
Cogley	Isabella	Waterloo Street	9	163
Cogley	Mark	Waterloo Street	19	163
Cole	Mrs Sarah	Elmwood Terrace	46	138
Cole	W. E.	Commercial Buildings		141
Cole	Andrew	The Rock	39	160
Coleman	Fanny	Bluebellhill Terrace	132	149
Coleman	H.	Shipquay Street		159
Colhoun	Hugh	Ann Street	1	126
Colhoun	Mrs	Charlotte Street	3	134
Colhoun	John	Clarendon Street	63	134
Colhoun	Captain James	Culmore Road	St. Elmo	136
Colhoun	Miss	Fairman Place	25	139
Colhoun	William	Ferguson Street	61	140
Colhoun	Adam	Fountain Street	21	140
Colhoun	Robert	Grafton Street	3	144
Colhoun	Andrew	Grove Place	18	145
Colhoun	Mrs E.	Hawkin Street	Grove House	146
Colhoun	William	Ivy Terrace	16	147
Colhoun	R. J.	Bluebellhill Terrace		149
Colhoun	William	Major's Row	6	151
Colhoun	Hugh	Marlborough Avenue	13	152
Colhoun	Miss	Marlborough Terrace	25	152
Colhoun	R.	North Edward Street	7	154
Colhoun	Mrs	Northland Road	Alt-an-Righ	155
Colhoun	Thomas	Park Avenue	19	156
Colhoun	John	Philips Street	29	156
Colhoun	Robert	Strand Road	22	161
Colhoun	William	Florence Street	16	167
Colhoun	William	Benvarden Avenue	36	169
Colhoun	William	Clooney Terrace	4	171
Colhoun	William	Cochrane's Row	3	172
Colhoun	Kate	Dungiven Road	8	173
Colhoun	William	Dungiven Road	20	173
Colhoun	John	Fountain Hill	68	174
Colhoun	George	Pine Street	17	176
Colhoun	Andrew	Pine Street	12	176
Colhoun	Miss	Spencer Road	126	177
Colhoun	John	Tamneymore		178
Colhoun	David	Violet Street Lower	21	178
Coll	Peter	Artillery Street		127
Coll	George	Governor Road	42	144
Coll	Hugh	Strand Road Lower		161

Surname	First Name	Street	House Number	Page Number
Coll	Charles	Westland Terrace	5	165
Coll	John	Cottage Row	42	168
Coll	Charles	Bridge Street	54	132
Coll	John	Cottage Row	34	168
Coll	Miss	Chapel Road	40	170
Coll	Gerorge	Margaret Street	6	175
Coll	Peter	De Burgh Square	10	136
Collins	Mrs	Brandywell Avenue	14	131
Collins	Edward	Collon Terrace		135
Collins	Mrs	Elmwood Terrace	4	138
Collins	Owen	Morrison's Close	1	139
Collins	P. & J.	Lecky Road	31	148
Collins	Anthony	William Street	10	165
Collins	Ellen	William Street	52	165
Collins	James	North Street	41	168
Collins	Daniel	Herbert Street	16	174
Collins	William	Margaret Street	9	175
Collins	Daniel	Mill Street	27	176
Collins	William	Spencer Road	56	177
Colquhoun & King		Shipquay Street	8	159
Conaghan	John	Bridge Street	15	131
Conaghan	James	Carrigans Lane	6	133
Conaghan	T. E.	New Market Street	5	154
Conaghan	Andrew	Orchard Row	32	155
Conaghan	Edward	Orchard Street	19	155
Conaghan	George	St. Joseph's Avenue	6	162
Conaghan	Neil	Chapel Road	27	170
Conaghan	Thomas	St. Mary's Terrace		170
Conaghan	Charles	Distillery Lane Lower	6	171
Conaghan	Neal	Duke Street	45	172
Conaghan	Joseph	Dunfield Terrace	27	172
Conaghan	Mrs	Margaret Street	3	175
Concannon	John	Deanery Street	56	136
Concannon	Robert	St. Columb's Wells	28	162
Condren	Constable John	Argyle Street	27	127
Conlan	Miss	Foyle Street		141
Conn	James	Abercorn Road	39	125
Conn	Robert	Ewing Street	3	139
Conn	Joseph	Stewart's Terrace	11	160
Conn	Mrs	Dunfield Terrace	3	172
Conner	Rev. W. G. S.	Clooney Terrace	4B	171
Connery	David	Bishop Street	52	130
Connolly	John	Northland Villas	2	127
Connolly	John	Foyle Street		141
Connolly	Mrs	Wesley Street	20	168
Connolly	Francis	Glendermott Road	10	174
Connor	Mrs F	Albert Street	4	126
Connor	George	Argyle Street	57	127
Connor	P	Butcher Street	9	132

Surname	First Name	Street	House Number	Page Number
Connor	Thomas	Ferguson Street	43	140
Connor	William	Foyle Terrace	117	142
Connor	Mrs	Great James Street	1	144
Connor	Patrick	Lecky Road	74	149
Connor	Patrick	Long Tower	27	150
Connor	William	Nassau Street Upper	4	153
Connor	Patrick	Philips Street	27	156
Connor	John	Princes Terrace	2	156
Connor	James S.	Princes Terrace	6	156
Connor	Mrs	Strand Road	29	160
Connor	John	Strand Road	88	161
Connor	Thomas	Wellington Street	33	164
Connor	Hugh	Artisan Street	1	166
Connor	Miss	Donegal Street	8	167
Connorly	Charles	Argyle Street	1	127
Conroy	John	Clooney Terrace	23	170
Conway	James	Francis Street	3	143
Conway	Peter	Little Diamond	6	150
Conwell	Patrick	Abbey Street	35	125
Conwell	Patrick	Union Street	31	163
Cooke	William	Bishop Street	85	129
Cooke	James	Bishop Street	62	130
Cooke	Robert & Co.	Butcher Street	14, 16	132
Cooke	Robert	Clarendon Street	37	134
Cooke	Dr J. G.	Clarendon Street	67	134
Cooke	H. J.	Culmore Road	Boomhall	136
Cooke	A. J.	Government House		143
Cooke	Robert	Howard Place	1	147
Cooke	Thomas	Meadowbank Avenue	29	152
Cooke	J & J	Queen's Quay		157
Cooke	Head-Constable	Strand Road	Victoria Barracks	161
Cooke	J. & J.	Strand Road		161
Cooke	J. & J.	Strand Road		161
Cooke	John & Co.	Waterloo Place		164
Cooke	John	Donegal Street	11	167
Cooke	T. F.	Caw	Caw House	170
Cooke	Thomas	Chapel Road		170
Cooley	Stephen	Bishop Street	73	129
Cooley	Edward	Deanery Place	3	136
Cooley	William	Friel's Terrace	2	153
Cooper	Miss	Abercorn Road	16	125
Cooper	Miss	Clarendon Street	48	135
Cooper	Norman	London Street	10	150
Cooper	Robert	Creggan Road	159	166
Cooper	Thomas	Emerson Street	24	173
Copland	William J.	Bishop Street	98	130
Corbett	David	Foyle Road		142
Corbett	John W. & Son	Shipquay Street		159
Corbett	J. D.	Deanfield		171

Surname	First Name	Street	House Number	Page Number
Cordiner	R K	Abercorn Road	6	125
Cordner	Mrs	Alexandra Place	28	126
Cordner	W.	Carlisle Road	73	133
Cordner	R. K.	John Street		147
Cordner	J & Sons	Ebrington Street Lower		173
Cordner	Joseph	Pine Street	16	176
Cordner	M.	Spencer Road	123	177
Corr	Patrick	Barry Street	41	128
Corr	Thomas	Elmwood Terrace	48	138
Corr	T.	Richmond Street	12	158
Corr	Constable J.	Benvarden Avenue	30	169
Corscaden	Albert	Little James Street	15	150
Corscaden	Mrs	Northland Road	Richmond	155
Corscaden	Mrs	Strand Road	Richmond	160
Cosgrove	George	Foyle Road	47	142
Cosgrove	Miss	Long Tower	9	150
Cosgrove & Co		Bishop Street	17, 19	129
Cosgrove & Co.		Society Street	2, 4	159
Coulter	James	Foyle View	4	143
Coulter	John	Westland Avenue	39	165
Coulter	John	Primrose Street	15	176
Courtney	Patrick	Mountjoy Street	22	153
Cousins	Mrs	Meehan's Row	7	176
Cowan	Robert	Abercorn Place	2	126
Cowan	Harold G S	Beechwood Avenue	59	128
Cowan	William	Florence Street	1	173
Cowan	William	York Street	1	179
Cowan	John	York Street	15	179
Cowan	William	York Street	14	179
Cowley	Michael	Brandywell Avenue	13	131
Cowley	Mrs	Ivy Terrace	25	147
Cowley	Alfred	Ivy Terrace	34	147
Cox	Daniel	Long Tower	79	150
Cox	Mrs	Moore Street	8	152
Coyle	Miss	Abbey Street	30	125
Coyle	John	Ann Street	5	126
Coyle	Neal	Ann Street	17	127
Coyle	Patrick	Bishop Street	41	129
Coyle	John	Blucher Street	3	131
Coyle	James	Bridge Street	27	132
Coyle	Bernard	Bridge Street	57	132
Coyle	James	Deanery Street	28	136
Coyle	John	Donegal Place	9	137
Coyle	John	Donegal Place	26	137
Coyle	Henry	Eden Place	4	138
Coyle	Charles	Eden Place	8	138
Coyle	Daniel	Elmwood Street	1	138
Coyle	Neal	Elmwood Street	20	138
Coyle	James	Fahan Street	91	139

Surname	First Name	Street	House Number	Page Number
Coyle	Mary	Fahan Street	92	139
Coyle	Robert senior	Fahan Street	96	139
Coyle	Mrs	Foyle Road	65	142
Coyle	Mrs	Glasgow Street	2	143
Coyle	William	Glasgow Terrace	25	144
Coyle	Andrew	Bluebellhill Terrace	184	149
Coyle	Edward	Magazine Street Upper	5	151
Coyle	James	Nassau Street Lower	7	153
Coyle	Daniel	Nassau Street Lower	21	153
Coyle	Denis	Nassau Street Lower	32	153
Coyle	John	Nassau Street Lower	46	153
Coyle	Mrs	Nelson Street	6	154
Coyle	Dan	Orchard Street	13	155
Coyle	Mrs	Richmond Street	Eglinton Hotel	158
Coyle	Mrs	Rossville Street	5	158
Coyle	Mrs	Rossville Street	42	158
Coyle	Edward	Rossville Street	44	158
Coyle	Manus	Stewart's Terrace	18	160
Coyle	Bridget	St. Columb's Wells	65	161
Coyle	James	Sugarhouse Lane	12	162
Coyle	John	Union Street	4	163
Coyle	Richard	Union Street	18	163
Coyle	J. P.	West-End Park	2	165
Coyle	William	William Street	119	165
Coyle	James	Windsor Terrace	7	166
Coyle	Daniel	Artisan Street	11	166
Coyle	William	Artisan Street	10	166
Coyle	Andrew	Creggan Road	133	166
Coyle	John	Creggan Road	165	167
Coyle	James	Creggan Road	62	167
Coyle	Henry	Donegal Street	23	167
Coyle	Richard	Epworth Street	23	167
Coyle	Daniel	North Street	17	168
Coyle	Mrs	Cochrane's Row	4	172
Coyle	James	Duke Street	78	172
Coyle	Sarah	Irish Street	5	174
Coyle	Constable P.	Spencer Road	111	177
Coyle	Charles	Spencer Road	118	177
Coyle	John	Strabane Old Road	23	177
Coyle	Alex	Union Street	13	178
Craig	William	Argyle Street	6	127
Craig	John	Beechwood Park	77	128
Craig	James	Governor Road	40	144
Craig	W. J.	Hawkin Street	36	146
Craig	Miss	Hawkin Street	37	146
Craig	William	Nicholson Square	5	154
Craig	Mrs	Northland Avenue	14	155
Craig	William J.	Pump Street	26	157

Surname	First Name	Street	House Number	Page Number
Craig	David	Queen Street	12	157
Craig	A. N.	Queen Street	15	157
Craig	T. H.	Society Street	11	159
Craig	Robert	Stewart's Terrace	1	160
Craig	Margaret	William Street		165
Craig	Charles	Bond's Hill	10	169
Craig	Miss	Distillery Lane Lower	8	171
Craig	James	Duke Street	22	172
Craig	Thomas	King Street	54	175
Craig	Dr. F. A.	Limavady Road	Ard-Cluan	175
Craig	Mrs	Limavady Road	Clooney cottage	175
Craig	Robert	St. Columb's Road		175
Craig	Joseph	Spencer Road	76	177
Craig	William	Strabane Old Road	46	178
Craig	James	Fountain Street	90	141
Craig	Dr James	Carlisle Terrace	2	133
Craig & Patton		Butcher Street	9	132
Craig & Wellwood Ltd		Ferryquay Street		140
Crainor	Mrs	Stanley's Walk	5	159
Crampsey	Mrs	Foyle Street		141
Craven	Eugene	Elmwood Terrace	35	138
Crawford	James	Bishop Street	128	130
Crawford	John H.	Clarendon Street	49	134
Crawford	William	Fountain Street	87	140
Crawford	Ernest	Foyle Road	61	142
Crawford	Robert	Nicholson Terrace	4	154
Crawford	Mrs Eva	Montrose Villas	2	154
Crawley	John	Caroline Place	23	133
Crawley	James	Fahan Street	36	139
Crawley	John	Lecky Road	11	148
Creany	Miss	Shipquay Street	10	159
Cregan	M. & Co.	Duke Street	12, 14	172
Cregan	Peter	Carlisle Road	75	133
Crerand	Denis	Rossville Street	43	158
Cresswell & Co.		Sackville Street	2	158
Creswell	John	Eden Place	16	138
Creswell	Andrew	Gordon Terrace	1	144
Creswell	D. A.	Great James Street	26	145
Creswell	Andrew	Hogg's Folly	4	146
Creswell	Andrew	Linenhall Street	25	149
Creswell	Alex	Marlborough Street	2	151
Creswell	Miss	Sloan's Terrace	36	159
Creswell	Annie Maria	Duke Street	1	172
Creswell & Co.		Linenhall Street	21	149
Crichton	Mrs	Kerr's Terrace	17	166
Crilley	V.	Spencer Road	82	177
Crilly	John	Edenmore Street	6	138
Cripps	Robert S.	Limavady Road	St. Kilda	175

Surname	First Name	Street	House Number	Page Number
Crockett	Robert	Barry Street	18	128
Crockett	William	Collon Terrace	20	135
Crockett	Miss	Glasgow Street	1	143
Crockett	Mrs	Glasgow Terrace	29	144
Crockett	E. C. & Co	Great James Street		145
Crockett	Ezekiel	Great James Street	68	145
Crockett	William	Nassau Street Lower	27	153
Crockett	William	Mount Street	10	168
Crockett	Mrs	Glendermott Road	28	174
Crockett	James	Spencer Road	71	177
Crockett	Andrew A.	Templemore Park		162
Crockett & Guy		Strand Road	1	160
Crolly	John	Bishop Street	157	130
Crook	George F.	West-End Park	5	165
Crooks	Samuel	Spencer Road	79	177
Crooks	Thomas	Spencer Road	4	177
Crooks	Thomas A.	Spencer Road	6	177
Crooks	Thomas	Spencer Road	16	177
Croom	Miss	Nicholson Terrace	7	154
Crosbie	Dr	Clarendon Terrace	1	134
Cross	James	Union Street	10	178
Crossan	Neal	Bishop Street	239, 241	130
Crossan	Paul	Brook Street Avenue	13	132
Crossan	Thomas	Cedar Street	8	133
Crossan	Neal	Eden Place		138
Crossan	E.	Fahan Street	75	139
Crossan	Charles	Fahan Street	90	139
Crossan	Charles	Fahan Street	94	139
Crossan	Miss	Foyle Road	121	142
Crossan	William	Harvey Street	8	146
Crossan	Edward	Little Diamond	13, 15	150
Crossan	J. J.	Mountjoy Street	7	152
Crossan	John	Princes Street	12	156
Crossan	Neal	Rossville Street	13	158
Crossan	Michael	Sloan's Terrace	2	159
Crossan	Annie	Walker's Place	15	163
Crossan	John	Alfred Street	15	168
Crossan	Ellen	Union Street	15	178
Crowe	Joseph	De Burgh Terrace	12	137
Crumlish	John	Brandywell Avenue	25	131
Crumlish	Michael	William Street	54	165
Culbert	Robert	Wellington Street	32	164
Culbert	Walter	Moore Street	29	176
Cullen	Fanny	Adam Street	3	126
Cullen	Miss	Argyle Street	49	127
Cullen	Elizabeth	Bishop Street	229	130
Cullen	Mrs	Chamberlain Street	27, 29	134
Cullen	D.	Harvey Street		146
Cullen	Philip	Infirmary Road	2	147
Cullen	John	Lecky Road	94	149

Surname	First Name	Street	House Number	Page Number
Cullen	William	Bluebellhill Terrace	222	149
Cullen	Charles	Lone Moor		150
Cullen	Patrick	Nailor's Row	32	153
Cullen	William	Nelson Street	57	154
Cullen & Allen		Princes Quay		157
Culley	James	Westland Avenue	13	165
Cullion	Mrs	St. Columb's Wells	110	162
Cullion	Michael	Westland Terrace	18	165
Cullion	James	Fountain Hill	32	174
Cully	Robert	Stewart's Terrace	10	160
Cumming	Mrs	Marlborough Park	61	166
Cummings	Frank	Miller Street	24	152
Cummings	Alex	Ashcroft Place	2	169
Cummings	Thomas	Ashcroft Place	5	169
Cunningham	Joseph	Abercorn Terrace	4	126
Cunningham	William	Argyle Street	23	127
Cunningham	Samuel	Blee's Lane		131
Cunningham	Miss	Butcher Street	15	132
Cunningham	David	Cedar Street	2	133
Cunningham	H. W.	Clarendon Street	35	134
Cunningham	Mrs	Hempton's Close		141
Cunningham	Mrs	Francis Street	49	143
Cunningham	Richard	Governor Road	38	144
Cunningham	John	Great James Street	40	145
Cunningham	Mrs	John Street	12	147
Cunningham	Patrick	Lecky Road	106	149
Cunningham	Andrew	Marlborough Avenue	4	152
Cunningham	R. A.	Queen Street	9	157
Cunningham	R. A.	Shipquay Place		159
Cunningham	Patrick	Walker's Place	45	163
Cunningham	Harriet	Clooney Terrace	7	170
Cunningham	Thomas	Pine Street	5	176
Cunningham	James	Primrose Street	17	176
Cunningham Bros.		William Street	58	165
Curless	John	Long Tower	42	150
Curley	Francis	Donegal Place	11	137
Curran	Anthony	Bishop Street	65	129
Curran	John	Carlisle Road	22	133
Curran	Patrick	New Street	6	133
Curran	Patrick	Corbett Street	11	135
Curran	Hugh	Fulton Place	7	143
Curran	Joseph	Hamilton Street	11	145
Curran	Anthony	Long Tower	44	150
Curran	Mrs	Long Tower	48	150
Curran	James	Nelson Street	21	153
Curran	Catherine	Rossville Street	20	158
Curran	Thomas	Sloan's Terrace	25	159
Curran	Henry	St. Columb's Wells	8	162
Curran	Miss	Victoria Street	20	163

Surname	First Name	Street	House Number	Page Number
Curran	Dan	Walker's Place	43	163
Curran	Francis	Waterloo Street	30	164
Curran	Mary	Wellington Street	36	164
Curran	William	Creggan Road	179	167
Curran	James	Donegal Street	33	167
Curran	Samuel	Cross Street	3	171
Curran	Isaac	Duke Street	15	172
Curran	Patrick	Glendermott Road	44	174
Curran	William	Meehan's Row	14	176
Curran	William	Union Street	12	178
Currie	W. J.	Melrose Terrace	2	175
Curry	Margaret	Albert Place	4	126
Curry	Mary	Alexandra Place	16	126
Curry	William	Elmwood Terrace	21	138
Curry	David	Fahan Street	70	139
Curry	James	Fountain Place	15	141
Curry	William	Mitchelburne Terrace	99½	142
Curry	James	Hawkin Street	24	146
Curry	Mrs	Dixon's Close	2	151
Curry	Miss	Miller Street	18	152
Curry	Mrs	Stewart's Terrace	14	160
Curry	Mrs	Windmill Terrace	15	166
Curry	William	Windmill Terrace	25	166
Curry	James	Bond's Place	10	170
Curry	Mrs	Emerson Street	2	173
Curry	Jacob	Emerson Street	22	173
Curry	Robert	Moore Street	24	176
Curry	Thomas	Strabane Old Road	52	178
Curtis	Miss	Victoria Terrace	8	127
Curtis	James	Princes Street	4	156
Curtis	Joseph	Violet Street Upper	3	179
Cusack	Robert	Elmwood Street	11	138
Cuthbert	Robert	Blucher Street	1	131
Cuthbert	James M.	Dungiven Road	103	173
Cuthbertson	Samuel	Eden Terrace		137
Dale	Samuel	Clooney Terrace	42	171
Dale	Samuel	Ebrington Terrace	1	173
Daley	Joseph	Lecky Road	61	148
Dallas	George	Rossville Street	52	158
Dalton	James	Bishop Street	219	130
Dalway	Mrs	Great James Street	57	145
Daly	Patrick	Beechwood Street	9	129
Daly	Thomas	Beechwood Street	21	129
Daly	Miss	Foyle Road	106	142
Daly	Joseph	Meave's Row	193	149
Daly	Philip	Orchard Street	6	155
Daly	Robert	St. Columb's Court	1	161
Daly	John	Thomas Street	42	162
Daly	Robert	West-End Terrace	8	165
Daly	Mrs	Dungiven Road	63	173

Surname	First Name	Street	House Number	Page Number
Dalzell	Mrs	Strabane Old Road	32	178
Dane	James J.	Mountjoy Street	1	152
Danker	Solomon	Moat Street	8	152
Darcus	Benjamin J.	Termonbacca		143
Darragh	Mrs	Dungiven Road	75	173
Darragh	David	Florence Street	11	173
Daulton	Eugene	Emerson Street	11	173
Davey	C. F.	Marlborough Street	32	151
Davidson	Robert	Bond's Hill	23	169
Davin	George	Aubrey Street	21	128
Davin	Thomas	Aberfoyle Terrace	21	160
Davis	Sergeant T.	Bishop Street	136	130
Davis	Thomas	Bishop Street	192	131
Davis	Robert J	Edenmore Street	28	138
Davis	Thomas	Ewing Street	33	139
Davis	Thomas	Ferguson Street	60	140
Davis	R. J.	Great James Street	30	145
Davis	James	Pitt Street	2	156
Davis	W. A.	Shipquay Street		158
Davis	William	Foyleview Terrace	6	160
Davis	Mrs	Victoria Street	9	163
Davis	John	Herbert Street	10	174
Davison	James	Riverview Terrace	1	176
Dawson	James	Chamberlain Street	33	134
Dawson	Michael	Sydney Terrace	3	145
Dawson	James	Pine Street	23	176
de Vere	Miss Enid	Castle Street	5	133
Deacon	Nurse	Great James Street	39	144
Deane	Catherine	Abbey Street	47	125
Deane	Arthur	Culmore Road	Kilroide	136
Deane	James	Nailor's Row	11	153
Deane	Sarah	Nailor's Row	13	153
Deane	George	St. Columb's Wells	38	162
Deane	David	West-End Park	19	165
Deane	J. T.	Bond's Hill	13	169
Deane	Robert	Cuthbert Street	3	171
Deane & Co.		Shipquay Street	21	159
Deans	Henry	Emerson Street	14	173
Deans	Hamilton	Strabane Old Road	44	178
Deehan	William	Bishop Street	216	131
Deehan	Thomas F.	Pump Street	22	157
Deehan	William	Rossville Street	11	158
Deehan	Neil	St. Columb's Wells	47	161
Deehan	James	St. Patrick Street	11	162
Deehan	Hugh	Cross Street	3	167
Deehan	Thomas	Osborne Street	20	168
Deehan	Mrs	Osborne Street	21	168
Deehan	George	Clooney Terrace	24	171
Deehan	Michael	Dungiven Road	16	173
Deehan	Mrs	Irish Street	7	174

Surname	First Name	Street	House Number	Page Number
Deehan	Thomas	King Street	3	175
Deehan	Hugh	Primrose Street	4	176
Deehan	William	Riverview Terrace	11	176
Deehan	Mrs	Violet Street Lower	32	178
Deeney	William	Beechwood Street	14	129
Deeney	Mrs	Creggan Street	15	135
Deeney	Mrs	Elmwood Terrace	20	138
Deeney	Philip	Cranagh Terrace	4	148
Deeney	Patrick	Lecky Road		148
Deeney	John	Linenhall Street	25	149
Deeney	John	Quarry Street	20	157
Deeney	Daniel	Strand Road	90	161
Deeney	Francis	Tyrconnell Street	6	163
Deeney	Robert	Bond's Street	16	170
Deeny	Charles	Beechwood Street	10	129
Deeny	John	Brandywell Road	26	131
Deeny	Mrs	Eden Place	10	138
Deeny	Patrick	Donaghy's Row	1	145
Deeny	John	Lower Road	13	151
Deeny	William	Pennyburn Terrace	14	156
Deeny	Patrick	Rossville Street	75	158
Deeny	David	Rossville Street	22	158
Deeny	James	New Row	1	160
Deeny	Miss	Creggan Road	64	167
Deeny	Miss	Benvarden Avenue	22	169
Deery	Patrick	Argyle Terrace	21	127
Deery	Maggie	Howard Place	4	147
Deery	Henry	Orchard Row	23	155
Deery	John	Matty's Lane	28	162
Deery	John	Walker's Place	42	163
Deery	Mrs	Chapel Road	1	170
Delpinto	S.	Waterloo Street	65	164
Delpinto	S.	Strand Road		160
Dennis	Mrs	Clooney Terrace	43	171
Dennison	Robert	Marlborough Villas	3	151
Desmond	John & Co.	Victoria Road		178
Devenny	Mrs	Glasgow Street	4	143
Devenny	Mrs	Lecky Road	135	148
Devenny	Henry	William Street	69	165
Devine	Catherine	Abercorn Road	10	125
Devine	Charles	Abercorn Terrace	2	126
Devine	Patrick	Argyle Street	61	127
Devine	Mrs	Bishop Street	118	130
Devine	John	Bishop Street	264	131
Devine	Hugh	Bridge Street	51	132
Devine	Mary	Millar's Close		132
Devine	Mary	Carrigans Lane	17	133
Devine	D. & Sons	Clarendon Street		134
Devine	William	Deanery Street	1	136
Devine	Charles	Deanery Street	46	136

Surname	First Name	Street	House Number	Page Number
Devine	Mrs	Elmwood Terrace	36	138
Devine	Robert	Fountain Place	11	141
Devine	Miss D.	Fountain Place	21	141
Devine	D. & Sons	Foyle Street		142
Devine	Robert	Francis Street	5	143
Devine	Michael	Linenhall Street	8	150
Devine	Timothy	Magazine Street Upper		151
Devine	Edward	Nailor's Row	33½	153
Devine	William	Richmond Street		158
Devine	Charles	Rossville Street	77	158
Devine	D. & Sons	Strand Road	59	160
Devine	Patrick	Walker's Place	3	163
Devine	Mrs	Alfred Street	4	168
Devine	William	Clooney Terrace	35	170
Devine	Charles	Dungiven Road	14	173
Devine	James	Fountain Hill	108	174
Devine	William	Riverview Terrace	13	176
Devine	Mrs S.	Strabane Old Road	47	178
Devlin	Arthur	Argyle Terrace	29	127
Devlin	James	Creggan Street	43	135
Devlin	Daniel	Edenballymore	4	137
Devlin	Henry	Glenbrook Terrace	7	143
Devlin	Edward	Governor Road	11	144
Devlin	Andrew	Long Tower	25	150
Devlin	John	Long Tower	18	150
Devlin	William	Nelson Street	67	154
Devlin	Hugh	Stanley's Walk	13	160
Devlin	Mrs	Strand Road Lower		161
Devlin	John	St. Columb's Wells	27	161
Devlin	Charles	St. Columb's Wells	33	161
Devlin	Rose Ann	Walker's Place	7	163
Devlin	Miss	Waterloo Place		164
Devlin	Re. Patrick	Chapel Road	Parochial House	170
Diamond	Edward	St. Columb's Wells	54	162
Diamond	Thomas	Wellington Street	68	164
Diamond	James	Alfred Street		168
Diamond	Daniel	Bond's Street	36	170
Diamond	Edward	Fountain Hill	122	174
Dick	Joseph	Ivy Terrace	22	147
Dickie	William E	Baronet Street	5	128
Dickson	Mrs	Alexandra Place	18	126
Dickson	William	Foyle Road	35	142
Dickson	John	Great James Street	36	145
Dickson	F. G.	Shipquay Street	33	159
Dickson	John	Victoria Street	1	163
Dickson	J. A.	Water Street		164
Dickson	Samuel	Alfred Street	11	168
Diffin	William	Windmill Terrace	32	166

Surname	First Name	Street	House Number	Page Number
Digby	William	Baronet Street	6	128
Dill	R F	Academy Road		126
Dillon	Sergeant R. J.	Creggan Road	155	166
Dillon	Mrs	Herbert Street	5	174
Dillon	James	Strabane Old Road	8	177
Dillon	Patrick	Strabane Old Road	10	178
Dingley	Miss	Church Wall	4	134
Dinsmore	William	Argyle Street	59	127
Dinsmore	James	Kennedy Street	5	148
Disher	Archibald S.	Duke Street	36	172
Diver	James	Barrack Street	4	128
Diver	Patrick	Millar's Close		132
Diver	David	St. Columb's Wells	69	161
Diver	Con	St. Columb's Wells	105	162
Diver	George	North Street	5	168
Diver	Mrs	King Street	40	175
Divin	Mrs	Bishop Street	72	130
Divin	Neal	Brook Street Avenue	17	132
Divin	John	Bluebellhill Terrace	196	149
Divin	Phlip	Long Tower	54	150
Divin	Lizzie	Violet Street Lower	44	178
Dixon	Robert J.	Alfred Street	13	168
Dixon	Alexander	Glendermott Road	58	174
Dixon	Robert	Glendermott Road	74	174
Doak	Mary A	Bennett Street Upper	23	129
Doak	John	Bishop Street	218	131
Doak	James	Howard Street	9	147
Doak	James	Creggan Road	121	166
Dobbins	Edward	Little Diamond	1	150
Docherty	Andrew	Magazine Street		151
Dodwell	David	Albert Place	15	126
Doherty	Patrick	Abbey Street	41	125
Doherty	Philip	Abbey Street	49	125
Doherty	John	Abbey Street	61	125
Doherty	James	Abbey Street	18	125
Doherty	Margaret	Abbey Street	24	125
Doherty	Thomas	Abbey Street	32	125
Doherty	Miss M	Abercorn Road	9	125
Doherty	William	Adair Street	3	126
Doherty	Mrs	Adam Street	5	126
Doherty	Edward	Adam Street	7	126
Doherty	John	Alexandra Place	31	126
Doherty	John	Ann Street	15	127
Doherty	Hugh	Ann Street	20	127
Doherty	Charles	Argyle Street	26	127
Doherty	Patrick	Argyle Street	28	127
Doherty	Patrick	Barry Street	1	128
Doherty	Thomas	Beechwood Avenue	1	128
Doherty	Hugh	Beechwood Street	5	128
Doherty	James	Beechwood Street	19	129

Surname	First Name	Street	House Number	Page Number
Doherty	Mrs	Bennett Street Upper	2	129
Doherty	Edward	Sunbeam Terrace	6	130
Doherty	Mrs	Sunbeam Terrace	10	130
Doherty	John	Bishop Street	141	130
Doherty	Annie	Bishop Street	147	130
Doherty	Mrs	Bishop Street	235	130
Doherty	David	Bishop Street	68	130
Doherty	Manasses	Bishop Street	80	130
Doherty	John	Bishop Street	82	130
Doherty	David	Bishop Street	102	130
Doherty	Miss	Bishop Street	114	130
Doherty	Frank	Bishop Street	116	130
Doherty	William	Bishop Street	130	130
Doherty	William	Bishop Street	134	130
Doherty	J.	Bishop Street	134	130
Doherty	Daniel	Bishop Street	208	131
Doherty	Mary	Bishop Street	210	131
Doherty	Joseph	Bishop Street	246	131
Doherty	John	Bishop Street	274	131
Doherty	Robert	Blucher Street	5	131
Doherty	Francis	Blucher Street	7	131
Doherty	John	Blucher Street	17	131
Doherty	Denis	Brandywell Avenue	2	131
Doherty	Christy	Brandywell Avenue	10	131
Doherty	Daniel	Brook Street Avenue	6	132
Doherty	Con	Brook Street Avenue	8	132
Doherty	Charles	Caroline Place	3	133
Doherty	Thomas	Caroline Place	9	133
Doherty	William	Caroline Place	17	133
Doherty	Margaret	New Street	2	133
Doherty	Susan	New Street	10	133
Doherty	W. J.	Castle Street		133
Doherty	Mrs	Chamberlain Street	23	134
Doherty	Michael	Chamberlain Street	31	134
Doherty	Ritchie	Clarence Place	7	134
Doherty	Patrick	Clarendon Street		134
Doherty	William	Corbett Street	16	135
Doherty	William	Creggan Street	5	135
Doherty	James	Creggan Street	11	135
Doherty	Richard	Creggan Street	25	135
Doherty	Rev John	Creggan Street	Parochial H	135
Doherty	Hugh	Creggan Terrace	7	135
Doherty	John	Creggan Terrace	15	135
Doherty	Miss	Deanery Street	23	136
Doherty	Daniel	Deanery Street	29	136
Doherty	Joseph	Deanery Street	33	136
Doherty	James	Deanery Street	54	136
Doherty	James	Demesne Terrace	3	137
Doherty	Patrick	Edenballymore		137
Doherty	Patrick	Edenballymore		137

Surname	First Name	Street	House Number	Page Number
Doherty	William	Eglinton Place	1a	138
Doherty	James	Eglinton Place	11	138
Doherty	William	Eglinton Place	8	138
Doherty	Daniel	Elmwood Terrace	30	138
Doherty	James	Elmwood Terrace	41	138
Doherty	Daniel	Elmwood Terrace	50	138
Doherty	Daniel	Elmwood Street	22	138
Doherty	Patrick	Fahan Street	43	139
Doherty	James	Fahan Street	45, 47	139
Doherty	Bernard	Fahan Street	73	139
Doherty	Mrs	Fahan Street	32	139
Doherty	John	Fahan Street	44	139
Doherty	James	Fahan Street	86	139
Doherty	Frank	Morrison's Close	3	139
Doherty	George	Fahan Street	134	139
Doherty	Patrick	Fahan Street	142	139
Doherty	Annie	Fahan Street	152	139
Doherty	James	Fountain Street	55	140
Doherty	James	Foyle Street	36	142
Doherty	James	Foyle Road	52	142
Doherty	John	Foyle Road	75	142
Doherty	Miss	Foyle Road	114	142
Doherty	Joseph	Foyle Road	116	142
Doherty	Patrick	Fox's Lane	9	143
Doherty	Mrs	Francis Street	41	143
Doherty	John	Frederick Street	5	143
Doherty	Mrs	Frederick Street	8	143
Doherty	John J.	Frederick Street	10	143
Doherty	James	Fulton Place	14	143
Doherty	Mary Ann	Gallagher's Square	4	143
Doherty	Bella	Glenbrook Terrace	11	143
Doherty	George	Glenbrook Terrace	15	143
Doherty	Henry	Glasgow Terrace	22	144
Doherty	Robert	Glasgow Terrace	28	144
Doherty	James	Great James Street		144
Doherty	George	Great James Street		145
Doherty	Mrs	Hamilton Street	1	145
Doherty	John	Hamilton Street	26	145
Doherty	Mrs	Hawthorn Terrace	5	146
Doherty	Edward	High Street	13	146
Doherty	Neal	Howard Street	22	147
Doherty	James	Hollywell Street	2	147
Doherty	Michael	Hollywell Street	11	147
Doherty	Matthew	Ivy Terrace	21	147
Doherty	Francis	Ivy Terrace	38	147
Doherty	John	Kennedy Street	18	148
Doherty	Mrs	Laburnum Terrace	4	148
Doherty	John	Lecky Road	13	148
Doherty	Elizabeth	Lecky Road	21	148
Doherty	Minnie	Lecky Road	25	148

Surname	First Name	Street	House Number	Page Number
Doherty	Miss	Lecky Road	37	148
Doherty	Henry	Lecky Road	49	148
Doherty	Richard	Hollywell Row	67	148
Doherty	Charles	Hollywell Row	69	148
Doherty	Charles	Lecky Road	107	148
Doherty	John	Lecky Road	113	148
Doherty	George	Lecky Road	127	148
Doherty	Patrick	Lecky Road	133	148
Doherty	Hugh	Foster's Terrace	163	148
Doherty	Joseph	Meave's Row	195	149
Doherty	William	Meave's Row	199	149
Doherty	Michael	Meave's Row	205	149
Doherty	John	Ann Street	3	149
Doherty	Hugh	Ann Street	7	149
Doherty	John	Lecky Road	24	149
Doherty	David	Lecky Road	34	149
Doherty	Patrick	Lecky Road	66	149
Doherty	John	Lecky Road	82	149
Doherty	Charles	Lecky Road	86	149
Doherty	William	Lecky Road	88	149
Doherty	Joseph	Lecky Road		149
Doherty	James	Bluebellhill Terrace	148	149
Doherty	Michael D.	Bluebellhill Terrace	154	149
Doherty	Edward	Bluebellhill Terrace	172	149
Doherty	Edward	Little Diamond	11	150
Doherty	John	Little James Street		150
Doherty	William	London Street	18	150
Doherty	Mrs	Long Tower	73	150
Doherty	David	Long Tower	40	150
Doherty	John	Lower Road	1	151
Doherty	Charles	Marlborough Street	43	151
Doherty	William	Marlborough Terrace	9	152
Doherty	Joseph	Miller Street	22	152
Doherty	Owen	Moore Street	13	152
Doherty	Joseph	Nailor's Row	12	153
Doherty	Michael	Nailor's Row	17	153
Doherty	James	Friel's Terrace	3	153
Doherty	James	Nailor's Row		153
Doherty	Hugh	Nassau Street Lower	43	153
Doherty	Owen	Nassau Street Lower	4	153
Doherty	Patrick	Nassau Street Upper	35	153
Doherty	Patrick	Nelson Street	15	153
Doherty	Bernard	Nelson Street	25	153
Doherty	Bernard	Nelson Street	35	154
Doherty	Eliza	Nelson Street	8	154
Doherty	Henry	Nelson Street	62	154
Doherty	Lizzie	Northland Terrace	4	155
Doherty	Mrs J.	Orchard Street	14	155
Doherty	Robert	Patrick Street	11	156
Doherty	Daniel	Quarry Street	6	157

Surname	First Name	Street	House Number	Page Number
Doherty	James	Rossville Street	7	158
Doherty	Michael	Rossville Street	49	158
Doherty	John	Rossville Street	65	158
Doherty	James	Rossville Street	71	158
Doherty	Patrick	Rossville Street	79	158
Doherty	Michael	Rossville Street	6	158
Doherty	Ellen	Rossville Street	16	158
Doherty	William	Rossville Street	36	158
Doherty	James	Rossville Street	64	158
Doherty	George	Rossville Street	72	158
Doherty	John	Sloan's Terrace	17	159
Doherty	John	Stanley's Walk	3	159
Doherty	Catherine	Stanley's Walk	20	160
Doherty	Ben	Stanley's Walk	32	160
Doherty	James	Stanley's Walk	33	160
Doherty	John	Stanley's Walk	47	160
Doherty	George	Rock Buildings		160
Doherty	John	Boating Club Road		161
Doherty	John	St. Columb's Wells	25	161
Doherty	William	St. Columb's Wells	39	161
Doherty	William	St. Columb's Wells	75	162
Doherty	James	St. Columb's Wells	99	162
Doherty	Patrick	St. Columb's Wells	24	162
Doherty	Joseph	St. Columb's Wells	26	162
Doherty	William	St. Columb's Wells	48	162
Doherty	James	St. Columb's Wells	62	162
Doherty	Joseph	St. Columb's Wells	100	162
Doherty	Edward	St. Columb's Wells	122	162
Doherty	William	St. Patrick Street	14	162
Doherty	Patrick	Sugarhouse Lane	10	162
Doherty	Hugh	Sugarhouse Lane	21	162
Doherty	Mrs	Matty's Lane	30	162
Doherty	Quinton	Thomas Street	9	162
Doherty	Daniel	Thomas Street	23	162
Doherty	Thomas	Tyrconnell Street	12	163
Doherty	Joseph	Union Street	11	163
Doherty	Mary	Union Street	8	163
Doherty	Mrs	Union Street	10	163
Doherty	Charles	Walker's Place	46	163
Doherty	Mrs	Walker's Place	48	163
Doherty	Patrick	Walker's Place	50	163
Doherty	William	Wapping Lane	9	163
Doherty	Ellen	Waterloo Street	21	163
Doherty	Mrs	Waterloo Street	35	164
Doherty	James	Waterloo Place		164
Doherty	John	Wellington Street		164
Doherty	John	Wellington Street	17	164
Doherty	Ellen	Wellington Street	61	164
Doherty	David	Wellington Street	66	164
Doherty	Bernard	Westland Terrace	6	165

Surname	First Name	Street	House Number	Page Number
Doherty	James	West-End Terrace	2	165
Doherty	James	William Street	17	165
Doherty	Mrs C.	William Street	29	165
Doherty	George	William Street	45	165
Doherty	Norah	William Street	71	165
Doherty	Patrick	William Street	83	165
Doherty	Lizzie	William Street	123	165
Doherty	John	William Street	127	165
Doherty	Con	William Street		165
Doherty	George & Co.	William Street	8	165
Doherty	Myles	William Street	70	166
Doherty	James	Windsor Terrace	6	166
Doherty	William	Artisan Street	12	166
Doherty	John	Marlborough Park	57	166
Doherty	Charles	Creggan Road	85	166
Doherty	James	Creggan Road	147	166
Doherty	Bernard	Creggan Road	177	167
Doherty	George	Creggan Road	2, 4	167
Doherty	James	Creggan Road	56	167
Doherty	Leo	Donegal Street	7	167
Doherty	Rose	Donegal Street	22	167
Doherty	Henry	Epworth Street	21	167
Doherty	Mrs	Florence Street	8	167
Doherty	Alex	North Street	15	168
Doherty	Mrs	North Street	27	168
Doherty	Anne	North Street	33	168
Doherty	Mrs	Osborne Street	13	168
Doherty	Henry	Osborne Street	14	168
Doherty	John	Benvarden Avenue	32	169
Doherty	David	Bond's Street	33	169
Doherty	Mary	Bond's Place	3	170
Doherty	David	Chapel Road		170
Doherty	Henry	Chapel Road	43	170
Doherty	Miss	Chapel Road	46	170
Doherty	Miss	Clooney Terrace	5	170
Doherty	Andrew	Cross Street	30	171
Doherty	Constable P.	Dervock Place	6	171
Doherty	Mrs	Cochrane's Row	8	172
Doherty	Miss R.	Dungiven Road	10	173
Doherty	Joseph	East Avenue	3	173
Doherty	James	Fountain Hill	112	174
Doherty	Forest	Glendermott Road	94	174
Doherty	Henry	Glendermott Road	98	174
Doherty	Andrew	Herbert Street	18	174
Doherty	Miss	Irish Street	6	174
Doherty	Mrs	King Street	19	175
Doherty	Robert	Margaret Street	23	175
Doherty	Mrs	Margaret Street	4	175
Doherty	James	Moore Street	21	176
Doherty	Mrs	Meehan's Row	8	176

Surname	First Name	Street	House Number	Page Number
Doherty	Mrs	Spencer Road	116	177
Doherty	Charles	Strabane Old Road	22	178
Doherty	Patrick	Union Street	11	178
Doherty	Andrew	Violet Street Lower	3	178
Doherty	John	Violet Street Lower	49	178
Doherty	John	Violet Street Lower	50	179
Doherty	Mrs	Walker's Street	3	179
Doherty	E & Co	Abercorn Road	39	125
Doherty & Co.		Butcher Street	4	132
Doherty & Son		Shipquay Street	2	159
Doherty Bros		Strand Road		160
Doherty Bros.		Ebrington Terrace	6	173
Dolan	Mrs	Strand Road Lower		161
Dolan	James	Bentley Street	8	169
Dolan	Constable M.	Spencer Road	10	177
Dolan	James	Dungiven Road	111	173
Doland	Thomas	Dungiven Road	33	172
Domnitz	Isaac	Fountain Street	27	140
Donaghey	Mrs	Barry Street	28	128
Donaghey	Michael	Bishop Street	204	131
Donaghey	Patrick	Bridge Street	47	132
Donaghey	Francis	Eglinton Place	25	138
Donaghey	James	Eglinton Terrace	11	138
Donaghey	John	McLaughlin's Close	1	140
Donaghey	Philip	Foyle Street	57	141
Donaghey	John	Ivy Terrace	37	147
Donaghey	Edward	Long Tower	35	150
Donaghey	Mrs	Strand Road	lodge	160
Donaghey	Edward	St. Patrick Street	1	162
Donaghey	J.	Waterloo Place		164
Donaghey	Francis	Wellington Street	47	164
Donaghey	Michael	Windsor Terrace	1	166
Donaghey	Bernard	Artisan Street	8	166
Donaghey	James	Creggan Road	115	166
Donaghey	William	Donegal Street	27	167
Donaghey	William	Benvarden Avenue	9	169
Donaghey	Stephen	Carlin Street	17	170
Donaghey	Patrick	Distillery Lane Lower	5	171
Donaghey	T. J.	Dunfield Terrace	35, 37	172
Donaghey	Michael	Dungiven Road	41	172
Donaghey	Joseph	Dungiven Road	69	173
Donaghey	James	Emerson Street	21	173
Donaghey	George	Fountain Hill	61	173
Donaghey	John	Moore Street	7	176
Donaghey	Hyland	Simpson's Brae	9	177
Donaghey	William	Violet Street Lower	5	178
Donaghey	John	Violet Street Lower	29	178
Donaghey & Robinson		Shipquay Street		159
Donaghy	Thomas	Fountain Street	42	141

Surname	First Name	Street	House Number	Page Number
Donaghy	Patrick	Northland Terrace	1	155
Donaghy	Robert	Duke Street	52	172
Donaghy	William	Moore Street	15	176
Donaghy	Miss	Violet Street Lower	36	178
Donaghy	Mrs	Strand Road	Avoca	160
Donaghy	Joseph	St. Columb's Wells	128	162
Donaldson	William	Aubrey Street	2A	128
Donaldson	William	Homefield		128
Donaldson	John	Beechwood Avenue	39	128
Donaldson	Henry	Beechwood Avenue	49	128
Donaldson	David	Bennett Street Lower	55	129
Donaldson	Mrs	Sunbeam Terrace	13	130
Donaldson	A.	Castle Street		133
Donaldson	William	Hawkin Street	30	146
Donaldson	Henry	Shipquay Street	8	159
Donnell	Patrick	Argyle Terrace	27	127
Donnell	James & Son	Castle Street		133
Donnell	James	Clarence Avenue	1	134
Donnell	Mrs	Crawford Square	5	135
Donnell	William J	Crawford Square	7	135
Donnell	William	Ferguson Street	39	140
Donnell	J.	Shipquay Place		159
Donnell	William	Foyleview Terrace	8	160
Donnell	Charles	Wapping Lane	35	163
Donnell	James	Waterloo Street	15	163
Donnell	Marshall	Caw	Owenmore	170
Donnell	Charles	Pine Street	9	176
Donnell	Mrs	Strabane Old Road	54	178
Donnell	James	Strabane Old Road	78	178
Donnell	Cunningham	Strabane Old Road		178
Donnell	Charles J.	Nicholson Terrace	14	154
Donnell	S. & W. J.	Castle Street		133
Donnell	Francis	Ivy Terrace	35	147
Donnell	Jane	Lower Road	14	151
Donnell	John	Strabane Old Road	14	178
Donnell	William	Victoria Park		178
Donnell	John	Glendermott Road	70	174
Donnellan	John	Mountroyal		155
Donnelly	Mrs	Bishop Street	278	131
Donnelly	Mrs	Clarence Avenue	6	134
Donnelly	Mrs M	Foyle Road		142
Donnelly	William	Henrietta Street	17	146
Donnelly	Mrs	John Street		147
Donnelly	Joseph	St. Columb's Terrace	91	148
Donnelly	William J.	Lecky Road	78	149
Donnelly	James	Nelson Street	45	154
Donnelly	Patrick	Sloan's Terrace	14	159
Donnelly	Michael	Sloan's Terrace	18	159
Donnelly	Mrs	Wells Street Terrace	3	164
Donnelly	Patrick	Glendermott Road	56	174

Surname	First Name	Street	House Number	Page Number
Donnelly	Mrs	Melrose Terrace	21	175
Donnelly	William	Pine Street	18	176
Donnelly	William	Union Street	6	178
Donohoe	Mrs Jane	Miller Street	19	152
Donohoe	Michael	Wellington Street	11	164
Donohue	Head-Constable	Strand Road	Victoria Barracks	161
Donohue	Thomas	Wellington Street	7	164
Donoughue	James F.	Brook Street	2	132
Doogan	James	Long Tower	49	150
Doogan	Sergeant B.	Marlborough Terrace	16	152
Doogan	Michael	St. Columb's Street	4	161
Dooley	Robert	Wells Street Terrace	2	164
Dooley	Mrs	William Street	56	165
Doority	Francis	King Street	42	175
Doran	Thomas	Linenhall Street	27	149
Doran	Patrick	Orchard Row	3	155
Doran	Daniel	Fountain Hill	5	173
Doran	Mrs	Fountain Hill	11	173
Doran	Mrs	Fountain Hill	19	173
Doran	Mrs	Spencer Road	65	177
Dorian	John	Artisan Street	16	166
Dornan	Mrs	Stanley's Walk	10	160
Dornan	Samuel	Emerson Street	10	173
Dorrans	H. S.	Carlisle Road	46	133
Dorrian	Arthur	Argyle Terrace	14	127
Dorrian	James	St. Columb's Terrace	93	148
Dorrian	Maurice	Strand Road	2	160
Dorrian	Maurice	Victoria Road	3	178
Dougan	Cassie	Bridge Street	46	132
Dougan	James A.	Ferryquay Street		140
Dougan	William	Great James Street	25	144
Dougan	James A.	Shipquay Place		159
Dougherty	Alfred	Argyle Terrace	39	127
Dougherty	James	Bishop Street	103	129
Dougherty	Henry	Nicholson Terrace	16	154
Dougherty	Alex	Park Avenue	2	156
Douglas	Joseph	Carlisle Road	67	133
Douglas	Thomas	Fountain Place	14	141
Douglas	Mrs	Francis Street	57	143
Douglas	William	Nicholson Square	11	154
Douglas	Mrs	Park Avenue	24	156
Douglas	James	Waterloo Street	31	163
Douglas	James	Creggan Road	125	166
Douglas	Mrs	Creggan Road	131	166
Douglas	James	Carlin Street	6	170
Douglas	William	Carlisle Chambers		172
Douglas	Robert	Melrose Terrace	14	175
Douglas	William	Spencer Road	133	177
Douglas	Henry	Spencer Road	135	177

Surname	First Name	Street	House Number	Page Number
Dowd	George T.	Hawkin Street	32	146
Dowds	George	Creggan Street	49	135
Dowds	William	Creggan Terrace	1	135
Dowds	Mrs	Foyle View	7	143
Dowds	James	Marlborough Park	65	166
Dowds	Ellen	Irish Street	1	174
Downes	William	Stewart's Terrace	15	160
Downes	James	Wesley Street	11	168
Downey	Thomas	Creggan Street	51	135
Downey	Michael	East Wall		137
Downey	William	Edenmore Street	14	138
Downey	Miss	Elmwood Terrace	14	138
Downey	George	Ewing Street	24	139
Downey	Michael	Governor Road	17	144
Downey	John	Lecky Road	7	148
Downey	Miss	Mountjoy Street	26	153
Downey	James	Nelson Street	5	153
Downey	Andrew	Orchard Row	8	155
Downey	James	Rossville Street	41	158
Downey	Margaret	St. Patrick Street	3	162
Downs	John	King Street	52	175
Doyle	John	Bridge Street	64	132
Doyle	Hugh	Nassau Street Lower	22	153
Driscoll	James	Westland Terrace	15	165
Duddy	Daniel	Caroline Place	15	133
Duddy	Michael	Corbett Street	14	135
Duddy	William	Eglinton Place	5	138
Duddy	William	Fahan Street	104	139
Duddy	Mrs	Fahan Street	116	139
Duddy	John	Fahan Street	126	139
Duddy	John	Fountain Place	7½	141
Duddy	Robert	High Street	10	146
Duddy	Bernard	Cranagh Terrace	2	148
Duddy	Mrs	Mary Street	24	152
Duddy	Patrick	Northland Avenue	4	155
Duddy	William	Thomas Street	16	162
Duddy	Michael	Emerson Street	33	173
Duddy	Mrs	King Street	25	175
Duddy	Patrick	King Street	8	175
Duddy	Michael	Mill Street	24	176
Duddy	James	Mill Street	28	176
Duddy	Joseph	Mountain View		176
Duddy	William	Pine Street	1	176
Duddy	Henry	York Street	11	179
Duff	Robert	Moore Street	11	176
Duff	Joseph	Moore Street	30	176
Duff	Joseph	Spencer Road	64	177
Duffy	Mrs	Argyle Street	31	127
Duffy	Patrick	Argyle Street	36	127
Duffy	Neil	Argyle Street	66	127

Surname	First Name	Street	House Number	Page Number
Duffy	Constable J P	Beechwood Street	8	129
Duffy	William	Fitters Row	261	130
Duffy	Miss	Cottage Row	5	131
Duffy	John	Brandywell Road	10	131
Duffy	James	Bridge Street	12	132
Duffy	Michael	Brook Street	3	132
Duffy	Arthur	Cable Street	19	132
Duffy	Miss	Caroline Place	11	133
Duffy	Joseph	Corbett Street	17	135
Duffy	James	Creggan Street	39	135
Duffy	Patrick	Creggan Terrace	3	135
Duffy	Mrs	Elmwood Terrace	47	138
Duffy	Thomas	Ferguson Street	12	140
Duffy	Edward	Foyle Street	107	141
Duffy	Miss	Foyle Road	34	142
Duffy	John	Foyle View	3	143
Duffy	John	Governor Road	1	144
Duffy	Michael	Hamilton Street	10	145
Duffy		High Street	16	146
Duffy	William	Howard Street	10	147
Duffy	Edward	Joseph Street	8	147
Duffy	Thomas	Lecky Road	123	148
Duffy	Isabella	Bluebellhill Terrace	142	149
Duffy	Hugh	Bluebellhill Terrace	164	149
Duffy	Con	Little Diamond	2	150
Duffy	John	Nassau Street Upper	25	153
Duffy	James	Philips Street	19	156
Duffy	Miss	Stanley's Walk	15	160
Duffy	Patrick	St. Columb's Wells	88	162
Duffy	Patrick	Thomas Street	27	162
Duffy	hugh	Union Street	9	163
Duffy	John H.	Union Street	26	163
Duffy	Thomas	Walker's Place	11	163
Duffy	Maria	Wellington Street	24	164
Duffy	Bernard	William Street	73	165
Duffy	William	Kerr's Terrace	9	166
Duffy	Mrs	Donegal Street	15	167
Duffy	Andrew	Lewis Street	24	167
Duffy	Charles	Cottage Row	26	168
Duffy	William	Violet Street Lower	10	178
Dugan	M J	Bishop Street	49	129
Dugan	Mrs	Carrigans Lane	13	133
Duggan	Sarah	Alma Place	13	126
Duggan	Mary A.	Laburnum Terrace	22	148
Duggan	Thomas	Nailor's Row	20	153
Duncan	Thomas	Albert Place	6	126
Duncan	A.	Commercial Buildings		141
Duncan	Thomas	Marlborough Street	31	151
Duncan	Robert	Miller Street	13	152

Surname	First Name	Street	House Number	Page Number
Duncan	Miss	St. Joseph's Avenue	5	162
Duncan	Mrs	Westland Avenue	33	165
Duncan	Thomas	Creggan Road	16	167
Duncan	James	Lewis Street	10	167
Duncan	William	Ebrington Gardens		170
Duncan	Archibald	Clooney Terrace	28	171
Dunleavy	Robert	Abercorn Terrace	1	126
Dunlevy	Samuel	Alfred Street	12	168
Dunlevy	Samuel	Spencer Road	forge	177
Dunlop	Nenian	Clarendon Street	45	134
Dunlop	Joseph	Creggan Terrace	10	135
Dunlop	Robert	Fairman Place	7	139
Dunlop	Cassie	Fountain Street	33	140
Dunlop	Robert E.	Grove Place	1	145
Dunlop	William	Marlborough Terrace	1	152
Dunlop	Mrs	Mountjoy Street	2	153
Dunlop	Mrs	Nicholson Square	22	154
Dunlop	John	Ashfield Terrace	31	166
Dunlop	Mrs	Lewis Street	14	167
Dunlop	James	Fountain Hill	56	174
Dunlop	Samuel	King Street	24	175
Dunlop	David	Violet Street Lower	41	178
Dunn	Mrs	Brandywell Road	30	131
Dunn	Mrs	Ferguson Street	37	140
Dunn	Joseph	Lawrence Hill		148
Dunn	James	Nicholson Square	18	154
Dunn	Robert	Cuthbert Street	29	171
Dunn	Mrs	King Street	41	175
Dunn	Joseph	Magazine Street		151
Dunne	William	Victoria Terrace	9	127
Dunne	Elizabeth	Foster's Terrace	165	148
Dunne	William	Orchard Row	9	155
Dunne	Mrs	Strand Road	36	161
Dunne	John	Sugarhouse Lane	11	162
Dunniece	Hugh	Bennett Street Lower	28	129
Dunniece	Jane	Frederick Street	12	143
Dunniece	Edward Hugh	Long Tower	62	150
Dunniece	Charles	Park Avenue	14	156
Dunniece	Mrs	Princes Street	6	156
Dunseath	John	Albert Place	7	126
Durey	R. J.	Bishop Street	92	130
Durnian	Cassie	Bishop Street	148	131
Durnian	James	Little James Street	9	150
Durnion	Edward	Waterloo Street	1	163
Dykes	Constable James	Hawkin Street	12	146
Eagleson	John	Melrose Terrace	11	175
Eakin	John	Fairman Place	18	140
Eakins	Constable T.	Fountain Hill	58	174
Earley	C.	Little James Street	1	150
Early	Henry	Deanery Street	12	136

Surname	First Name	Street	House Number	Page Number
Eason	John	Queen Street		157
Eaton	Thomas	Argyle Terrace	8	127
Eaton	Alexander	Stewart's Terrace	12	160
Eaton	John	Rosemount Avenue	6	168
Eaton & Co.		Duke Street	2, 4	172
Eddleston	John W.	College Terrace	10	135
Edgar	John	Gordon Place	6	144
Edgar	Samuel	Windmill Terrace	16	166
Edgar	John	Maple Street	5	175
Edmiston	J. J.	Maybrook House		135
Edmiston	Wallace	Crawford Square	8	135
Edmiston & Co.		Shipquay Street	35, 37	159
Edwards	John	Aubrey Street	16	128
Edwards	John	Clarendon Street	5	134
Edwards	Thomas	Corbett Street	7	135
Edwards	Robert J R	East Wall	2	137
Edwards	James	Eden Place	17	138
Edwards	William	Ivy Terrace	19	147
Edwards	Mrs	Lawrence Hill		148
Edwards	Richard	Marlborough Avenue	19	152
Edwards	Mrs	Bond's Street	40	170
Elder	John	Foyle Street	55	141
Elder	Miss	Grove Place	16	145
Elder	William	Nailor's Row	19	153
Elder	Robert	Duke Street	21	172
Elkin	H. L.	De Burgh Terrace	16	137
Elkin	James	Gordon Terrace	14	144
Elliott	Annie	Aubrey Street	6	128
Elliott	Thomas	Bishop Street	56	130
Elliott	Mrs	College Terrace	11	135
Elliott	R. T.	Collon Terrace		135
Elliott	Sergeant Acting J	Elmwood Terrace	7	138
Elliott	James	Ferguson Street	34	140
Elliott	James	Grafton Street	7	144
Elliott	William	Henry Street	20	146
Elliott	P. H.	Magazine Street		151
Elliott	Mrs	Friel's Terrace	4	153
Elliott	Mary	Orchard Lane	3	155
Elliott	Patrick H.	Queen Street	3	157
Elliott	James	Lewis Street	8	167
Elliott	Laurence	Chapel Road	6	170
Elliott	Hugh	Duke Street	56	172
Elliott	James	Fountain Hill	forge	173
Elliott	James	Irish Street	21	174
Elliott	John	King Street	20	175
Elliott	William	Spencer Road	33	177
Ellis	Philip	Baronet Street	8	128
Ellis	George	Carlisle Road	44	133
Ellis	Philip	Glasgow Terrace	34	144

Surname	First Name	Street	House Number	Page Number
Ellis	Samuel	Clooney Terrace	45	171
Elvin	Mrs	Argyle Terrace	28	127
Elvin	Matilda	Chapel Road	54	170
Emerson	Mrs	Great James Street	65	145
Emery	Andrew & Son	Carlisle Road	11	132
Emery	William	Clooney Terrace	34E	171
English	Miss	Francis Street	47	143
English	John G.	Marlborough Street	5	151
English	Charles	The Rock	23	160
Englishby	Constable C.	Dungiven Road	79	173
Epstein	J.	Richmond Street	13	158
Evans	William	Lone Moor		150
Ewing	E W	Baronet Street	7	128
Ewing	Miss	Marlborough Street	16	151
Fagan	Thomas	Fairman Place	13	139
Fagan	Richard	Westland Terrace	9	165
Fairman	James	Waterloo Street	43	164
Fairweather	George	Cuthbert Street	22	171
Falkoner	George	Victoria Place	1	163
Faller	William	Orchard Street	11	155
Faller	William	Market Buildings		161
Fanning	Charles	Bishop Street	260	131
Fanning	Richard	Long Tower	19	150
Fanning	Mrs Mary	Long Tower	21	150
Farrell	Christopher	Elmwood Terrace	5	138
Farrell	W. J.	Great James Street		145
Farren	Michael	Bishop Street	43	129
Farren	John	Bishop Street	288	131
Farren	Patrick	Mitchelburne Terrace	94	142
Farren	Edward	Glasgow Street	5	144
Farren	John	Hamilton Street	16	145
Farren	Mrs	High Street	1	146
Farren	Michael	Bluebellhill Terrace	180	149
Farren	Michael	Bluebellhill Terrace	204	149
Farren	John	Mary Street	10	152
Farren	Michael	Wells Street Terrace	5	164
Farren	Mrs	Florence Street	27	173
Faulkiner	Miss	Bridge Street	34	132
Faulkiner	James	Bond's Street	8	169
Faulkiner	Thomas	Violet Street Lower	18	178
Faulkner	James	Long Tower	80	150
Faulkner	Robert	Princes Street	17	156
Faulkner	Thomas	The Rock	29	160
Faulkner	Rev. George	Victoria Place	Parochial House	163
Faulkner	Robert	Violet Street Lower	22	178
Fee	Margaret	Abercorn Road	14	125
Fee	William J. D.	Bishop Street	36	130
Fee	William J. D.	Melrose Terrace	4	175
Feeney	Denis	Friel's Terrace	7	153

Surname	First Name	Street	House Number	Page Number
Feeney	James	Violet Street Lower	9	178
Feeny	Luke	Abercorn Road	40	125
Feeny	M. C.	Castle Street		133
Ferguson	Noble	Albert Place	1	126
Ferguson	Alfred	Argyle Street	16	127
Ferguson	Robert	Aubrey Street	26	128
Ferguson	Edward	Baronet Street	2	128
Ferguson	Miss	Bellevue Avenue	3	129
Ferguson	John	Sunbeam Terrace	18	130
Ferguson	Alexander	Bishop Street	64	130
Ferguson	William	Blucher Street	Stables	131
Ferguson	Maggie	Brandywell Avenue	7	131
Ferguson	William	Butcher Street	9	132
Ferguson	Mrs	Fairman Place	11	139
Ferguson	John	Fountain Street	workshop	141
Ferguson	William	Fountain Street	82	141
Ferguson	William	Foyle Street	43	141
Ferguson	Thomas	Foyle Road	45	142
Ferguson	James	Foyle Road	103	142
Ferguson	Mrs	George Street	12	143
Ferguson	Thomas	Great James Street	46	145
Ferguson	James	Hollywell Street	4	147
Ferguson	Thomas	Magazine Street	7	151
Ferguson	John	Nelson Street	58	154
Ferguson	Mary	Nelson Street	60	154
Ferguson	John	Aberfoyle Terrace	31	160
Ferguson	Rev. S.	Caw		170
Ferguson	James	Dunfield Terrace	23	172
Ferguson	J.	Dunfield Terrace	39	172
Ferrier	James	Mountjoy Street	16	153
Ferris	Joseph	Bishop Street	142A	131
Ferris	Miss	Elmwood Terrace	1	138
Ferris	William Ltd	Foyle Street	41	141
Ferris	Andrew	Lower Road	5	151
Ferris	Joseph	Lower Road	12	151
Ferris	Robert	Lower Road	26	151
Ferry	Edward	Creggan Terrace	2	135
Ferry	Mrs	Foster's Terrace	159	148
Ferry	Daniel	Nassau Street Lower	18	153
Ferry	James	Nassau Street Lower	52	153
Ferry	James	Pennyburn		156
Ferry	Samuel	Donegal Street	14	167
Findlay	N. R.	Florence Terrace	3	154
Findlay	G. P.	Strand Road		161
Finlay	William	Argyle Street	34	127
Finlay	William	Argyle Street	40	127
Finlay	Ernest	Edenmore Street	39	138
Finlay	John	Kennedy Street	1	148
Finlay	Thomas	Kennedy Street	17	148
Finlay	Robert	Linenhall Street	17	149

Surname	First Name	Street	House Number	Page Number
Finlay	Robert J.	The Rock	27	160
Finlay	Alex	Bentley Street	10	169
Finlay	John	Cochrane's Row	5	172
Finlay	John	Moore Street	4	176
Finlay Bros.		Linenhall Street		149
Finn	Thomas	Lecky Road	121	148
Fisher	Joseph	Bishop Street	182	131
Fisher	Charles	Bridge Street	20	132
Fisher	Michael L.	Great James Street	41	144
Fisher	Bros	Prince Arthur Street		156
Fisher	Patrick	Sloan's Terrace	24	159
Fitzgerald	Gerald F.	Marlborough Street	30	151
Fitzgerald	G. F.	Shipquay Street		159
Fitzpatrick	Mrs	Edenmore Street	22	138
Fitzpatrick	Francis	Dungiven Road	51	172
Fitzpatrick	Mrs	Violet Street Lower	16	178
Fitzsimmons	Mrs	Ann Street	7	126
FItzsimmons	John	Ann Street	22	127
Flanagan	John	Argyle Street	73	127
Flanagan	Bernard	Grafton Avenue	51	127
Flanagan	Mrs	Bennett Street Upper	3	129
Flanagan	Mrs	Charlotte Street	9	134
Flanagan	Bernard	Great James Street	5	144
Flanagan	Lizzie	Henry Street	2	146
Flanagan	John	Kildarra Terrace	9	146
Flanagan	Sergeant J.	Clooney Terrace	13	170
Flanagan	P. J.	Clooney Terrace	20	171
Flannagan	Daniel	Foyle Road	119	142
Flannagan	James	London Street	20	150
Flannagan	Mrs	Cross Street	39	171
Flannery	Sergeant John	De Burgh Square	5	136
Fleming	Richard	Elmwood Terrace	24	138
Fleming	Mary	Lower Road		151
Fleming	William	Moore Street	9	152
Fleming	William J.	Rossville Street	83	158
Fleming	Sam	Bond's Street	15	169
Fleming	William	Cuthbert Street	2	171
Fleming	William	Spencer Road	107	177
Fleming	George	Spencer Road	52	177
Fleming & Co.		Strand Road	37	160
Fleming & Moore		Waterloo Place		164
Fletcher	Daniel	Clarendon Street	33	134
Fletcher	Henry J.	Harding Street	19	145
Fletcher	John B. A.	Northland Avenue	17	155
Fletcher	Daniel	Queen's Quay		157
Fletcher	Mrs	Benvarden Avenue	47	169
Fletcher	A.	Victoria Park	gate lodge	178
Flood	Anthony	Fahan Street	100	139
Floyd	Robert R. A.	Pump Street	7	156

Surname	First Name	Street	House Number	Page Number
Flynn	Mrs	Abercorn Road	11	125
Flynn	Francis	Abercorn Road	53	125
Flynn	Thomas	Brandywell Avenue	5	131
Flynn	James	Marlborough Avenue	15	152
Flynn	Thomas	Park Avenue	7	156
Flynn	Michael	Westland Terrace	19	165
Flynn	John	Osborne Street	23	168
Flynn & Co.		Butcher Street	2	132
Foley	Constable	Northland Avenue	10	155
Forbes	Constable	Fairman Place	19	139
Forbes	Samuel	Governor Road	44	144
Forbes	Andrew	Spencer Road	14	177
Forde	Robert	Edenmore Street	31	138
Forester	Mrs	Grove Place	10	145
Forrester	John	Strand Road	33	160
Forster	William	Richmond Street	7	158
Forster	Rev. W. H.	Deanfield		171
Forsythe	Miss	Asylum Road	5	127
Forsythe	John James	Beechwood Avenue	4	128
Forsythe	John	Marlborough Terrace	8	152
Forsythe	Robert	Meadowbank Avenue	31	152
Forsythe	Miss	Bond's Street	51	169
Forte	G.	Foyle Street	101	141
Foster	William	Academy Terrace	4	126
Foster	James W	Bishop Street	11	129
Foster	George	Edenballymore		137
Foster	Mrs	Richmond Street	9	158
Foster	William	Richmond Street	4	158
Foster	Miss	Stewart's Terrace	7	160
Foster	James	Sugarhouse Lane	5	162
Foster	John H.	Waterloo Place		164
Foster	John	William Street	39	165
Fowler	Thomas	Sloan's Terrace	6	159
Fox	John	Howard Street	25	147
Fox	Patrick	Hollywell Row	73	148
Fox	Edward	William Street	48	165
Francis	James	Bishop Street	133	130
Francis	David	Bishop Street	258	131
Francis	John	Patrick Street	2	156
Franklin	John T.	Marlborough Street	33	151
Fraser	David	Charlotte Street	5	134
Frazer	A E A	Edenballymore	Creggan	137
Frazer	Alfred E.	Marlborough Street	4	151
Frazer	John	Wapping Lane	31	163
Fredlander	M.	Orchard Street		155
Fredlander	Michael	Victoria Road	7	178
Fredlander & Co.		Foyle Street		142
Fredlander & Silver		Carlisle Road	31	132

Surname	First Name	Street	House Number	Page Number
Frew	A. H.	Carlisle Road	1	132
Friel	John	Abbey Street	37	125
Friel	James	Abbey Street	20	125
Friel	Michael	Abbey Street	22	125
Friel	Daniel	Abercorn Road	42	125
Friel	Daniel	Bennett Street Upper	25	129
Friel	James	Bishop Street	42	130
Friel	Bernard	Carlisle Road	1	132
Friel	William	Caroline Place	1	133
Friel	Henry	Chamberlain Street	12	134
Friel	William	Fahan Street	97	139
Friel	Bella	Fahan Street	144	139
Friel	Justin	Fahan Street	154	139
Friel	Charles	Fulton Place	11	143
Friel	Maggie	Hollywell Street	14	147
Friel	William	Laburnum Terrace	3	148
Friel	Patrick	Hollywell Row	71	148
Friel	Francis	Ann Street	5	149
Friel	John	Nelson Street	3	153
Friel	James	Nelson Street	49	154
Friel	Bernard	Nelson Street	50	154
Friel	Catherine	Orchard Street	5	155
Friel	John P.	Rossville Street	14	158
Friel	James	Stanley's Walk	30	160
Friel	Patrick	Market Buildings		161
Friel	Mrs	Matty's Lane	32	162
Friel	Manasses	Thomas Street	36	162
Friel	James	Union Street	5	163
Friel	Mrs	Waterloo Street	18	164
Friel	Ellen	Donegal Street	26	167
Friel	Thomas	Wesley Street	18	168
Friel	Edward	Bond's Place	6	170
Friel	Patrick	Clooney Terrace	53	171
Friel	Michael	Duke Street	48	172
Friel	James	Ebrington Street	7	173
Friel	John	Fountain Hill	21	173
Friel	Robert	Osborne Street	2	168
Friell	James	Lewis Street	26	167
Friesland	Isaac	Moat Street	3	152
Frizell	W A (M.D)	Woodleigh Terrace	3	127
Frizell	W. A. & Co.	Shipquay Place		159
Fullerton	Thomas	College Terrace	4	135
Fullerton	John	Foyle Street	52	142
Fullerton	James	Wellington Street	29	164
Fulton	Robert	Bishop Street	3	129
Fulton	Robert	Clarence Place	3	134
Fulton	Thomas	Edenmore Street	34	138
Fulton	Mrs	Kennedy Street	13	148
Fulton	R. Victor	Northland Avenue	16	155
Fulton	W. J.	Northland Avenue	18	155

Surname	First Name	Street	House Number	Page Number
Fulton	Joseph	St. Columb's Wells	60	162
Fulton	Robert	Wapping Lane	10	163
Fulton	J. A.	Deanfield		171
Fulton	D. J.	Duke Street	53	172
Fulton	William D.	Glendermott Road	60	174
Fulton	Andrew	King Street	21	175
Funston	Henry	Hawkin Street	25	146
Furey	John	Dungiven Road	47	172
Gabler	Adolphe	Shipquay Street	21	159
Gaff	Robert	Edenballymore	Creggan	137
Gailey	Mrs	Waterloo Place		164
Galbraith	Mrs	Beechwood Avenue	27	128
Galbraith	Joseph	Gordon Terrace	12	144
Galbraith	Mrs	Great James Street	21	144
Galbraith	J.	Magazine Street		151
Galbraith	William	Dungiven Road	31	172
Galbraith	Fitzgerald F.	King Street	18	175
Gallagehr	Daniel	St. Columb's Wells	120	162
Gallagher	James	Argyle Terrace	1	127
Gallagher	John	Aubrey Street	22	128
Gallagher	Daniel	Barry Street	37	128
Gallagher	John	Beechwood Street	11	129
Gallagher	Matilda	Bellevue Avenue	23	129
Gallagher	Andrew	Bennett Street Upper	9	129
Gallagher	Hugh	Bishop Street	129	130
Gallagher	Mary	Bishop Street	131	130
Gallagher	William	Bishop Street	34	130
Gallagher	John	Bishop Street	202	131
Gallagher	Hugh	Bishop Street	282	131
Gallagher	Michael	Bishop Street	284	131
Gallagher	John	Bishop Street	296	131
Gallagher	John	Brandywell Road	1	131
Gallagher	Edward	Brandywell Avenue	23	131
Gallagher	John	Brandywell Avenue	8	131
Gallagher	Anthony	Bridge Street	17	132
Gallagher	Michael	Butcher Street	7	132
Gallagher	Mrs	Carrigans Lane	7	133
Gallagher	John	Alexander Cottages	5	133
Gallagher	William	Chamberlain Street	16	134
Gallagher	Edward	Clarendon Street	39	134
Gallagher	John	Creggan Street	41	135
Gallagher	Joseph	Deanery Place	4	136
Gallagher	Mrs	Edenmore Street	23	138
Gallagher	Charles	Edenmore Street	33	138
Gallagher	Pat	Eglinton Place	16	138
Gallagher	George	Elmwood Street	3	138
Gallagher	Daniel	Elmwood Street	7	138
Gallagher	John	Fahan Street	57	139
Gallagher	William G.	Fahan Street	132	139
Gallagher	William	Fountain Street	49	140

Surname	First Name	Street	House Number	Page Number
Gallagher	Robert	Fountain Street	59	140
Gallagher	William	Fountain Street	81	140
Gallagher	Robert	Fountain Street	83	140
Gallagher	Samuel	Fountain Street	86	141
Gallagher	Mrs	Fountain Street	96	141
Gallagher	Nancy	Foyle Road	66	142
Gallagher	Patrick	Foyle Road	70	142
Gallagher	Charles	Foyle Road	72	142
Gallagher	Thomas	Foyle Road	79A	142
Gallagher	James	Foyle Terrace	118	142
Gallagher	Theobald	Foyle View	8	143
Gallagher	Richard	Francis Street	15	143
Gallagher	Sarah	Frederick Street	11	143
Gallagher	William	Glasgow Terrace	17	144
Gallagher	Matthew	Gordon Terrace	5	144
Gallagher	Mrs	Governor Road	22	144
Gallagher	Dominick	Hamilton Street	19	145
Gallagher	Thomas	Howard Place	6	147
Gallagher	William	Ivy Terrace	23	147
Gallagher	William	Laburnum Terrace	10	148
Gallagher	Edward	St. Columb's Terrace	99	148
Gallagher	William	Foster's Terrace	183	148
Gallagher	Hugh	Meave's Row	191	149
Gallagher	James	Lecky Road	257	149
Gallagher	Josephine	Ann Street	1	149
Gallagher	Daniel	Lecky Road	64	149
Gallagher	John	Bluebellhill Terrace	134	149
Gallagher	Hugh	Lundy's Lane	3	150
Gallagher	Winifred	Long Tower	76	150
Gallagher	Patrick	Stewart's Close	2	151
Gallagher	Mrs	Miller Street	10	152
Gallagher	Miss	Friel's Terrace	6	153
Gallagher	James	Friel's Terrace	9	153
Gallagher	William	Nassau Street Lower	16	153
Gallagher	James	Nelson Street	56	154
Gallagher	William	Orchard Row	31	155
Gallagher	Hugh	Pennyburn		156
Gallagher	T.	Queen's Quay		157
Gallagher	Daniel	Quarry Street	15	157
Gallagher	Joseph	Quarry Street	10	157
Gallagher	James	Rossville Street	19	158
Gallagher	Bridget	Rossville Street	61	158
Gallagher	William	Sackville Street	9	158
Gallagher	John	Sloan's Terrace	15	159
Gallagher	James	Sloan's Terrace	38	159
Gallagher	James & Sons	Strand Road		161
Gallagher	Patrick	St. Columb's Wells	77	162
Gallagher	Edward	St. Columb's Wells	76	162
Gallagher	Dominick	St. Columb's Wells	80	162
Gallagher	Mrs	St. Columb's Wells	104, 106	162

Surname	First Name	Street	House Number	Page Number
Gallagher	James	Thomas Street	2	162
Gallagher	Daniel	Union Street	15	163
Gallagher	William J.	Wellington Street	28	164
Gallagher	John E.	West-End Park	20	165
Gallagher	Joseph	William Street	66	166
Gallagher	Edward	Artisan Street	3	166
Gallagher	Joseph	Creggan Road	103	166
Gallagher	George	Donegal Street	21	167
Gallagher	Mrs	Epworth Street	19	167
Gallagher	William	Lewis Street	17	167
Gallagher	Mrs	North Street	21	168
Gallagher	James	North Street	31	168
Gallagher	Charles	Cottage Row	14	168
Gallagher	Mrs	Park Villas	1	168
Gallagher	Alex	Bentley Street	9	169
Gallagher	William	Bond's Place	11	170
Gallagher	William	Florence Street	17	173
Gallagher	Isabel	Fountain Hill	40	174
Gallagher	Mrs	Fountain Hill	102	174
Gallagher	Elizabeth	Fountain Hill	114	174
Gallagher	John	Fountain Hill	118	174
Gallagher	Mrs	Herbert Street	13	174
Gallagher	William	Herbert Street	17	174
Gallana	James	Castle Gate		133
Gallen	Miss	Butcher Street	15	132
Gallick	Robert	Collon Terrace		135
Gallinagh	Bridget	Waterloo Street	26	164
Gallivan	Daniel	Barrack Street		128
Gallivan	Daniel	Bishop Street	107	129
Gallivan	Daniel	Glendermott Road	11	174
Gallon	Elizabeth	Marlborough Terrace	10	152
Galloway	George P.	Marlborough Terrace	19	152
Galway	Miss	St. Columb's Court	6	161
Gamble	Mary	Abbey Street	51	125
Gamble	John	Ann Street	3	126
Gamble	Samuel T.	Chamberlain Street	34	134
Gamble	Wilson	College Terrace	6	135
Gamble	Robert	Collon Terrace		135
Gamble	Andrew	Frederick Street	6	143
Gamble	John	Hamilton Street	12	145
Gamble	Sarah	Thomas Street	35	162
Gamble	Miss	Westland Avenue	25	165
Gamble	Thomas	Ebrington Street Lower	1	173
Gamble	Mrs	Limavady Road		175
Gardiner	William	Glasgow Terrace	31	144
Gardiner	Thomas	Barnewall Place	11	169
Gardner	Charles	McLaughlin's Close	5	140
Garland	Mrs	Dungiven Road	55	172
Garmany	Robert	Charlotte Crescent		160

Surname	First Name	Street	House Number	Page Number
Garmany	William	William Street	59	165
Garrow	Mrs	Florence Street	19	173
Garvan	Henry	Charlotte Crescent		160
Gash	Richard	Beechwood Avenue	65	128
Gash	R. M.	Shipquay Street		158
Gasser	Joseph	Bennett Street Upper	21	129
Gault	Nathaniel	Melrose Terrace	8	175
Gavigan	Thomas	Ferguson Street	51	140
Gavigan	Hugh	King Street	22	175
Gavin	Patrick	Riverview Terrace	2	176
Gay	George	Butcher Street	3	132
Gedye	Samuel	Clooney Terrace	52	171
Genner	Frank	Bond's Hill	4	169
Geoghan	Henry V	Beechwood Park	81	128
Gibbons	Thomas	Baronet Street	3	128
Gibbons	Mrs	Bishop Street	51	129
Gibbons	Martha	Fahan Street	156	139
Gibbons	James	Fountain Street	108	141
Gibbons	John	Laburnum Terrace	14	148
Gibbons	Charles	Marlborough Avenue	20	152
Gibbons	Samuel	Chapel Road	23	170
Gibbons	Hugh	King Street	32	175
Gibson	Mrs	Custom House Street		136
Gibson	William	Edenmore Street	19	138
Gibson	John	Fahan Street	1	139
Gibson	William James	Orchard Lane	2	155
Gibson	T.	Rossville Street	2	158
Gibson	Mrs	Shipquay Place		159
Gibson	Miss	Union Street	19	163
Gibson	Daniel	Emerson Street	29	173
Gibson	William	Emerson Street	18	173
Giff	George	Rosemount Terrace	6	168
Giffen	Miss	Diamond		137
Gilbey	W. & A.	Shipquay Street		159
Gilchrist	Thomas J	Woodleigh Terrace	4	127
Gilchrist	Joseph	Dark Lane	3	136
Gilchrist	Thomas J.	Shipquay Place		159
Gildea	Edward	Sunbeam Terrace	19	130
Gildea	Edward	John Street	15, 17	147
Gildea	Edward	John Street	21	147
Gildea	Patrick	Bluebellhill Terrace	130	149
Gilfillan	James	Aubrey Street	28	128
Gilfillan	Mrs	Collon Terrace	16	135
Gilfillan	Miss	Foyle View	9	143
Gilfillan	W. J.	Rossville Street	4	158
Gilfillan	J. A.	Bond's Hill	20	169
Gilfillan	Mrs	Melrose Terrace	15	175
Gill	John	Linenhall Street	33	149
Gill	Edward	Violet Street Lower	25	178
Gillan	William	Bridge Street	53	132

Surname	First Name	Street	House Number	Page Number
Gillen	Michael	Abbey Street	34	125
Gillen	Hugh	Caroline Place	19	133
Gillen	Edward	Ferguson Street	54	140
Gillen	John	Harvey Street	12	146
Gillen	James	William Street	21	165
Gillen	Thomas	Dungiven Road	59	173
Gillen	Mrs	Primrose Street	14	176
Gillespie	James	Academy Terrace	6	126
Gillespie	Patrick	Bishop Street	188	131
Gillespie	Hugh	Blucher Street	15	131
Gillespie	Hugh	Bridge Street	14	132
Gillespie	Edward	Deanery Street	32	136
Gillespie	Daniel	Elmwood Terrace	45	138
Gillespie	Robert	Fairman Place	12	140
Gillespie	Miss	Ferryquay Street		140
Gillespie	Mrs	Fountain Place	12	141
Gillespie	William	Mitchelburne Terrace	96	142
Gillespie	William	Fox's Lane	6	143
Gillespie	Daniel	Glenbrook Terrace	1	143
Gillespie	James	Long Tower	16	150
Gillespie	James	Marlborough Terrace	21	152
Gillespie	John	Orchard Row	27	155
Gillespie	Daniel	Philips Street	15	156
Gillespie	Daniel	Richmond Street	17	158
Gillespie	James	Foyleview Terrace	15	161
Gillespie	Miss	Westland Avenue	7	164
Gillespie	Thomas	Ashfield Terrace	47	166
Gillespie	Daniel	Rosemount Avenue	1	168
Gillespie	Thomas	Fountain Hill	33	173
Gillian	Michael	Cuthbert Street	17	171
Gillies	J. B.	Clarendon Street	23	134
Gillies	Mrs	Crawford Square	10	135
Gilliland	John	Argyle Terrace	33	127
Gilliland	R. K.	Culmore Road	Ardcaen	136
Gilliland	Mrs	Culmore Road	Brookhall	136
Gilliland	Alex	Grove Place	5	145
Gilliland	S. & Sons	Queen's Quay		157
Gilliland	S. & Sons Ltd	Strand Road		161
Gilliland	Frank	Rock Villas	1	161
Gilliland	Mrs	Cuthbert Street	27	171
Gilliland	Miss	Limavady Road	Friarsfield	175
Gilliland	E. Catherine	Limavady Road	Eshcol	175
Gilmour	James	Aubrey Street	20	128
Gilmour	Mrs	Clarendon Street	3	134
Gilmour	Bryce	Hawkin Street	18	146
Gilmour	Mary	Hogg's Folly	11	146
Gilmour	Samuel	Mary Street	22	152
Gilmour	Miss	Spencer Road	124	177
Given	Thomas	Long Tower	30	150
Given	Alex	Nelson Street	27	153

Surname	First Name	Street	House Number	Page Number
Givins	William T.	Marlborough Street	20	151
Glacken	John	Wesley Street	16	168
Glackin	Edward	Carrigans Lane	21	133
Glass	James	Carlisle Road	65	133
Glass	Robert P	Edenballymore		137
Glass	Joseph	Alma Terrace	40	142
Glass	Miss	Nicholson Square	20	154
Glass	D.	Orchard Street		155
Glass	Hannah	Waterloo Street	63	164
Glass	William	King Street	38	175
Glass	David	Spencer Road	129	177
Glendinning	James	Clarendon Street	14	134
Glendinning	J. C.	Crawford Square	11	135
Glendinning	James	Ewing Street	22	139
Glendinning	James	Waterloo Place		164
Glenn	Richard	Albert Place	18	126
Glenn	Robert	Fountain Street	57	140
Glenn	John	Glasgow Terrace	37	144
Glenn	Cassie	Howard Street	20	147
Glenn	John	Lecky Road	119	148
Glenn	Charles	Lecky Road	137	148
Glenn	John	St. Joseph's Avenue	3	162
Glenn	Patrick	Union Street	16	163
Glenn	Mrs	Windsor Terrace	5	166
Glenn	William	Creggan Road	22	167
Glenn	Mrs	Bond's Street	17	169
Glenn	Thomas	Dungiven Road	35	172
Glenn	William	Dungiven Road	43	172
Glenn	John	Emerson Street	19	173
Glenn	Henry	Fountain Hill	84	174
Glenn	David	Herbert Street	12	174
Glenn	Joseph A.	Violet Street Lower	1	178
Glenn	Mrs	Lower Road		151
Glenn & Hay		Linenhall Street	19	149
Glenn & Hay		Richmond Street		158
Glenn & McClafferty		Waterloo Street	8	164
Glover	Arthur	Bridge Street	52	132
Godfrey	Edward	Windmill Terrace	33	166
Godfrey	Mrs	Clooney Terrace	50	171
Godfrey	Alex	Emerson Street	20	173
Golden	W. J.	Chamberlain Street	28	134
Goligher	Mrs	Clarendon Street	20	134
Goligher	James	London Street	14	150
Goligher	J. H.	Templemore Park		162
Goligher	A. T.	Ebrington Terrace	8	173
Goodman	Wesley	Collon Terrace	6	135
Goodman	Alban	Collon Terrace	19	135
Gordon	William	Alexandra Place	20	126
Gordon	Ephraim	Sunbeam Terrace	12	130

Surname	First Name	Street	House Number	Page Number
Gordon	Thomas R.	Diamond		137
Gordon	Thomas	Friel's Terrace	8	153
Gordon	E.	New Market Street	7, 8	154
Gordon	C. W.	Alexandra Terrace	1	154
Gordon	R. D.	St. Joseph's Avenue	2	162
Gordon	Joe	Bond's Street	38	170
Gordon	James	Cedar Street	11	133
Gordon & Co.		Carlisle Road	6	133
Gorman	James	Brandywell Road	18	131
Gorman	Thomas	Fahan Street	32	139
Gorman	Thomas	Fahan Street	38	139
Gorman	Rachel	John Street		147
Gorman	William	Barnewall Place	12	169
Gorman	Mrs	King Street	30	175
Gorman	Sam	Margaret Street	13	175
Gormley	John	Carrigans Lane	1	133
Gormley	Miss	Harvey Street	15	146
Gormley	James	Park Avenue	16	156
Gormley	John	Carlin Street	4	170
Gormley	Edward	Strabane Old Road	18, 20	178
Goss	John	London Street	22	150
Goss	Patrick	William Street	115	165
Goss	Herbert	Cochrane's Row	2	172
Goulding	David	Foyle Street		141
Goulding	James	St. Columb's Wells	82	162
Goulding	William	Westland Terrace	13	165
Gourlay	William	Glendermott Road	24	174
Gourley	John	Irish Street	4	174
Gourley	Alex	Meehan's Row	11	176
Graham	Samuel	Albert Place	13	126
Graham	John	Aubrey Street	11	128
Graham	T. D.	Butcher Street	6	132
Graham	Mrs	Alexander Cottages	6	133
Graham	Alex	Claremont Street		134
Graham	Mrs	Clarence Place		134
Graham	Bernard	Corbett Street	10	135
Graham	Daniel	Fahan Street	14	139
Graham	Sarah	Foyle View	2	143
Graham	Mrs	Kennedy Place	6	147
Graham	David	Little James Street	3	150
Graham	Miss	Claremount Villas	Claremont	154
Graham	Francis	Philips Street	40	156
Graham	Alexander	Strand Road	41	160
Graham	Peter	Walker's Place	36	163
Graham	Thomas	Clooney Terrace	27	170
Graham	George	Clooney Terrace	26	171
Graham	Robert	Dungiven Road	53	172
Graham	David	Fountain Hill	86	174
Graham	William	Spencer Road	94	177
Graham	John	Spencer Road	120	177

Surname	First Name	Street	House Number	Page Number
Granado	Mrs	Ebrington Terrace	11	173
Gransden	Robert	Sunbeam Terrace	3	130
Gransden	S. H.	St. Columb's Court	2	161
Grant	James A.	Clarence Avenue	5	134
Grant	Edward	Foyle Street	105	141
Grant	Col. Pharic, T.D.	Spring Grove		143
Grant	Con	Meave's Row	187	149
Grant	Mrs	Victoria Place	3	163
Grant	A. B. & Sons	Park Villas		168
Grant	James A.	Foyle Street	50	142
Grant	John	Sunbeam Terrace	15	130
Grant	William & Co.	Bishop Street	104	130
Grant	William	Bishop Street	108	130
Grant	Patrick	Bishop Street	142	131
Grant Brothers		Barrack Street		128
Gray	Adam	Sunbeam Terrace	7	130
Gray	Joseph	Edenballymore		137
Gray	Robert	Glenbrook Terrace	3	143
Gray	Robert	Alexandra Terrace	3	154
Gray	Robert	Lewis Street	6	167
Gray	Fanny	Benvarden Avenue	27	169
Gray	John	Benvarden Avenue	33	169
Greaves	Thomas	Spencer Road	32	177
Green	Patrick	Blucher Street	21	131
Green	Bridget	Carrigans Lane	9	133
Green	Thomas	Fahan Street	48	139
Green	James	Fahan Street	118	139
Green	John	Fahan Street	122	139
Green	Dan	St. Columb's Terrace	83	148
Green	Patrick	St. Columb's Wells	59	161
Green	George	Walker's Place	47	163
Green	Peter	Fahan Street	32	139
Greenway	Henry	Edenmore Street	4	138
Greer	Stewart	Woodleigh Terrace	1	127
Greer	Thomas	Carlisle Road	38	133
Greer	William	Cedar Street	7	133
Greer	Mrs	Fahan Street	28	139
Greer	Alex	Henry Street	12	146
Greer	Rev. J. C.	Edenbank		154
Greer	Thomas	Shipquay Street	8	159
Greer	Sergeant A.	Florence Street	7	173
Greer	Mrs M.	Limavady Road	gate lodge	175
Greer	Robert	Fountain Street	11	140
Gregory	Frederick	Sunbeam Terrace	16	130
Gregson	R. H.	Rock Buildings		160
Greives	Miss	Foyle Road	30	142
Grieve	William	Bishop Street	93	129
Grieve	Henry	Clifton Street	8	170
Griffeths	Miss	Primrose Street	27	176

Surname	First Name	Street	House Number	Page Number
Griffin	A. J.	Fountain Street	37	140
Griffin	Peter	Gallagher's Square	9	143
Griffin	Miss	Great James Street	75	145
Griffin	Peter	William Street	117	165
Griffith	Mrs	Donegal Place	1	137
Griffith	John	Chapel Road	42	170
Griffiths	James	Beechwood Avenue	5	128
Griffs	Henry H.	Clooney Terrace	57	171
Grimes	William B.	Benvarden Avenue	23	169
Grimshaw	Sergeant J J	Bishop Street	127	130
Grumley	Thomas	Elmwood Terrace	39	138
Gurney	Hugh	Charlotte Street	18	134
Gurney	Hugh	Nassau Street Upper	13	153
Gurney	Isaac	Park Avenue	9	156
Gurney	John	Creggan Road	143	166
Gurney	Hugh	Creggan Road		167
Gurney	Hugh	Lewis Street	1	167
Gurney	William	Lewis Street	3	167
Gurney	Mrs	Cottage Row	18	168
Gurney	James	Cottage Row	20	168
Guthrie	Thomas	Duncreggan Road	Meadowbank	137
Guthrie	William	Alma Terrace	42	142
Guthrie	Edward	Lecky Road	129	148
Guthrie	Bridget	Long Tower	36	150
Guy	Andrew	Aubrey Street	19	128
Hagan	Mrs	Edenmore Street	18	138
Hagan	Miss	Fox's Lane	1	143
Hagan	William	Glasgow Street	4	143
Hagan	Joseph	Long Tower	38	150
Hagan	Denis	Foyleview Terrace	5	160
Hagan	James	Donegal Street	9	167
Hagan	Charles	Donegal Street	16	167
Hagan	George	Florence Street	20	167
Hagan	John	Osborne Street	19	168
Hagan	Daniel	Duke Street	63	172
Haire	Samuel	Argyle Street	69	127
Haire	Edward	Edenballymore	Glen Cottages	137
Haire	Thomas	St. Mary's Terrace	35	170
Haire	Samuel	King Street	50	175
Haire	Samuel	Melrose Terrace	16	175
Halferty	Edward	Alexandra Place	26	126
Halferty	Miss	Long Tower	81	150
Hall	Miss	Asylum Road	6	127
Hall	James H	Asylum Road	7	127
Hall	J. H.	Great James Street	2, 3	144
Hamill	Robert	Bellevue Avenue	2	129
Hamill	Henry	Cottage Row	7	131
Hamill	William J.	Ferguson Street	24	140
Hamill	Trafford	Fountain Place	6	141

67

Surname	First Name	Street	House Number	Page Number
Hamill	Michael	Linenhall Street	13	149
Hamill	James	Windmill Terrace	18	166
Hamilton	Thomas	Abercorn Road	13	125
Hamilton	James	Albert Street	19	126
Hamilton	Charles	Albert Place	14	126
Hamilton	James	Alexandra Place	14	126
Hamilton	Miss	Beechwood Avenue	11	128
Hamilton	Samuel R	Bellevue Avenue	5	129
Hamilton	Mrs	Bellevue Avenue	26	129
Hamilton	James	Bennett Street Lower	51	129
Hamilton	Thomas	Bishop Street	86	130
Hamilton	James	Blee's Lane		131
Hamilton	Joseph	Charlotte Street	7	134
Hamilton	James	Charlotte Street	11	134
Hamilton	Miss	Clarence Avenue	2	134
Hamilton	S.	Culmore Road	Fairymount	136
Hamilton	Miss	Diamond		137
Hamilton	James	Fountain Street	77	140
Hamilton	James	Fountain Street	76	141
Hamilton	Miss	Fountain Street	92	141
Hamilton	Henry S. & Co	Foyle Street	24	142
Hamilton	William	Frederick Street	2	143
Hamilton	Robert E.	Great James Street	47	144
Hamilton	William	Great James Street	53	144
Hamilton	Andrew	Hawkin Street	34	146
Hamilton	David	Henry Street	16	146
Hamilton	James	John Street	6	147
Hamilton	James	Lawrence Hill		148
Hamilton	Mrs	Lawrence Hill	Fairview	148
Hamilton	Robert	Major's Row	5	151
Hamilton	William	Marlborough Avenue	28	152
Hamilton	John A.	Shipquay Street		159
Hamilton	A.	Aberfoyle Terrace	19	160
Hamilton	Thomas	Wapping Lane	41	163
Hamilton	Joseph	Wellington Street	12	164
Hamilton	William	West-End Park	4	165
Hamilton	William & Co.	William Street	43	165
Hamilton	Matthew	William Street	111	165
Hamilton	Charles	Creggan Road	75	166
Hamilton	John	Caw	Bayview House	170
Hamilton	Robert	Cuthbert Street	9	171
Hamilton	William	Fountain Hill	48	174
Hamilton	John	Fountain Hill	64	174
Hamilton	W. J.	Spencer Road		177
Hamilton	Robert	Termon Street	3	178
Hamilton	Ellen	Violet Street Upper	19	179
Hampsey	Bernard	Bluebellhill Terrace	140	149
Hampsey	William	Spencer Road	67	177
Hampsey	James	Dunfield Terrace	29	172

Surname	First Name	Street	House Number	Page Number
Hampsey & Co.		Duke Street	8	172
Hampton	John	Fountain Street	75	140
Hand	John	Horace Street		146
Handcock	Mrs	Benvarden Avenue	26	169
Hanlon	Mrs	The Rock	37	160
Hanna	Constable D	Argyle Street	30	127
Hanna	John	Edenballymore	Glen Cottages	137
Hanna	Lewis	Ferguson Street	14	140
Hanna	James L.	Ivy Terrace	26	147
Hanna	Robert	Philips Street	20	156
Hanna	Miss	Emerson Street	4	173
Hanna	Miss	Spencer Road	36	177
Hannaway	William	Brandywell Road	11	131
Hannaway	James	Brandywell Road	22	131
Hannaway	Francis	Stanley's Terrace	4	150
Hannigan	William	New Row	2	160
Hannigan	Edward	Florence Street	4	167
Hannigan	William	Cochrane's Row	7	172
Hants	Mrs	High Street	2	146
Haran	Catherine	Lecky Road	128	149
Harding	John	Abbey Street	36	125
Hargan	Miss	Hamilton Street	6	145
Harkin	Mrs	Abercorn Road	39	125
Harkin	James	Argyle Street	8	127
Harkin	John	Barry Street	9	128
Harkin	James	Bishop Street	113	130
Harkin	Catherine	Bishop Street	143	130
Harkin	James A.	Castle Gate		133
Harkin	Cornelius	Fahan Street	87	139
Harkin	Mrs	Francis Street	13	143
Harkin	Patrick	Howard Street	21	147
Harkin	Patrick	Hollywell Street	9	147
Harkin	Mrs	Joseph Street	10	147
Harkin	William	Lecky Road	51	148
Harkin	Patrick	Lecky Road		148
Harkin	Miss	Lecky Road	76	149
Harkin	Joe	Nailor's Row	45	153
Harkin	Thomas	North Edward Street	9	154
Harkin	James	Northland Avenue	9	155
Harkin	F. J. & M. H.	Shipquay Street	26	159
Harkin	Patrick	Sir E. Reid's Market	4	159
Harkin	William	Sloan's Terrace	22	159
Harkin	Patrick	Stanley's Walk	6	159
Harkin	Mrs	Stanley's Walk	9	160
Harkin	John	St. Columb's Wells	97	162
Harkin	James	St. Patrick Street	5	162
Harkin	James	Thomas Street	12	162
Harkin	Hugh	Waterloo Street	45	164
Harkin	James	Waterloo Street	24	164

Surname	First Name	Street	House Number	Page Number
Harkin	Daniel	Wellington Street	26	164
Harkin	James	Donegal Street	35	167
Harkin	Bernard	Donegal Street	41	167
Harkin	Mrs	Lewis Street	30	167
Harkin	James	Cottage Row	38	168
Harkin	Michael	Farney Terrace	1	168
Harley	Robert	Barry Street	23	128
Harley	John	Grove Place	3	145
Harley	Robert	Creggan Road	89	166
Harold	Patrick	Walker's Place	31	163
Harper	Robert J	Alexandra Place	19	126
Harper	W. J.	Ferguson Street	10	140
Harper	John	Foyle Road		142
Harper	John	Great James Street	29	144
Harper	Hugh	Bond's Street	23	169
Harper	Paul	Clooney Terrace	18	171
Harper	James Ltd	Duke Street	37	172
Harran	James	Great James Street		145
Harran	Catherine	Walker's Place	49	163
Harries	Ernest G	Bishop Street	3	129
Harrigan	John	Alma Place	7	126
Harrigan	James	Beechwood Street	16	129
Harrigan	William	Bishop Street	183	130
Harrigan	John	Infirmary Road		147
Harrigan	Annie	Sloan's Terrace	21	159
Harrigan	Mrs	Sloan's Terrace	4	159
Harrigan	James	St. Patrick Street	4	162
Harrigan	Robert	Chapel Road	4	170
Harrigan	Patrick	Dungiven Road	24	173
Harrington	Herbert	Shipquay Street		158
Harrington	Michael	St. Columb's Wells	17	161
Harris	Joseph	Fountain Place	26	141
Harris	William J.	North Edward Street	10	154
Harris	William J.	Strand Road		160
Harris	John	Kerr's Terrace	25	166
Harris & Cochrane		John Street	11, 13	147
Harris & Cochrane		John Street	19	147
Harrison	David	Alexandra Place	13	126
Harrison	William	Spencer Road	26	177
Harrison	Marcus	Violet Street Upper	17	179
Harron	George	Lower Road	29	151
Harron	Mrs	Meehan's Row	13	176
Harte	Robert	Beechwood Street	26	129
Harte	William	Foyle Road	57	142
Harte	Maggie	Waterloo Street	25	163
Harte	John	Windmill Terrace	19	166
Harte	William	Mount Street	12	168
Hartin	William	George Street	7	143

Surname	First Name	Street	House Number	Page Number
Hartin	John	Henry Street	4	146
Harvey	J. G. M. & Son	Custom House Street		136
Harvey	J. W.	Great James Street		145
Harvey	John	Ivy Terrace	24	147
Harvey	F. R.	Magazine Street		151
Harvey	Daniel	Miller Street	12	152
Harvey	J. G. M.	Northland Road	Creglorne	154
Harvey	Miss	Northland Road	Hilden	155
Harvey	Mrs	Epworth Street	5	167
Haslett	Thomas	Bishop Street	214	131
Haslett	Robert	Rosemount Avenue	Fairview	168
Haslett	John	Clooney Terrace	37	170
Haslett	Ralph	Duke Street	61	172
Haslett	Mrs	Limavady Road	Elmhurst	175
Haslett	Mrs	Maple Street	2	175
Haslett Brothers		Abercorn Road		125
Hassan	Isabel	Carrigans Lane	11	133
Hassan	Miss	Deanery Street	13, 15	136
Hassan	Mrs	Union Street	22	163
Hassen	James	Bishop Street	179	130
Hassen	James	Creggan Terrace	16	135
Hassen	James	Ivy Terrace	28	147
Hassen	Henry	Bluebellhill Terrace	226	149
Hassen	Ellen	Moore Street	16	152
Hassen	Eliza	Chapel Road	21	170
Hassen	Samuel	Glendermott Road	13	174
Hasson	Thomas	Bishop Street	270	131
Hasson	Daniel	Bridge Street	55	132
Hasson	Catherine	Long Tower	53½	150
Hasson	Patrick	Moore Street	10	152
Hastings	John	Beechwood Street	22	129
Hastings	J. R. & Co. Ltd	Foyle Street	61, 63, 65	141
Hastings	Mrs	Foyle Road	62	142
Hastings	Thomas	Mitchelburne Terrace	80	142
Hastings	J. R.	Caw	Foyle view	170
Hastings	Mrs Ross	Queen Street	16	157
Haswell	Mrs	Primrose Street	12	176
Hatrick	James	Edenballymore	Creggan	137
Hatrick	Alex	Bond's Street	2	169
Haughey	Robert	Barry Street	17	128
Havlin	William	Foster's Terrace	169	148
Hawkins	Frederick	Gordon Terrace	15	144
Hawthorne	Mrs M	Abercorn Road	27	125
Hawthorne	Miss	Princes Terrace	9	156
Hawthorne	John	Windmill Terrace	2	166
Hay	Philip	Edenmore Street	13	138
Hay	Miss	Fairman Place	15	139
Hay	William	Clooney Terrace	2	170
Hay	Rev. David	Victoria Park		178

Surname	First Name	Street	House Number	Page Number
Hayden	Quartermaster W. T. A.	Melrose Terrace	13	175
Hayes	Dean	Bishop Street	Deanery	130
Hayes	Rev. W. A.	Bishop Street		130
Hayes	Thomas	Lecky Road	209	149
Hayes	Joseph	Northland Road	21	155
Hayes	W. J.	Spencer Road	68	177
Hayward	Joseph	Bond's Street	35	169
Hazlett	Alex	Nassau Street Lower	38	153
Healy	William	Barry Street	30	128
Healy	James	Lecky Road	43	148
Healy	Patrick	Wellington Street	9	164
Healy	Joseph	Pine Street	6	176
Heaney	Patrick	Governor Road	15	144
Heaney	Miss	Harding Street	35	145
Heaney	W. J.	Mountjoy Terrace	2	153
Heaney	William	Benvarden Avenue	25	169
Heaney	Denis	Benvarden Avenue	4	169
Heaney	John	Benvarden Avenue	18	169
Heaney	Miss	Clooney Terrace	11	170
Heaney	Joseph	Clooney Terrace	44	171
Heaney	E. C.	Dungiven Road	99	173
Heaney	Patrick	King Street	56	175
Heaney	Bernard	Margaret Street	11	175
Heaney	James J.	Moore Street	37	176
Heaney	Bernard	Spencer Road	23	177
Heaney	Miss	Spencer Road	44	177
Heany	Miss M.	Strand Road		160
Heatley	Samuel	Fountain Street	107	140
Heatley	George	Great James Street	28	145
Heatley	S.	Society Street		159
Hegarty	William	Adam Street	6	126
Hegarty	Charles	Brook Street Avenue	16	132
Hegarty	Mrs D. M.	Carlisle Road	71	133
Hegarty	Hugh	Corbett Street	1	135
Hegarty	Rev Laurence	Creggan Street	Parochial H	135
Hegarty	Mrs	Eglinton Place	1	138
Hegarty	Charles	Eglinton Terrace	9	138
Hegarty	Patrick	Fahan Street	150	139
Hegarty	William	Ferguson Street	52	140
Hegarty	Patrick	Foyle Street		141
Hegarty	Miss E.	Foyle Street	53	141
Hegarty	Thomas	Foyle Street	66	142
Hegarty	Thomas	Harding Street	6	145
Hegarty	Bella	Howard Street	2	147
Hegarty	Mrs	St. Columb's Terrace	81	148
Hegarty	William	Lecky Road	92	149
Hegarty	James	Lecky Road	122	149
Hegarty	Frank	Long Tower	52	150
Hegarty	Miss	Long Tower	68	150

Surname	First Name	Street	House Number	Page Number
Hegarty	Mrs	Lower Road	35	151
Hegarty	Peter	Nailor's Row	4, 5	153
Hegarty	William	Nelson Street	66	154
Hegarty	Hugh	St. Columb's Wells	31	161
Hegarty	James	St. Columb's Wells	85	162
Hegarty	John	Walker's Place	41	163
Hegarty	John	Waterloo Street	32	164
Hegarty	John	Waterloo Street	36	164
Hegarty	Patrick	Westland Avenue	3	164
Hegarty	Hugh	William Street	73½	165
Hegarty	Mrs	Artisan Street	14	166
Hegarty	John	Creggan Road	169	167
Hegarty	Hugh	Donegal Street	4	167
Hegarty	John	Cottage Row	22	168
Hegarty	William	Alfred Street	6	168
Hegarty	George	Chapel Road	52	170
Hegarty	Joseph	Ebrington Street Lower	4	173
Hegarty	John	Strabane Old Road		178
Hempton	James & Co.	Shipquay Street	13	158
Henderson	S. & Son	Chamberlain Street	5	134
Henderson	John	Clarendon Street	26	134
Henderson	Robert	Cunningham Row	2	136
Henderson	Hudson	Demesne Terrace	7	137
Henderson	James	Foyle Road	108	142
Henderson	Hugh	Foyle Road	122	142
Henderson	John	Lecky Road	33	148
Henderson	Samuel	Moat Street	2	152
Henderson	Constable W. C.	Nicholson Square	2	154
Henderson	Hugh	Claremount Villas	Cul Edan	154
Henderson	John	Sackville Street	7	158
Henderson	D.	Sackville Street	11	158
Henderson	Robert	Society Street	9	159
Henderson	Constable	Chapel Road	61	170
Henderson	Samuel	Duke Street	67	172
Henderson	Mrs	Spencer Road	91	177
Henderson	George	Strabane Old Road	49	178
Heney	Robert	Rossville Street	26	158
Henry	Mrs	Beechwood Avenue	2	128
Henry	James	Bishop Street	95	129
Henry	Robert	Carlisle Road	31A	132
Henry	Mrs	Carlisle Pass		132
Henry	Robert	Collon Terrace	4	135
Henry	Eliza	Diamond		137
Henry	Hugh	Edenmore Street	29	138
Henry	William	Kennedy Street	20	148
Henry	John	Lower Road	2	151
Henry	William	Lower Road	4	151
Henry	James	Nassau Street Upper	21	153
Henry	Robert	Quarry Street	19	157

Surname	First Name	Street	House Number	Page Number
Henry	David	Wapping Lane	23	163
Henry	Thomas	Creggan Road	Ivy Cottage	167
Henry	James	Duke Street	90	172
Henry	John J.	Moore Street	5	176
Henry	Robert	Olive Terrace	5	176
Henry & Co.		Duke Street	96	172
Hepburn	William	Shipquay Street	8	159
Herbert	James	Ferguson Street	1	140
Heron	Margaret K.	Ferguson Street	58	140
Heron	G. C.	Francis Street	63	143
Heron	Mrs	Orchard Row		155
Herr	Louis	Shipquay Street	4	159
Hetherington	Doctor	Lawrence Hill		148
Hetherington	D.	Northland Road	gate lodge	155
Hetherington	J. J.	Dungiven Road	1, 3	172
Hetherington	J. J.	Spencer Road	140	177
Hickey	Mrs	Laburnum Terrace	15	148
Higgins	Lizzie	Bishop Street	111	130
Higgins	Mrs	Fulton Place	9	143
Higgins	David	Henry Street	8	146
Higgins	Sergeant John	Marlborough Avenue	16	152
Higgins	John	Nelson Street	55	154
Higgins	Mary	Orchard Row	39	155
Higgins	James	St. Patrick Street	8	162
Higgins	Edward	Wellington Street	52	164
Higgins	Matthew J.	Westland Terrace	7	165
Higgins	James	Alfred Street	32	168
Higgins	Constable K.	Duke Street	102	172
Higgins	James	Florence Street	13	173
Hill	Constable H	Academy Terrace	7	126
Hill	Miss	Marlborough Street	22	151
Hill	Robert	Mount Street	20	168
Hill & Co.		Spencer Road	27, 29	177
Hillen	Charles	Ann Street	10	127
Hillen	Alexander	Ann Street	16	127
Hinds	Walter	Carlin Street	9	170
Hipps Ltd		Market Buildings		161
Hipwell	William	Abercorn Road	43	125
Hobson	James	Bellevue Avenue	37	129
Hogan	Laurence	Great James Street		144
Hogan	William	Howard Street	19	147
Hogan	Patrick	Stanley's Walk	44	160
Hogan	John	Spencer Road	31	177
Hogan	Laurence	Victoria Park		178
Hogg	Robert	Mitchelburne Terrace	82	142
Hogg	Mrs	Glasgow Street	6	144
Hogg	Mrs	Limavady Road	Lisowen	175
Hogg & Mitchell		Great James Street		144

Surname	First Name	Street	House Number	Page Number
Hogg & Mitchell		Little James Street		150
Hogg & Mitchell		Sackville Street	10, 12, 14	158
Holland	Mrs	Albert Street	2	126
Holland	Thomas	Kennedy Street	2	148
Hollingsworth	Almur	Dunfield Terrace	19	172
Hollingsworth	John	Spencer Road	98	177
Hollingworth	Elizabeth	Fulton Place	13	143
Holloway	William	Orchard Row	22	155
Holman	William H	Argyle Street	68	127
Holmes	William	Abercorn Road		125
Holmes	John	Bishop Street	199	130
Holmes	Robert	Charlotte Street	12	134
Holmes	Mrs	Clarendon Street	24	134
Holmes	John	Fountain Street	13	140
Holmes	David	Gordon Place	8	144
Holmes	Miss	Lone Moor		150
Holmes	Robert	Lower Road	39	151
Holmes	Samuel	Northland Terrace	10	155
Holmes	James	Windmill Terrace	17	166
Holmes	George	Cross Street	34	171
Holmes	William	Dunfield Terrace	1	172
Holmes	Hugh	King Street	17	175
Holmes, Mullin & Dunn		Magazine Street		151
Holmes, Mullin & Dunn		Princes Quay		157
Holmes, Mullin & Dunn		William Street		165
Holmes. Mullin & Dunn		Waterloo Place		164
Hone	Bridget	Nelson Street	40	154
Hone	Thomas	Cross Street	13	171
Hone	William	Riverview Terrace	12	176
Honeyford	Charles	Dungiven Road	29	172
Horgan	John	Deanery Street	20	136
Horner	Mrs Marian	Mountjoy Terrace	5	153
Horner	William	Shipquay Street	2	159
Horner	William	Chapel Road		170
Houghton	Mrs	London Street	11	150
Houlihan	John	Clarendon Street	53	134
Hourihane	J.	Custom House Street		136
Houston	Patrick	Alexandra Place	23	126
Houston	John	Alexandra Place	25	126
Houston	Robert	Barry Street	3	128
Houston	Mary	Bishop Street	163	130
Houston	William	Elmwood Street	13	138
Houston	Daniel	Elmwood Street	16	138
Houston	David	Miller Street	30	152
Houston	Joyce	Northland Avenue		155

Surname	First Name	Street	House Number	Page Number
Houston	Robert	Shipquay Street		159
Houston	John	Windmill Terrace	24	166
Houston	Elizabeth	Bond's Street	4	169
Houston	Miss	Ebrington Terrace	13	173
Houston	Charles	Fountain Hill	98	174
Houston	Mrs	Limavady Road		175
Howard	Charles	Hamilton Street	13	145
Howard	Caldwell	Barnewall Place	6	169
Howatson	Mrs	Cedar Street	1	133
Howatson	George & Co	Foyle Street		142
Howatson	George & Co.	Abercorn Quay		157
Howatt	John	Great James Street	34	145
Howes	A. J. W.	Deanfield	Beechmount	171
Huey	William	De Burgh Square	9	136
Huey	William	Foyle Road	48	142
Huey	Alex	Gordon Terrace	10	144
Huey	R. J.	Pine Street	7	176
Huey	Rev. J.	Victoria Park		178
Huffington	William	Miller Street	7	152
Hughes	Stewart	Barry Street	25	128
Hughes	Samuel	Fountain Street	17	140
Hughes	John	Fountain Street	78	141
Hughes	Catherine	Lecky Road	19	148
Hughes	Edward J.	Nicholson Square	14	154
Hughes	John & Co.	Orchard Street		155
Hughes	Edward	Orchard Street		155
Hughes	Edward	Farney Terrace	5	168
Hughes	Jack	Cochrane's Row	1	172
Hughes	Robert	Olive Terrace	2	176
Hughes	Patrick	Park Terrace	1	144
Hughes' Academy		Foyle Street		141
Hume	John	Chamberlain Street	14	134
Hume	William	Farney Terrace	3	168
Humes	John	Nassau Street Lower	20	153
Humphreys	Sarah	Mill Street	35	176
Hunter	Mrs	Albert Street	25	126
Hunter	Andrew G	Barry Street	14	128
Hunter	S	Bishop Street	Caretaker	130
Hunter	David	Edenmore Street	37	138
Hunter	Samuel	Ferguson Street	35	140
Hunter	John	Fountain Street	95	140
Hunter	Mrs	Fountain Place	31	141
Hunter	Thomas J.	Guildhall Street		145
Hunter	W. B.	Hawkin Street	40	146
Hunter	James	Miller Street	5	152
Hunter	John	Moat Street	7	152
Hunter	Hugh	Northland Avenue	7	155
Hunter	Samuel	St. Columb's Court		161
Hunter	Douglas	Victoria Street	18	163

Surname	First Name	Street	House Number	Page Number
Hunter	Charles H.	Waterloo Place		164
Hunter	John	Lewis Street	29	167
Hunter	Mrs	Ebrington Street	5	173
Hunter	Miss S.	Ebrington Terrace	7	173
Hunter	Walter	Glendermott Road	1	174
Hunter	Hugh G.	Spencer Road	128	177
Hurst	Miss	Lawrence Hill		148
Huston	W. E.	Marlborough Street	18	151
Hutchinson	William A	Beechwood Park	69	128
Hutchinson	Rev W. W.	Dacre Terrace		133
Hutchinson	John	Nassau Street Lower	54	153
Hutchinson	Mrs	Victoria Street	4	163
Hutchinson	Daniel	Wapping Lane	29	163
Hutchinson	James	Creggan Road		167
Hutchinson	Jacob	Creggan Road	Rosemount Cottage	167
Hutchinson	James	Spencer Road	73	177
Hutchinson	John	Spencer Road	75	177
Hutchison	Frank	Barrack Street	10	128
Hutchison	Thomas	Lower Road	16	151
Hutchison	James	Lower Road	24	151
Hutchison	James	Violet Street Upper	6	179
Hutchman	Alexander	Glasgow Terrace	21	144
Hutton	Michael	Abercorn Road	46	125
Hutton	Peter	Bishop Street	103	129
Hutton	Peter	Bishop Street	96	130
Hutton	John	Foyle Road	46	142
Hutton	John	Kildarra Terrace	7	146
Hutton	Mrs	Mountjoy Street	13	152
Hutton	Daniel	Nailor's Row	46	153
Hutton	Edward	Stanley's Walk	12	160
Hutton	James	Thomas Street	34	162
Hutton	Mrs	Donegal Street	39	167
Hutton	Henry	Donegal Street	2	167
Huxley & Postlethwaite		Lecky Road		149
Hyland	J. & F.	Clarendon Street Lower		135
Hyland	Fred	Shipquay Street	6	159
Hyndman	William E	Albert Place	10	126
Hyndman	Mrs	Edenballymore	Glen Cottages	137
Hyndman	Samuel	Ferryquay Street		140
Hyndman	R. J.	Fountain Place	9	141
Hyndman	William	Kennedy Street	7	148
Hyndman	Samuel	Linenhall Street		149
Hyndman	James	Moat Street	1	152
Hyndman	William	Northland Road	Carrickmore House	155
Hyndman	Caldwell	Philips Street	30	156

Surname	First Name	Street	House Number	Page Number
Hyndman	John	Duke Street	62	172
Hyndman	John	Fountain Hill	1	173
Hyndman & Smith		Bank Place		128
Hynes	Mrs	Windsor Terrace	4	166
Hynes	Mrs	Emerson Street	17	173
Irons	William M.	Northland Road		154
Irvine	D.	Waterloo Street		164
Irvine	Robert	Cross Street	31	171
Irvine	David S.	Mountroyal		155
Irvine & Co		Linenhall Street	4	149
Irvine & Co.		Ferryquay Street		140
Irvine & Co.		Ferryquay Street		140
Irwin	Patrick	Fahan Street	83	139
Irwin	Mrs	Foyle Road	60	142
Irwin	William	High Street	3	146
Irwin	Robert	Lower Road	31	151
Irwin	James	Lower Road	33	151
Irwin	John	Nelson Street	23	153
Irwin	Mrs	Rossville Street	68	158
Irwin	John	Union Street	30	163
Irwin	Robert	Duke Street	77	172
Irwin	Alexander	Fountain Hill	34	174
Irwin	Samuel	King Street	23	175
Irwin	John	Spencer Road	103	177
Jack	Miss	Clarendon Street		134
Jack	Captain William H	Eden Terrace		137
Jack	Robert	Marlborough Terrace	24	152
Jack	William	Rosemount Terrace	12	168
Jack	Samuel	Melrose Terrace	5	175
Jack	William J.	Marlborough Avenue	6	152
Jack	Mrs	Park Avenue	15	156
Jackson	Mrs	Albert Street	38	126
Jackson	Mrs	Fahan Street	9	139
Jackson	George	Fountain Street	50	141
Jackson	Mrs	Glasgow Terrace	8	144
Jackson	George	Grafton Street	12	144
Jackson	John & Son	Little James Street	8	150
Jackson	Charles	Stewart's Close	4	151
Jackson	John	Miller Street	34	152
Jackson	A.	Nicholson Terrace	9	154
Jackson	William	Orchard Row	11	155
Jackson	J. & Son	Prince Arthur Street		156
Jackson	Patrick	Sloan's Terrace	7	159
Jackson	William G.	St. Columb's Wells	52	162
Jackson	Denis	William Street	50	165
Jackson's Ltd		Ferryquay Street	20	140
Jacob	Moses	Bishop Street	244	131
James	Thomas	Great James Street	56	145

Surname	First Name	Street	House Number	Page Number
James	Elizabeth	Epworth Street	13	167
Jamieson	Miss	Abercorn Place	12	126
Jamieson	William	Bayview Terrace	6	128
Jamieson	William & Co.	Corporation Street		135
Jamieson	Mrs	Ewing Street	15	139
Jamieson	Lizzie	Lewis Street	13	167
Jamieson	Mrs	Olive Terrace	3	176
Jamieson	David	Spencer Road	83	177
Jamieson & Sons		Duke Street	29, 31	172
Jamieson & Sons		Walker's Street		179
Jefferson	Robert J.	Gordon Terrace	13	144
Jeffrey	Thomas	Abercorn Road	8	125
Jeffreys	Miss	Fountain Street	48	141
Jervis	William	Fountain Place	4	141
Jervis	Andrew	Tamneymore		178
Johnson Bros		Ferryquay Street		140
Johnston	James	Argyle Street	71	127
Johnston	James	Argyle Terrace	11	127
Johnston	Mrs	Bishop Street	206	131
Johnston	Francis	Cable Street	17	132
Johnston	J. V.	Castle Street		133
Johnston	F.	Diamond		137
Johnston	J B & Co	Edward Street		138
Johnston	J. B. & Co.	Great James Street	2	145
Johnston	Samuel G.	Great James Street	60	145
Johnston	James	Harding Street	10	145
Johnston	Michael	Linenhall Street	29	149
Johnston	Samuel	Stewart's Close	3	151
Johnston	R.	Marlborough Street	41	151
Johnston	J. V.	Marlborough Street		151
Johnston	Eliza	Nassau Street Upper	18	153
Johnston	Richard	Nelson Street	44	154
Johnston	T.	New Market Street	1	154
Johnston	T.	New Market Street	2	154
Johnston	Andrew	Northland Road	Westbank	154
Johnston	Thomas	Aberfoyle Terrace	5	160
Johnston	Patrick	St. Columb's Wells	43	161
Johnston	Fred	Westland Terrace	8	165
Johnston	Anthony	Marlborough Park	55	166
Johnston	James	Creggan Road	69	166
Johnston	Mrs	Rosemount Terrace	4	168
Johnston	Mrs	Bond's Street	47	169
Johnston	Mrs	Mill Street	30	176
Johnston	Robert	Fountain Street	112	141
Johnston H.		Ferryquay Street		140
Jolliffe	Robert A.	Grafton Street	17	144
Jones	Frederick W.	Diamond		137
Jones	William	Edenmore Street	7	138

Surname	First Name	Street	House Number	Page Number
Jones	Thomas E.	Creggan Road	161	167
Jones	John E.	Dungiven Road	81	173
Jones & Lowther		Bishop Street	109	130
Jordan	William	Great James Street	43	144
Jordan	Thomas L.	London Street	15	150
Joyce	Thomas	De Burgh Terrace	10	137
Judd	David	Wesley Street	3	168
Kane	Joseph	Barry Street	4	128
Kane	John	Bishop Street	211	130
Kane	Mrs	Ferguson Street	44	140
Kane	James	Glasgow Street	5	144
Kane	John	Glasgow Terrace	32	144
Kane	Henry	Hamilton Street	2	145
Kane	John	Gresham's Row	1	145
Kane	John	Magazine Street		151
Kane	George	Stanley's Walk	34	160
Kane	Morgan	The Rock	33	160
Kane	Mary J.	Wellington Street	56	164
Kane	George	Chapel Road	16	170
Kane	Patrick	Dungiven Road	109	173
Kane	Charles	King Street	12	175
Kane	Hugh	Primrose Street	5	176
Kane	Michael	Violet Street Lower	38	178
Kavanagh	James	New Street	11	133
Kavanagh	James	Fox's Lane	3	143
Kavanagh	Edward	Lecky Road	90	149
Kavanagh	Mrs	Pennyburn		156
Kealey	Mrs	Glendermott Road	9	174
Kearney	Maggie	Bishop Street	63	129
Kearney	Patrick	Chamberlain Street	9	134
Kearney	Mrs	Deanery Street	38	136
Kearney	John	Philips Street	23	156
Kearney	Mrs	Thomas Street	32	162
Kearney	Hugh	Creggan Road	181	167
Kearns	Thomas	Fahan Street	129	139
Kearns	Mrs	Artisan Street	13	166
Keely	Michael	Chapel Road	56	170
Keen	S & Co.	Pump Street	3	156
Keenan	James	St. Columb's Street	8	161
Keenan	Daniel	St. Columb's Wells	44	162
Keenan	Lance-Corporal	Emerson Street	28	173
Keeney	Mrs	Edenballymore	Glen Cottages	137
Kellett	James F.	Princes Terrace	1	156
Kellock	Mrs	Lorne Terrace	45	125
Kellock	Edwin D.	Marlborough Avenue	12	152
Kelly	Joseph	Albert Place	2	126
Kelly	Thomas	Argyle Street	9	127
Kelly	Robert	Argyle Street	35	127

Surname	First Name	Street	House Number	Page Number
Kelly	Michael	Argyle Street	2	127
Kelly	Edward	Argyle Terrace	7	127
Kelly	Ernest	Aubrey Street	17	128
Kelly	Miss	Beechwood Avenue	17	128
Kelly	Joseph	Bennett Street Upper	17	129
Kelly	Robert	Brook Street Avenue	20	132
Kelly	Philip	Carlisle Road	19	132
Kelly	Patrick	New Street	5	133
Kelly	Hugh	New Street	13	133
Kelly	James	Creggan Street	1	135
Kelly	Michael	Creggan Terrace	18	135
Kelly	Miss	Custom House Street		136
Kelly	Daniel	Eglinton Place	9	138
Kelly	Charles	Eglinton Place	13	138
Kelly	Margaret	Eglinton Place	10	138
Kelly	Francis	Fahan Street	25	139
Kelly	James	Fahan Street	112	139
Kelly	John	Foyle Alley	2	141
Kelly	Daniel	Foyle Road	107	142
Kelly	Alex	Governor Road	35	144
Kelly	Robert	Governor Road	2B	144
Kelly	Mrs	Great James Street	54	145
Kelly	Miss	Guildhall Street		145
Kelly	Hugh	Henrietta Street	9	146
Kelly	Edward	Laburnum Terrace	13	148
Kelly	P. J.	Marlborough Street	11	151
Kelly	Thomas	Miller Street	32	152
Kelly	James	Moore Street	2	152
Kelly	Robert	Mountjoy Street	18	153
Kelly	William	Nailor's Row	31	153
Kelly	William	North Edward Street	2	154
Kelly	James	Rossville Street	29	158
Kelly	Edward	Rossville Street	30	158
Kelly	Thomas	Shipquay Street	8	159
Kelly	James	Stanley's Walk	19	160
Kelly	James	St. Columb's Wells	67	161
Kelly	James	St. Columb's Wells	130	162
Kelly	James	Thomas Street	33	162
Kelly	Patrick	Thomas Street	22	162
Kelly	J.	Water Street		164
Kelly	William	Wellington Street	31	164
Kelly	James J.	West-End Park	14	165
Kelly	Mrs	West-End Terrace	9	165
Kelly	Mrs	William Street	53	165
Kelly	Henry	William Street	56	165
Kelly	Mrs	Creggan Road	163	167
Kelly	Edward	Lewis Street	32	167
Kelly	Daniel	Benvarden Avenue	7	169
Kelly	Rev. P.	Chapel Road	Parochial House	170

Surname	First Name	Street	House Number	Page Number
Kelly	William	Chapel Road	60	170
Kelly	Mrs	Deanfield		171
Kelly	Mrs	Derry View Terrace	4	171
Kelly	Mrs	Duddy's Row	5	172
Kelly	Hugh M.	Duke Street	99	172
Kelly	Mrs	Ebrington Street	9	173
Kelly	James	Fountain Hill	67	174
Kelly	Denis	Irish Street	8	174
Kelly	John	King Street	35	175
Kelly	Patrick	Spencer Road	25	177
Kelly	Margaret	Strabane Old Road	13	177
Kelly	James	Strabane Old Road	80	178
Kelly	Mrs	Strabane Old Road	96	178
Kelly	Hugh	Strabane Old Road	98	178
Kelly	Miss	Violet Street Lower	45	178
Kelpey	Mrs	Ferguson Street	42	140
Kelpie	Joseph	Carrigans Lane	27	133
Kendall	Thomas	Clarence Avenue	9	134
Kendell	Thomas	Custom House Street		136
Kendell	Thomas	Queen's Quay		157
Kenendy	James	Simpson's Brae	11	177
Kenna	Mrs	Nicholson Square	24	154
Kennedy	Caldwell	Abercorn Road	57	125
Kennedy	James	Alexandra Place	8	126
Kennedy	Francis	Ann Street	8	127
Kennedy	William J	Argyle Street	18	127
Kennedy	Robert	Bennett Street Lower	45	129
Kennedy	Hugh	Bridge Street	42	132
Kennedy	James	Bridge Street	44	132
Kennedy	Sergeant S	Edenballymore	Glen Cottages	137
Kennedy	John	Fahan Street	136	139
Kennedy	Andrew D.	Foyle Street	39	141
Kennedy	James	Governor Road	26	144
Kennedy	S. M. & Co	Great James Street	4	145
Kennedy	Marshall	Great James Street	22	145
Kennedy	Mrs Isabel	Kennedy Place	9	147
Kennedy	S. M. & Co.	Magazine Street	16	151
Kennedy	Miss	Marlborough Street	34	151
Kennedy	Miss M.	Sloan's Terrace	20	159
Kennedy	Joseph	Thomas Street	26	162
Kennedy	Sergeant S.	Creggan Road	155	166
Kennedy	Joseph	Epworth Street	9	167
Kennedy	Mrs	Ashcroft Place	7	169
Kennedy	Robert	Benvarden Avenue	45	169
Kennedy	David	Duke Street	7	172
Kennedy	Matthew	Henry Street	24	146
Kennedy-Skipton	H. S.	Limavady Road		175
Kenney	John	Thomas Street	10	162

Surname	First Name	Street	House Number	Page Number
Kenny	Constable M.	Ferguson Street	5	140
Kent	Richard	John Street		147
Keogh	William	Abbey Street	53	125
Keogh	Andrew	Linenhall Street		149
Keown	D. R.	Rock Villas	3	161
Keown	M. & Co.	William Street	38	165
Kerlin	Patrick	Rossville Street	23	158
Kerlin	Rev. C. H.	Victoria Place	Parochial House	163
Kernaghan	Joseph	Aberfoyle Terrace	15	160
Kerr	Matthew	Abercorn Road	37	125
Kerr	Matthew	Abercorn Road	48	125
Kerr	Robert	Argyle Street	48	127
Kerr	Miss	Carlisle Road	51	132
Kerr	Robert	Eglinton Terrace	13	138
Kerr	John	Kennedy Street	8	148
Kerr	Miss	Miller Street	1	152
Kerr	Mrs	Nassau Street Upper	11	153
Kerr	Robert	Northland Avenue	15	155
Kerr	Mrs	Waterloo Place		164
Kerr	Mrs	William Street	36	165
Kerr	John	North Street	19	168
Kerr	James N.	Emerson Street	15	173
Kerr	Andrew	Mitchelburne Terrace	83	142
Kerr	Miss	Great James Street	48	145
Kerr & Co		Foyle Street		141
Kerr, Lang & Jackson		Great James Street		145
Kerr, Lang & Jackson Ltd		Strand Road	31	160
Kerr, Ramsay & Simpson		Strand Road		160
Kerrigan	John	Bluebellhill Terrace	220	149
Kerrigan	Mrs	Bond's Hill	9	169
Kerrigan	Edward	Spencer Road	112	177
Kerrigan	Michael	Violet Street Lower	57	178
Kewell	Mrs	Pine Street	25	176
Keys	James	Bishop Street	266	131
Keys	James	Caroline Place	7	133
Keys	Robert Fleming	Clarendon Street	71	134
Keys	Thomas	Fahan Street	99	139
Keys	R. & Co.	Queen's Quay		157
Keys	R. & Co.	Strand Road		161
Keys	R. & Co.	Strand Road		161
Keys	Robert & Co.	Waterloo Place		164
Keys	James	Lewis Street	15	167
Keys	Miss	Lewis Street	18	167
Keys	William	Bond's Street	19	169
Keys	Alex	Dervock Place	1	171
Keys	Robert	Fountain Hill	104	174

Surname	First Name	Street	House Number	Page Number
Keys	John	Spencer Road	136	177
Keys	Joseph	Strabane Old Road	15	177
Keys	David	York Street	20	179
Kidd	Mrs	Bennett Street Lower	53	129
Kidd	James	Dunfield Terrace	33	172
Kilby	George	Wapping Lane	51	163
Kildea	Thomas	Blee's Lane		131
Kildea	Patrick	Blee's Lane		131
Kildea	James	Hamilton Street	5	145
Kildea	Patrick	Westland Terrace	3	165
Kilfillan	William J.	Rosemount Terrace	11	168
Kilgore	William	Argyle Street	54	127
Kilgore	James E	Bennett Street Lower	35	129
Kilgore	Richard	Ferguson Street	50	140
Kilgore	Mrs	Hogg's Folly	3	146
Kilgore	Samuel	Mary Street	18	152
Kilgore	Mrs	Barnewall Place	2	169
Kilgore	John	Bentley Street	7	169
KIlgore	William	Bond's Street	34	170
Kilgore	Alex	Cochrane's Row	6	172
Kilgore	Mrs	Primrose Street	7	176
Kilgore	Joseph	Primrose Street	2	176
Kilkey	George	Brandywell Road	5	131
Kilkie	James	Violet Street Lower	13	178
Killen	James	Bennett Street Upper	23	129
Killen	Dr. J. W.	Mountroyal		155
Kilpatrick	Robert	Argyle Street	42	127
Kilpatrick	Robert	Edenballymore	Creggan	137
Kilpatrick	Joseph	King Street	29	175
Kimmitt	E.	Shipquay Street		159
Kincade	James	Fountain Street	72	141
Kincade	George	Strand Road		161
Kincaid	Mrs	Fairman Place	21	139
Kincaid	William	Grafton Street	10	144
Kincaid	John	Grafton Terrace	3	144
Kincaid	Andrew	Grove Place	9	145
Kincaid	John	Harding Street	14	145
Kincaid	John	Nicholson Square	16	154
Kincaid	John	Rosemount Avenue	2	168
King	R. A.	Bishop Street	186	131
King	Patrick	Nelson Street	17	153
King	John	Society Street	13	159
King	William	York Street	2	179
Kinnear	Robert	Strand Road		160
Kinnear	Robert	Rosemount Terrace	5	168
Kinnear	James	Duke Street	104	172
Kinnear	Joseph	Spencer Road	72	177
Kinsella	Michael	Lecky Road	59	148
Kirby	Miss	Abercorn Road	35	125
Kirby	Luke	Duncreggan Road	Meadowbank	137

Surname	First Name	Street	House Number	Page Number
Kirby	Mrs	Marlborough Street	17	151
Kirke	Samuel A.	Fountain Street	105	140
Kirke	Mrs A.	Nicholson Square	9	154
Kirkland	George	Marlborough Avenue	1	151
Kitchen	Michael	St. Columb's Wells	50	162
Kitson	Mrs	Barry Street	19	128
Kitson	Robert J.	Ashcroft Place	1	169
Knox	S D	Academy Road	1	126
Knox	William	Argyle Street	62	127
Knox	Rev W F	Sunbeam Terrace	9	130
Knox	J M C	East Wall	2	137
Knox	James	Gordon Place	3	144
Knox	Thomas	Harding Street	1	145
Knox	E. C. H.	Templemore Park		162
Knox	Hugh	Clarence Avenue	3	134
Knox, Gilliland & Babington		Castle Street		133
Kydd	Ernest	Edenmore Street	5	138
Kyle	William	Woodleigh Terrace	5	127
Kyle	Mrs	Governor Road	13	144
Kyle	Ellen	Joseph Street	2	147
Kyle	Miss	Lawrence Hill		148
Kyle	Robert	New Row		160
Kyle	James	Dungiven Road	34	173
Kyle	Bella	Spencer Road	89	177
Kyle	William	Spencer Road	58	177
Kyle	James	Violet Street Upper	1	179
Kyle	William	Nassau Street Upper		153
Kyle	Miss	Northland Road	St. Lurach College	155
Kyle	Mrs	Philips Street	1	156
Ladley	William	Meadowbank Avenue	23	152
Lafferty	Daniel	Bishop Street	240	131
Lafferty	Miss A.	Bridge Street	7	131
Lafferty	Mrs	Eglinton Place	2	138
Lafferty	John	Pitt Street	6	156
Lafferty	John	Rossville Street	37	158
Lafferty	Daniel	St. Columb's Wells	58	162
Lafferty	Mrs	Clooney Terrace	8½	171
Laird	John	Little James Street	12	150
Laird	James	Nicholson Square	6	154
Laird	Robert	Creggan Road	66	167
Laird	James	Lewis Street	23	167
Laird	S.S. Co.	Princes Quay		157
Lamb	George	Bayview Terrace	3	127
Lamb	J. & Co.	Spencer Road	119	177
Lamberton	Robert	Nelson Street	51	154
Lamberton	James	Park Avenue	11	156
Lamberton	Charles	Osborne Street	22	168
Lambie	William	Barry Street	10	128

Surname	First Name	Street	House Number	Page Number
Landreth	Joseph	Governor Road	20	144
Lane	Henry & Co.	Princes Quay		157
Lane	H & Co.	Cochrane's Row		172
Lang	Mrs	Clooney Terrace	41	170
Langan	Mrs	Waterloo Street	37	164
Langham	Patrick	Donegal Street	31	167
Lappin	John	Alfred Street	19	168
Lapsley	John	Aubrey Street	3	128
Lapsley	William	Aubrey Street	13	128
Lapsley	David	Mountjoy Street	17	152
Large	George	Orchard Row	5	155
Larkey	Constable Michael	College Terrace	13	135
Larkey	Mrs	Long Tower	75	150
Larkin M. & M.		Richmond Street		158
Larmor	Professor A.	College Avenue		155
Larmour	John	Nailor's Row	1, 2	153
Larmour	James	Nailor's Row	3	153
Laughlin	John	Bellevue Avenue	7	129
Laughlin	James	Moore Street	13	176
Laverty	Patrick	Bishop Street	209	130
Laverty	Margaret	Church Wall	3	134
Laverty	George	Lecky Road	111	148
Laverty	George	Mary Street	6	152
Lavery	Joseph	Philips Street	3	156
Lawrence	Mrs	Orchard Row	21	155
Lawry & Porter		Bishop Street	109	129
Leach	William	Herbert Street	11	174
Leavy	Mrs	Epworth Street	27	167
Lecky	Henry	Culmore Road	The Farm	136
Lecky	James & Co.	William Street	26, 28	165
Lee	Joseph	Abercorn Road	28	125
Lee	John	Argyle Street	7	127
Lee	Robert	William Street	81	165
Leebody	Professor J. R.	College Avenue		155
Leeke	George	Great James Street		145
Leeke	Robert	Ebrington Street	21	173
Leeke	Joseph	Olive Terrace	4	176
Leeper	John	Foyle Road	36	142
Leinster	John	Sunnyside House		131
Leinster Brothers		Bellevue Avenue		129
Lemon	Samuel	Beechwood Park	67	128
Lemon	Joseph	Ferryquay Street		140
Lennon	Mrs	Abercorn Road	29	125
Leonard	Arthur	Foyle Road	68	142
Leonard	John	Marlborough Street	15	151
Leonard	Margaret	Nelson Street	32	154
Leonard	Constable T.	Park Avenue	13	156
Leslie	James	Dark Lane	18	136

Surname	First Name	Street	House Number	Page Number
Leslie	John	Clooney Terrace	34	170
Leslie	Mrs	Moore Street	14	176
Leslie	Marshall	Spencer Road		177
Leslie	James	Spencer Road	121	177
Lewis	Hugh	Howard Street	4	147
Lewis	Robert	Nelson Street	20	154
Lewis	T. G.	Orchard Street	25	155
Liddle	Adam	Argyle Terrace	26	127
Liddy	Mrs	Creggan Terrace	17	135
Lilley	William	Barnewall Place	23	169
Lily	Miss	Adair Street	1	126
Lindsay	William	Barry Street	31	128
Lindsay	William	De Burgh Square	3	136
Lindsay	Miss	Edenmore Street	2	138
Lindsay	David	Infirmary Road		147
Lindsay	William	Lone Moor		150
Lindsay	David	Park Avenue	Avonmore	156
Lipton Ltd		Bishop Street	5	129
Little	William J	Abercorn Place	7	126
Little	Henry	Grafton Street	29	144
Little	John	Howard Place	3	147
Little	Mrs	Long Tower	17	150
Little	Miss	Princes Street	10	156
Little	Thomas	Strand Road		160
Little	Robert	Barnewall Place	1	169
Little	John	Cuthbert Street	8	171
Little	Mrs	Cuthbert Street	10	171
Little	Alexander	Robert Street	4	176
Little	W. J. & Co.	Carlisle Road	73	133
Livingstone	Daniel	Woodleigh Terrace	2	127
Livingstone	William	Spencer Road	45	177
Lloyd, Attree & Smith		Great James Street		145
Loagh	William	Dervock Place	3	171
Lobb	Rebecca J.	Clarendon Street	32	135
Lobb	John H.	Marlborough Street	35	151
Lochhead	Jane	Clooney Terrace	38	170
Lochrie	Edward	Sunbeam Terrace	5	130
Lodge	G. F. S.	Queen Street	10	157
Logan	William	Abercorn Road	54	125
Logan	John	Foyle Road	43½	142
Logan	Mrs	Governor Road	28	144
Logan	James	Grafton Street	1	144
Logan	Joseph W.	Grafton Street	25	144
Logan	James	Victoria Street	16	163
Logan	Robert	William Street	67	165
Logier	Joseph A.	Harding Street	18	145
Logue	Robert junior	Albert Place	17	126
Logue	John	Alexandra Place	9	126
Logue	Mrs	Argyle Street	44	127

Surname	First Name	Street	House Number	Page Number
Logue	James	Beechwood Street	17	129
Logue	H	Sunbeam Terrace	19	130
Logue	Robert	Bishop Street	84	130
Logue	Robert	Bishop Street	138	131
Logue	Andrew	Bishop Street	138	131
Logue	Daniel	Deanery Street	6	136
Logue	Daniel	Deanery Place	stables	136
Logue	Charles	Fountain Street	19	140
Logue	James	Foyle Road	73	142
Logue	John	Gresham's Row	2	145
Logue	Joseph	Harding Street	15	145
Logue	Mrs	Harvey Street	19	146
Logue	Mrs	Bluebellhill Terrace	152	149
Logue	Mrs	Marlborough Avenue	18	152
Logue	James	Friel's Terrace	5	153
Logue	Mrs	Orchard Lane	5	155
Logue	Mrs	Waterloo Street	33	164
Logue	Rose	Waterloo Street	14	164
Logue	James	Westland Terrace	4	165
Logue	William	Creggan Road	12	167
Logue	Sam	Lewis Street	27	167
Logue	James	Alfred Street	38	168
Logue	John	Bond's Hill	16	169
Logue	John	Chapel Road	10	170
Logue	Mrs	Clooney Terrace	39	170
Logue	James	Cuthbert Street	26	171
Logue	Mrs	Herbert Street	9	174
Logue	William	King Street	39	175
Logue	John	Spencer Road	store	177
Logue	John	Spencer Road	40	177
Logue	John	Spencer Road	106	177
Logue	George	Spencer Road	110	177
Logue	John	Union Street	24	178
Long	Robert	Albert Street	9	126
Long	Alexander	Alma Place	14	126
Long	John	Collon Terrace	5	135
Long	Samuel	Dark Lane	22	136
Long	Hugh	Donegal Place	7	137
Long	John	Fahan Street	18	139
Long	George	Fountain Street	63	140
Long	Joseph	Fountain Place	27	141
Long	Mrs	Foyle View	10	143
Long	William	George Street	6	143
Long	Mrs	Kennedy Street	15	148
Long	William	Miller Street	36	152
Long	George	Walker's Place	40	163
Long	Edward	Wapping Lane	3	163
Long	William	Wapping Lane		163
Longwell	John	Commercial Buildings		141

Surname	First Name	Street	House Number	Page Number
Longwell	John	Kennedy Street	12	148
Longwell	John	Water Street		164
Longwell	David	Duke Street	30	172
Looney	Martin	Miller Street	3	152
Lorimer	John	Albert Street	15	126
Loughead	Robert	Magazine Street	5	151
Loughlin	Robert	Braeside		128
Loughlin	Robert	Charlotte Street	24	134
Loughlin	Andrew T.	Gordon Place	9	144
Loughlin	John	Ivy Terrace	17	147
Loughlin	Robert	Wapping Lane	6	163
Loughlin	John	Alexander Terrace	2	176
Loughnan	John	Aberfoyle Terrace	27	160
Loughrey	Andrew	Bishop Street	159	130
Loughrey	Francis	Deanery Street	8	136
Loughrey	Edward	Elmwood Terrace	42	138
Loughrey	Dan	Francis Street	53	143
Loughrey	James	North Edward Street	8	154
Loughrey	Joseph	Richmond Street	1	158
Loughrey	Patrick	Rossville Street	46	158
Loughrey	Joseph	Shipquay Street		158
Loughrey	Mrs	Sloan's Terrace	31	159
Loughrey	Joseph	Caw	Rosslyn	170
Love	A.	Magazine Street Upper		151
Love	Alex	Victoria Street	12	163
Love	Mrs	Wapping Lane	27	163
Love	William	Wapping Lane	8	163
Love	James	North Street	13	168
Love	Robert	Glendermott Road	25	174
Lowry	Mrs	Princes Street	13	156
Lowry	William	Windmill Terrace	30	166
Lowry	John	Clooney Terrace	19	170
Lowry	G. R.	Columba Terrace	4	171
Lowther	Nixon	Bennett Street Lower	24	129
Lowther	Mrs	Bishop Street	109	130
Lowther	James	Carrigans Lane	10	133
Lowther Bros		Richmond Street		158
Lowthers	John	Clooney Terrace	10	171
Lowthers	Thomas	Derry View	1	171
Lumsden	David	Ivy Terrace	6	147
Lumsden	Henry	Orchard Row	2	155
Lund	Charles J.	Strand Road		161
Lymburn	Robert	Wesley Street	8	168
Lynas	William T.	Clooney Terrace	14	171
Lynch	Edward	Abbey Street	29	125
Lynch	Samuel	Albert Place	11	126
Lynch	Mrs	Bishop Street	58	130
Lynch	Joseph	Clarendon Street	29	134
Lynch	Hugh	Donegal Place	17	137

Surname	First Name	Street	House Number	Page Number
Lynch	Charles	Fahan Street	95	139
Lynch	James	Fahan Street	82	139
Lynch	Thomas	Fahan Street	160	139
Lynch	John	Hawthorn Terrace	7	146
Lynch	Joseph	Henrietta Street	10	146
Lynch	Hugh	Hogg's Folly	17	146
Lynch	John	Foster's Terrace	171	148
Lynch	William	Lecky Road	259	149
Lynch	Hugh	Ann Street	9	149
Lynch	Patrick	Bluebellhill Terrace	202	149
Lynch	James	Little James Street		150
Lynch	Mrs	Lower Road	6	151
Lynch	David	Major's Row	8	151
Lynch	Patrick	Miller Street	28	152
Lynch	John	Nassau Street Lower	44	153
Lynch	James	Edenbank		154
Lynch	James & Co.	Sackville Street	23	158
Lynch	Patrick	Sloan's Terrace	1	159
Lynch	James	Sloan's Terrace	3, 5	159
Lynch	John	Stanley's Walk	1	159
Lynch	James	St. Columb's Wells	81	162
Lynch	Michael	St. Columb's Wells	30	162
Lynch	Susan	St. Columb's Wells	42	162
Lynch	Robert	Walker's Place	5	163
Lynch	Joseph & Co.	Waterloo Street	39	164
Lynch	George	William Street	77	165
Lynch	William	William Street	82	166
Lynch	James	Creggan Road	171	167
Lynch	Matilda	Creggan Road	173	167
Lynch	Robert J.	Bentley Street	2	169
Lynch	D. J.	Bond's Street	25	169
Lynch	Joseph Orr	Columba Terrace	5	171
Lynch	William	Derry View	3	171
Lynch	Joseph Orr	Duke Street	4	172
Lynch	Robert Rankin	Dunfield Terrace	13	172
Lynch	John	Ebrington Street	19	173
Lynch	John James	Florence Street	23	173
Lynch	Joseph	Fountain Hill	74	174
Lynch	Patrick	Simpson's Brae	23	177
Lyndsay	David	Foyle Street		142
Lyndsay	Hugh	Windmill Terrace	13	166
Lyndsay	Mrs	Lewis Street	19	167
Lynn	Mrs	Carlisle Road	34	133
Lynn	R. J.	Carlisle Road	34	133
Lynn	James	Ferguson Street	55	140
Lynn	James R.	Rockmount Villas	2	154
Lynn	Michael	Creggan Road	111	166
Lynn	Denis	Fountain Hill	63	173
Lynn	Denis	Spencer Road	31	177
Lyons	James	Bridge Street	17	132

Surname	First Name	Street	House Number	Page Number
Lyons	Miss	Castle Street		133
Lyons	James	Lawrence Hill	Rosebank	148
Lyons	John	Philips Street	33	156
Lyons	James	Princes Quay		157
Lyons	Teresa	Shipquay Street	6	159
Lyons	Robert	Shipquay Street		159
Lyttle	Thomas	Argyle Street	22	127
Lyttle	Robert	Charlotte Street	20	134
Lyttle	R.	Great James Street		145
Lyttle	Robert	Richmond Crescent	2	157
Macari	T. & Co.	Bridge Street	8	132
Macari	Luci	William Street	27	165
Macari T. & Co.		Carlisle Road	1	132
Macartney	Robert	King Street	31	175
Macaulay	Miss	De Burgh Terrace	14	137
Macaulay	David	Fountain Street	15	140
Macdevette & Donnell		Foyle Street		141
Macdonald	Alex	Sunbeam Terrace	4	130
Macdonald	Mrs I.	Bishop Street	74	130
Macdonald	John	Kennedy Place	4	147
Macdonald	Miss M. C.	Whittaker Street	City Hotel	165
Macdonnald	Mrs	Crawford Square	2	135
MacFeely	Rev. W. B.	Chapel Road	Parochial House	170
Machett	Andrew	Pine Street	31	176
Mack	Akexander B	Abercorn Road	1	125
Mackay	David	Society Street	15	159
Mackey	Mrs M.	Aberfoyle Terrace	9	160
MacKillip	Miss	Crawford Square	16	135
MacKillip	Miss J.	Crawford Square	18, 19	135
MacKillip	John	Victoria Park		178
Macky	William	Bennett Street Upper	10	129
Macky	Mrs	Culmore Road	Belmont	136
Macky	Miss	Great James Street	19	144
Macky	Joseph	Foster's Terrace	179	148
Macky	William	Bond's Place	14	170
MacLaughlin	Dr. Thomas	Shipquay Street	9	158
MacLaughlin & Allan		Waterloo Place		164
Maclean	Alexander	Victoria Park		178
Maclean & Reaper		Carlisle Road	46	133
Maclean & Reaper		East Wall	6	137
MacLehose	James	Abercorn Place	3	126
MacLellan	Mrs	Columba Terrace	6	171
MacLoughlin	Mark	Demesne Terrace	10	137
MacMahon	Mrs	East Wall	3	137
MacMillan	A.	Foyle Street		141

Surname	First Name	Street	House Number	Page Number
MacMillan	Alexander	Market Street	1	152
MacMillan	A.	Claremount Villas	Ardavon	154
MacMillan	Alex	Strand Road	35	160
MacMillan	Alexander	Strand Road	42	161
MacMillan	William	Victoria Park		178
MacNeary	T. A. & Co.	Bishop Street	16	130
Maconnachie	John	Fountain Street	69	140
Macourt	Rev. W. T.	Myrtle Terrace		154
MacPherson	Miss	Clarendon Street	42	135
MacQuaide	Rev Canon J. W.	Crawford Square	20	135
Macready	John	King Street	27	175
Macrory	John	Philips Street	36	156
Macrory	R. V.	Limavady Road	Woodville	175
Madden	Bros	Patrick Street	8	156
Madden	Patrick	Princes Street	16	156
Madden Bros		Commercial Buildings		141
Madden Bros		Shipquay Place		159
Madden Brothers		Waterloo Place		164
Madill	Mrs	Ferryquay Street		140
Madill	Joseph	West-End Park	10	165
Magee	John	Abbey Street	16	125
Magee	J. Gilbert	Castle Street	7	133
Magee	Mrs	De Burgh Terrace	4	136
Magee	Patrick	Foyle Road	67	142
Magee	Patrick	Frederick Street	7	143
Magee	Doctor J. R.	Magazine Street	20	151
Magee	Terence	Magazine Street	21	151
Magee	Mrs Annie	Richmond Street	16	158
Magee	Thomas	Barnewall Place	19	169
Magee	Simon	Bond's Street	39	169
Magee	John	Chapel Road	15	170
Magee	John	Glendermott Road	4	174
Magee	Patrick	Mill Street	26	176
Magee	Mrs	Pine Street	22	176
Maginnis	Thomas	Mill Street	25	176
Magirr	Mrs	Bridge Street	61	132
Magrory	Miss	Donegal Street	36	167
Maguire	Joseph	Bellevue Avenue	31	129
Maguire	James	Sunbeam Terrace	14	130
Maguire	Charles	Dark Lane	6	136
Maguire	Dr E A	East Wall	4	137
Maguire	William	Fulton Place	1	143
Maguire	Sergeant F.	Harding Street	8	145
Maguire	Bridget	Joseph Street	9	147
Maguire	John	Long Tower	29	150
Maguire	Edward	St. Columb's Wells	124	162
Maguire	R.	Spencer Road	74	177

Surname	First Name	Street	House Number	Page Number
Magwood	Mrs	Foyle Road	44	142
Mahaffey	Samuel	Lewis Street	11	167
Mahon	James A	Abercorn Road	7	125
Mahon	Rodger	Bishop Street	120	130
Mahon	Joseph	Deanery Street	3	136
Mahon	Thomas	Donegal Place	5	137
Mahon	Annie	Hogg's Folly	16	146
Mahon	Miss	Hogg's Folly	22	146
Mahon	Thomas	Quarry Street	4	157
Mahon	Rev. P.	Chapel Road	Parochial House	170
Mailey	William	Carlisle Chambers		172
Mailey	William J.	Strabane Old Road	68	178
Mallett	Jeremiah	Fahan Street	123	139
Mallett	Sarah	Lecky Road	35	148
Mallett	Michael	Wellington Street	19	164
Malley	Patrick & Son	Great James Street	55	145
Malley	P. L.	Great James Street		145
Mallon	James	Foyle Road	74	142
Malseed	Doctor	Bond's Hill	28	169
Malseed	R. C. & Co.	Duke Street		172
Malseed	Mrs	Limavady Road	Edendale	175
Manning	Mary	Donaghy's Row	2	145
Manning	James	Orchard Row	15	155
Manning	Thomas	Benvarden Avenue	53	169
Manning	Mrs	York Street	18	179
Marchini	Armandra	Fountain Place	20	141
Margey	Hugh	Argyle Terrace	17	127
Margey	John	Eglinton Place	7	138
Margey	Patrick	Eglinton Place	6	138
Margey	Mrs	Fahan Street	127	139
Margey	Henry	Governor Road	7	144
Marks	E & Co	Bishop Street	18	130
Marley	John	Argyle Street	29	127
Marley	John	Deanery Street	17	136
Marley	Mrs	Bluebellhill Terrace	160	149
Marley	Richard	Quarry Street	17	157
Marley	Mark	Wesley Street	13	168
Marshall	John	Governor Road	5	144
Marshall	Mrs	Charlotte Crescent		160
Marshall	Robert	Park Villas	2	168
Marshall	Mrs	Dungiven Road	91	173
Marshall	Thomas	Dungiven Road	101	173
Martin	W G	Abercorn Road	21	125
Martin	James	Alma Place	9	126
Martin	John	Aubrey Street	14	128
Martin	Charles	Barry Street	5	128
Martin	James	Brandywell Avenue	9	131
Martin	Mary	Brandywell Avenue	4	131
Martin	Patrick	Bridge Street	49	132

Surname	First Name	Street	House Number	Page Number
Martin	Denis	Bridge Street	40	132
Martin	Samuel	Brook Street Avenue	18	132
Martin	Frederick	Edenballymore	Glen Cottages	137
Martin	Patrick	Fahan Street	12	139
Martin	Richard	Ferguson Street	7	140
Martin	Denis	Foyle Street	68	142
Martin	Denis	Foyle Road	29	142
Martin	William	Fox's Lane	8	143
Martin	Mrs	Glasgow Terrace	9	144
Martin	John	Great James Street	77	145
Martin	Thomas	Lecky Road	10	149
Martin	Daniel	Stanley's Terrace	3	150
Martin	Samuel	Lower Road	22	151
Martin	Robert	Nassau Street Upper	19	153
Martin	John	Nelson Street	38	154
Martin	Samuel	Orchard Row	12	155
Martin	Hugh	Union Street	28	163
Martin	Denis	Wellington Street	74	164
Martin	Robert	William Street	55½	165
Martin	Frank	Rosemount Terrace	2	168
Martin	Charles	Bond's Street	24	170
Martin	Francis	Chapel Road	62	170
Martin	W. J.	Herbert Street	6	174
Martin	John	Bishop Street	232	131
Martin & McGrory		Bishop Street	29	129
Mason	William	Sunbeam Terrace	1	130
Mason	Miss	Marlborough Street	45	151
Mason	Mrs	Nicholson Terrace	5	154
Mason	David	Victoria Street	14	163
Mason	John	Donegal Street	43	167
Masterson	Laurence	Bishop Street	122	130
Masterson	Miss	Elmwood Terrace	49	138
Masterton	Edward	Wapping Lane	7	163
Mathews	R H	East Wall	2	137
Matthews	Robert J.	Mountjoy Terrace	8	153
Matthews	Mrs	Bond's Street	41	169
Matthews & Co.		Sackville Street	6	158
Matthewson	William	Donegal Place	3	137
Maultsaid	Mrs	Aberfoyle Terrace	13	160
Maultsaid	Lizzie	Strabane Old Road	60	178
Maultsiad	Patrick	Rossville Street	73	158
Maxwell	Mrs	Bennett Street Lower	14	129
Maxwell	J.	Duncreggan Road	Meadowbank	137
Maxwell	Mrs	East Wall	8, 9	137
Maxwell	William	Great James Street	37	144
Maxwell	Mrs	Wapping Lane	4	163
May	Thomas	Clarendon Street	59	134
May	William	Dark Lane	17	136

Surname	First Name	Street	House Number	Page Number
May	Thomas	Great James Street	33	144
McAdams	Thomas	Brandywell Road	32	131
McAdams	John	Carlisle Road	77	133
McAdams	John	Pennyburn Terrace	12	156
McAdams	Rev. J.	Victoria Park		178
McAdoo	Mrs	Crawford Square	15	135
McAleer	Mrs	Long Tower	46	150
McAleney	Patrick	Lecky Road	110	149
McAlinden	H. & T.	Orchard Street		155
McAlister	Con	Benvarden Avenue	15	169
McAllister	Con	Bridge Street	48	132
McAllister	Andrew	Henry Street	13	146
McAllister	Robert	Marlborough Terrace	15	152
McAllister	W. J.	Spencer Road		177
McAnair	John	Creggan Road	32	167
McAnair	Mrs	Creggan Road	42	167
McAnair	James	Creggan Road	44	167
McAnaney	Robert	Bishop Street	245	130
McAnaney	Thomas H.	Foyle Road	59	142
McAnaul	Mrs	York Street	3	179
McAnee	John	Deanery Street	11	136
McAnee	John	Bluebellhill Terrace	188	149
McArthur	William	Barrack Street	9	128
McAteer	Hugh	William Street	76	166
McAuley	David	King Street	1	175
McAuley	J. L.	Spencer Road	102	177
McBane	James	Cuthbert Street	11	171
McBey	William James	Argyle Terrace	20	127
McBirney	William	George Street	8	143
McBirney	Mrs	Gordon Terrace	3	144
McBirney	James	Marlborough Terrace	5	152
McBrearty	Patrick	Beechwood Street	2	129
McBrearty	Patrick	Deanery Street	10	136
McBrearty	Joseph	Elmwood Street	14	138
McBrearty	Patrick	Gallagher's Square	7	143
McBrearty	Daniel	Lecky Road	109	148
McBrearty	Patrick	Lecky Road	100	149
McBrearty	Charles	Quarry Street	2	157
McBrearty	Edward	North Street	35	168
McBride	John	Beechwood Street	24	129
McBride	Mrs	Bishop Street	215	130
McBride	James	Bridge Street	23	132
McBride	John	Bridge Street	18	132
McBride	Patrick	Charlotte Place	6	134
McBride	Mrs	Eden Place	2½	138
McBride	James	Fountain Place	17	141
McBride	Mrs	Fox's Lane	7	143
McBride	James	Harvey Street	5	146
McBride	Robert	Henry Street	14	146
McBride	James	Hogg's Folly	20	146

Surname	First Name	Street	House Number	Page Number
McBride	Mrs	Howard Street	6	147
McBride	John H.	Howard Street	8	147
McBride	John	Lecky Road	249	149
McBride	Hamilton sen	Nassau Street Lower	31	153
McBride	Thomas	Philips Street	34	156
McBride	Edward	Foyleview Terrace	1	160
McBride	James	St. Columb's Wells	51	161
McBride	Catherine	St. Columb's Wells	72	162
McBride	James	Thomas Street	18	162
McBride	Mrs	William Street	19	165
McBride	Samuel	Creggan Road	99	166
McBride	William	Rosemount Terrace	8	168
McBride	John	Wesley Street	17	168
McBride	Catherine	Chapel Road	49	170
McBride	Edward	Florence Street	29	173
McBrien	James	Spencer Road	19	177
McBrien	William	Spencer Road	37	177
McCabe	Charles	Bishop Street	112	130
McCabe	William	Bishop Street	180	131
McCafferty	Neal	Donegal Place	21	137
McCafferty	James	Donegal Place	2	137
McCafferty	Neil	Elmwood Terrace	16	138
McCafferty	Bartholomew	Elmwood Terrace	18	138
McCafferty	Patrick	Elmwood Terrace	25	138
McCafferty	John	Elmwood Street	8	138
McCafferty	Catherine	Ferguson Street	2	140
McCafferty	Catherine	Foyle Road		142
McCafferty	William	Foyle Road	111	142
McCafferty	Patrick	Francis Street	25	143
McCafferty	John	Henrietta Street	11	146
McCafferty	Annie	Henrietta Street	13	146
McCafferty	Patrick	Henrietta Street	16	146
McCafferty	John	Lecky Road	60	149
McCafferty	James	Lecky Road		149
McCafferty	James	Bluebellhill Terrace	182	149
McCafferty	James	Long Tower	56	150
McCafferty	Reps A.	Magazine Street	3	151
McCafferty	J. D.	Magazine Street		151
McCafferty	W. J.	Marlborough Street	39	151
McCafferty	James	Mountjoy Street	11	152
McCafferty	Patrick	Nassau Street Upper	10	153
McCafferty	Edward	Northland Avenue	11	155
McCafferty	Patrick	Sackville Street	2	158
McCafferty	David	Sloan's Terrace	27	159
McCafferty	George	Stanley's Walk	23	160
McCafferty	Robert	Waterloo Street	28	164
McCafferty	Robert	Waterloo Street	38	164
McCafferty	Charles	Wellington Street	43	164
McCafferty	Patrick	William Street	61	165
McCafferty	John	Alfred Street	10	168

Surname	First Name	Street	House Number	Page Number
McCafferty	William	Gortfoyle Place	4	174
McCafferty	James	Strabane Old Road	2	177
McCafferty	Robert	Strabane Old Road	58	178
McCafferty	John	York Street	4	179
McCaffrey	Rev. John	Melrose Terrace	6	175
McCaig	James	Glendermott Road	104	174
McCallion	Patrick	Abbey Street	7	125
McCallion	Patrick	Argyle Street	4	127
McCallion	James	Barry Street	11	128
McCallion	George	Beechwood Street	7	129
McCallion	John	Beechwood Street	15	129
McCallion	Patrick	Beechwood Street	18	129
McCallion	Charles	Bishop Street	154	131
McCallion	Thomas	Bishop Street	156	131
McCallion	Mrs	Cottage Row	8	131
McCallion	Patrick	Bishop Street	228, 230	131
McCallion	Thomas	Blee's Lane		131
McCallion	William	Brook Street Avenue	9	132
McCallion	John	Chamberlain Street	36	134
McCallion	James	Creggan Terrace	8	135
McCallion	Margaret	Fahan Street	5	139
McCallion	John	Ivy Terrace	31	147
McCallion	Michael	Stanley's Terrace	2	150
McCallion	Edward	Nassau Street Lower	14	153
McCallion	Joseph	Nassau Street Upper	14	153
McCallion	Mrs	Pennyburn		156
McCallion	William	Princes Terrace	8	156
McCallion	Mrs	St. Columb's Wells	19	161
McCallion	Patrick	Kerr's Terrace	7	166
McCallion	William	Creggan Road	149	166
McCallion	Joseph	Creggan Road	30	167
McCallion	George	Cross Street	1	167
McCallion	Daniel	Cross Street	2	167
McCallion	George	Cross Street	5	167
McCallion	James	Donegal Street	10	167
McCallion	Alex	Osborne Street	7	168
McCallion	James	Osborne Street	15	168
McCallion	Joseph	Osborne Street	17	168
McCallion	Mary	Duke Street	19	172
McCallum	Daniel	Aberfoyle Terrace	25	160
McCallum	John	Foyleview Terrace	3	160
McCallum	William	Strand Road	22A	161
McCandless	Mrs	Bridge Street	20	132
McCandless	W. H. B.	Clarendon Street	61	134
McCandless	Mrs	Clarendon Street	28	134
McCandless	H. S.	College Terrace	1	135
McCandless	William A.	Grafton Terrace	1	144
McCandless	Sergeant J.	Northland Avenue	8	155
McCandless	W. H. B.	Strand Road	32	161
McCandless	Mrs	Clooney Terrace	56	171

Surname	First Name	Street	House Number	Page Number
McCann	Miss	Bishop Street	40	130
McCann	Mrs	Bridge Street	15	131
McCann	Miss Mary	Lecky Road	102	149
McCann	Bernard	Queen Street	6	157
McCann	Thomas	Clyde Street	1	157
McCann	Thomas	Rossville Street	10	158
McCann	James	New Row	3	160
McCann	Joseph	Walker's Place	39	163
McCann	Hugh	Waterloo Street	3	163
McCann	James	Waterloo Street		164
McCann	Mrs	Creggan Road	175	167
McCann	John	Creggan Road	58	167
McCann	Thomas	Donegal Street	20	167
McCann	Michael	Osborne Street	11	168
McCann	Nathaniel	Benvarden Avenue	16	169
McCann	James	Riverview Terrace	15	176
McCarrall	A. B.	Myrtle Terrace		154
McCarroll	James E.	Waterloo Street	2	164
McCarron	Miss	Albert Place	16	126
McCarron	Mrs	Bellevue Avenue	1	129
McCarron	Neal	Bellevue Avenue	6	129
McCarron	Robert	Bennett Street Upper	4	129
McCarron	John	Bishop Street	149	130
McCarron	Mrs	Bridge Street	15	131
McCarron	John	Fahan Street	67	139
McCarron	Neal (store)	Ferguson Street	47	140
McCarron	Miss	Foyle Road	110	142
McCarron	Mrs	Frederick Street	13	143
McCarron	James	Hogg's Folly	13	146
McCarron	Thomas	Orchard Row	35	155
McCarron	Thomas	Templemore Terrace	2	156
McCarron	William	Philips Street	11	156
McCarron	John	Wapping Lane	21	163
McCarron	Daniel	Waterloo Street	51	164
McCarron	Neil	Wellington Street	37	164
McCarron	John	Artisan Street	5	166
McCarron	William	Creggan Road	71	166
McCarron	Owen	Wesley Street	2	168
McCarter	William	Alexandra Place	30	126
McCarter	Robert	Culmore Road		136
McCarter	Mrs	Demesne Terrace	6	137
McCarter	William	Duncreggan Road	Meadowbank	137
McCarter	William	Marlborough Avenue	5	151
McCarter	Miss	Nicholson Terrace	1	154
McCarter	John	Pitt Street	3	156
McCarter	William	Princes Quay		157
McCarter	William	Queen's Quay		157
McCarter	William & Son	Duke Street	41	172
McCarter	James	Florence Street	21	173
McCarter	Alex	Glendermott Road	64	174

Surname	First Name	Street	House Number	Page Number
McCarter	Matthew	King Street	28	175
McCarter	Lizzie	Mill Street	34	176
McCartney	John	Alexandra Place	22	126
McCartney	Catherine	Bishop Street	47	129
McCartney	Hugh	Bishop Street	221	130
McCartney	William	Bishop Street	88	130
McCartney	Neil	Mitchelburne Terrace	97	142
McCartney	Bridget	High Street	6	146
McCartney	James	Sloan's Terrace	16	159
McCartney	Henry	St. Columb's Wells	36	162
McCaughey	John	Abercorn Road	34	125
McCaughey	Bernard	Bishop Street	137	130
McCaughey	Bernard	Marlborough Terrace	22	152
McCaughey & Co.		Carlisle Road	36	133
McCaul	John	Lecky Road		149
McCaul	John	Lecky Road	63	148
McCaul	James	Tyrconnell Street	4	163
McCaul	Francis	Deanery Street	25	136
McCauley	James	Abbey Street	26	125
McCauley	William	Alma Place	3	126
McCauley	Daniel	Argyle Street	33	127
McCauley	Mary	Barrack Street	7	128
McCauley	Thomas	Barry Street	6	128
McCauley	D.	Castle Street		133
McCauley	Miss	Cunningham Row	3	136
McCauley	William	Eglinton Place	23	138
McCauley	Patrick	Mitchelburne Terrace	85	142
McCauley	Thomas	Harvey Street	2	146
McCauley	John	Meave's Row	189	149
McCauley	James	Philips Street	39	156
McCauley	Mrs	Pump Street	21	156
McCauley	Sarah	Stanley's Walk	39	160
McCauley	Andrew	Foyleview Terrace	7	160
McCauley	John	Donegal Street	13	167
McCauley	Mrs Mary	Donegal Street	19	167
McCauley	Thomas	Donegal Street	25	167
McCauley	William	Donegal Street	37	167
McCauley	Nelis	Donegal Street	32	167
McCauley	William	Lewis Street	16	167
McCauley	William	Cottage Row	24	168
McCauley	Miss	King Street	36	175
McCauley	Mrs	Violet Street Lower	46	179
McCauley	James	York Street	13	179
McCay	Mrs	Asylum Road	2	127
McCay	Daniel	Bishop Street	67	129
McCay	William	Bishop Street	290	131
McCay	John	Carlisle Road	44	133
McCay	Mrs	Creggan Terrace	6	135
McCay	Mrs	Culmore Road	Troy Hall	136

Surname	First Name	Street	House Number	Page Number
McCay	James A	Edenballymore	Creggan	137
McCay	James	Fahan Street	72	139
McCay	Alexander & Co.	Ferryquay Street		140
McCay	Miss	Hollywell Street	17	147
McCay	Elijah	Lecky Road	27	148
McCay	Owen	Lundy's Lane	5	150
McCay	Miss	Marlborough Terrace	23	152
McCay	David	Meadowbank Avenue	1	152
McCay	Alexander	Claremount Villas	2	154
McCay	Alex & Co.	Pump Street	8	157
McCay	William	Rossville Street	45	158
McCay	Henry Crawford	Shipquay Street	27	158
McCay	William	Stanley's Walk	45	160
McCay	Thomas	Thomas Street	21	162
McCay	Mrs	Wellington Street	22	164
McCay	Mrs	Clooney Terrace	31	170
McCay	James	Duke Street	42	172
McCay	Peter	King Street	7	175
McCay	John	Spencer Road	7	177
McCay	John	Spencer Road	13	177
McChrystal	Michael	Clooney Terrace	9	170
McClafferty	Hugh	Rossville Street	21	158
McClafferty	Philip	Rossville Street	25	158
McClafferty	John	Wellington Street	40	164
McClatchie	J	Bank Place	1	128
McClatchie	J.	Shipquay Street		159
McClay	David L.	College Terrace	2	135
McClay	Mary A.	Howard Street	17	147
McClay	Robert G.	Barnewall Place	15	169
McClay	Thomas	East Avenue	1	173
McClay	Stephen	Fountain Hill	44	174
McClay	William James	Moore Street	32	176
McClay	Henry	Robert Street	2	176
McClay	John	Spencer Road	34	177
McClay	Allan	Strabane Old Road	21	177
McClay	John	Strabane Old Road	25	177
McClean	David	Barry Street	24	128
McClean	James	Carlisle Road	24	133
McClean	A.	Demesne Terrace	5	137
McClean	James	Rossville Street	4	158
McClean	James	Walker's Place	21	163
McClean	James	William Street	store	165
McClean	Mrs	William Street	21½	165
McClean	Mrs	Windmill Terrace	22	166
McClean	Robert	Osborne Street	16	168
McClean	Albert	Rosemount Terrace	3	168
McClean	Patrick	Hollywell Row	75	148
McClean	Mary	Meave's Row	203	149
McClean	James	Little James Street	11	150

Surname	First Name	Street	House Number	Page Number
McClean	James	Little James Street	13	150
McClean A. & Reaper		Grove Place		145
McCleary	Charles	Iona Terrace		174
McCleery	Samuel	Argyle Street	14	127
McCleery	Mrs	Clarendon Street	12	134
McCleery	J. R.	Mountjoy Terrace	9	153
McCleery	William	Templemore Terrace	3	156
McCleery	James	Park Avenue	22	156
McClellan, Smyth & Co.		Duke Street	47	172
McClelland	Henry	Bennett Street Lower	31	129
McClelland	W. J. G.	De Burgh Terrace	1	136
McClelland	Thomas	Horace Street	1	146
McClelland	W. J. G.	Magazine Street	10	151
McClelland	W. J.	Northland Avenue	6	155
McClelland	William	Ashcroft Place	8	169
McClelland	Robert	Bond's Street	11	169
McClelland	Mrs	Fountain Hill	57	173
McClelland	William	Irish Street	17	174
McClelland	Francis	Strabane Old Road	1	177
McClelland	Jane	Violet Street Lower	17	178
McClelland	Robert	Dark Lane	4	136
McClelland	John	Fountain Place	25	141
McClelland & Graham		Carlisle Road	2	133
McClelland & Graham		Fountain Street		140
McClements	John	Bishop Street	75	129
McClements	Robert	Charlotte Place		134
McClements	Robert	London Street	13	150
McClements	Mrs	Bond's Street	18	170
McClements	Hamilton	Limavady Road	Wellington Villa	175
McClenaghan	Charles	Bishop Street	242	131
McClenaghan	William	Fountain Street	113	141
McClenaghan	John	St. Columb's Wells	90	162
McClenaghan	James	Windmill Terrace	5	166
McClenaghan	John	Fountain Hill	29	173
McClintock	Thomas	Hamilton Street	3	145
McClintock	Mrs	St. Columb's Terrace	87	148
McClintock	James	Long Tower	43	150
McClintock	John	Nailor's Row	35	153
McClintock	Catherine	Nelson Street	13	153
McClintock	Mary	St. Columb's Wells	41	161
McClintock	Mrs	Pine Street	33	176
McCloskey	Thomas	Alma Place	2	126
McCloskey	Catherine	Bridge Street	39	132
McCloskey	George	Brook Street Avenue	10	132
McCloskey	John	Clarendon Street	22	134

Surname	First Name	Street	House Number	Page Number
McCloskey	Mary	Creggan Street	9	135
McCloskey	Mrs	Creggan Terrace	19	135
McCloskey	Frank	East Wall		137
McCloskey	John	Fahan Street	124	139
McCloskey	John	Ferguson Street	33	140
McCloskey	William	Foyle Street	109	141
McCloskey	Patrick	Harding Street	33	145
McCloskey	Mary A.	Kildarra Terrace	1, 2	146
McCloskey	John	Hollywell Street	5	147
McCloskey	Mrs	Laburnum Terrace	2	148
McCloskey	Joseph	Laburnum Terrace	11	148
McCloskey	Charles	Lecky Road	84	149
McCloskey	Catherine	Bluebellhill Terrace	136	149
McCloskey	John	Bluebellhill Terrace	138	149
McCloskey	Bernard	Long Tower	7	150
McCloskey	James	Nassau Street Lower	3	153
McCloskey	William	Philips Street	38	156
McCloskey	John	Sackville Street	9	158
McCloskey	John	Stanley's Walk	11	160
McCloskey	Michael	Stanley's Walk	25	160
McCloskey	W. & Son	Stanley's Walk	50, 51	160
McCloskey	Thomas	Townsend Street	3	162
McCloskey	James	West-End Terrace	5	165
McCloskey	Andrew	William Street	68	166
McCloskey	Mrs	Creggan Road	127	166
McCloskey	William	Bond's Street	9	169
McCloskey	R. J.	Columba Terrace	8	171
McCloskey	P.	Duke Street	75	172
McCloskey	Patrick	Dungiven Road	65	173
McCloskey	John	Dungiven Road	83	173
McCloskey	Isaac	King Street	6	175
McCloskey	Patrick	Meehan's Row	19	176
McCloskey	James	Spencer Road	77	177
McCloskey	Mrs	Spencer Road	50	177
McCloskey	M.	Spencer Road	80	177
McCloskey	Mrs	Tamneymore		178
McCloud	Miss	Rossville Street	39	158
McCloud	William	Benvarden Avenue	37	169
McCloud	William	Primrose Street	11	176
McClune	James	Claremont Street		134
McClung	John	Simpson's Brae	21	177
McClure	Mrs	Beechwood Avenue	8	128
McClure	Francis	Myrtle Terrace		154
McClure	James	Cross Street	40	171
McClure	John	Glendermott Road	50	174
McClure	John	Maple Street	1	175
McClure & Co.		Ferryquay Street		140
McCoach & Co.		Shipquay Place		159
McColgan	Thomas	Abbey Street	57	125
McColgan	Patrick	Abbey Street	28	125

102

Surname	First Name	Street	House Number	Page Number
McColgan	John & Co.	Bishop Street	16	130
McColgan	John & Co.	Bishop Street	18	130
McColgan	Mrs	Demesne Terrace	4	137
McColgan	Robert	Joseph Street	5	147
McColgan	Mrs	Lower Road	27	151
McColgan	Mrs	Marlborough Street	50	151
McColgan	Mrs	Mary Street	26	152
McColgan	John	Walker's Place	20	163
McColgan	Michael	Wellington Street	34	164
McColgan	James	West-End Park	16	165
McColgan	James	Carlin Street	3	170
McColl	John	King Street	33	175
McComb	John	Alma Place	10	126
McComb	Mrs	Cedar Street	13	133
McComb	William	George Street	10	143
McComb	Thomas	Bentley Street	6	169
McComb	Samuel	May Street	8	175
McComb	James	Moore Street	3	176
McCombe	Samuel	Beechwood Avenue	19	128
McConachie	William	Distillery Brae Lower		171
McConaghey	Mrs	Asylum Road	12	127
McConaghey	Matthew	York Street	9	179
McConaghy	James	Park Avenue	23	156
McConnachie	James	Abercorn Road	59	125
McConnell	John	Albert Street	1	126
McConnell	John James	Albert Street	6	126
McConnell	Charles H	Beechwood Park	83	128
McConnell	Thomas	Bennett Street Lower	27	129
McConnell	Charles	Brandywell Road	17	131
McConnell	James	Charlotte Street	4	134
McConnell	Mrs	Collon Terrace	2	135
McConnell	Miss	Crawford Square	12	135
McConnell	J. H.	Culmore Road	Tripoli	136
McConnell	Robert	Gordon Place	4	144
McConnell	Moses	Harding Street	5	145
McConnell	Thomas & Co.	Pump Street	6	156
McConnell	Mrs	Queen Street	8	157
McConnell	John	St. Patrick Street	10	162
McConnell	Miss	Bond's Street	18	170
McConnell	Mrs	Margaret Street	22	175
McConnell	Hugh	Meehan's Row	21	176
McConnell	John	Mountain View		176
McConnell	James	Violet Street Upper	25	179
McConnell	Thomas	Marlborough Avenue	17	152
McConnell	Michael	Nelson Street	7	153
McConnell	Mrs	Fountain Street	92A	141
McConnell & Co.		Foyle Street		141
McConnell Bros. & Co.		William Street		165

Surname	First Name	Street	House Number	Page Number
McConnellogue	Daniel	Fitters Row	263	130
McConnellogue	Mrs	Creggan Street	13	135
McConnellogue	Andrew	Eden Place	14	138
McConnellogue	Denis	Francis Street	35	143
McConnellogue	Denis	Great James Street	64	145
McConnellogue	John	Kildarra Terrace	5	146
McConnellogue	Michael	Park Avenue	5	156
McConnelogue	Michael	Thomas Street	31	162
McConnelogue	Daniel	Wellington Street	10	164
McConnollogue	William J.	Meadowbank Avenue	17	152
McConomy	Charles	Patrick Street	15	156
McConomy	James	York Street	19	179
McConomy	John	York Street	25	179
McConoway	Mrs	Fahan Street	130	139
McConway	James	Fahan Street	105	139
McConway	William	Great James Street	73	145
McCool	Miss	Bishop Street	247	130
McCool	William	Creggan Street	33	135
McCool	John	Elmwood Terrace	34	138
McCool	Frank	Foster's Terrace	155	148
McCool	John	Orchard Row	25	155
McCool	Mrs	Pennyburn Terrace	13	156
McCool	Rose	Quarry Street	3	157
McCool	George	Quarry Street	13	157
McCool	William	Sackville Street	2	158
McCool	William	Strand Road	17	160
McCool	William	William Street		165
McCorkell	George	New Street	12	133
McCorkell	Mrs	Culmore Road	Ballynagard	136
McCorkell	James	Dark Lane	1	136
McCorkell	Mrs	Fountain Street	116	141
McCorkell	W. H. & Co.	Queen's Quay		157
McCorkell	W. & Co.	Strand Road	8	161
McCorkell	William	Ashfield Terrace	37	166
McCorkell	Joseph	Creggan Road	10	167
McCorkell	William J.	Dark Lane	8	136
McCorkell & Co.		Shipquay Place		159
McCormack	Sydney	Bentley Street	11	169
McCormick	Mrs	Aubrey Street	5	128
McCormick	George	Bishop Street	171	130
McCormick	Catherine	Millar's Close		132
McCormick	Charles	Castle Street	3	133
McCormick	H.	Clarendon Street	25	134
McCormick	John	Fahan Street	131	139
McCormick	Daniel	Foyle Road	33	142
McCormick	Charles	Francis Street	27	143
McCormick	Mrs	Francis Street	29	143
McCormick	John	Bluebellhill Terrace	216	149
McCormick	Henry	Nailor's Row	22	153

Surname	First Name	Street	House Number	Page Number
McCormick	Mrs	Nailor's Row	22½	153
McCormick	Dr. Hugh	Northland Road		155
McCormick	Frank	Wellington Street	46	164
McCormick	Mrs	Windsor Terrace	9	166
McCormick	Charles	Creggan Road	93	166
McCormick	Miss	Dungiven Road	4	173
McCourt	Annie	Beechwood Street	12	129
McCourt	Henry	Bellevue Avenue	19	129
McCourt	Daniel	Eden Place	15	138
McCourt	Jeremiah	Francis Street	31	143
McCourt	Denis	Francis Street	43	143
McCourt	James	Fulton Place	2	143
McCourt	James & Sons	Henrietta Street		146
McCourt	Henry	Howard Street	18	147
McCourt	Edward	St. Columb's Terrace	97	148
McCourt	Patrick	Lower Road	15	151
McCourt	Elizabeth	Lower Road	8	151
McCourt	James & Sons	Strand Road		161
McCourt	Patrick	St. Columb's Wells	126	162
McCourt	John	Walker's Place	33	163
McCourt	John	Walker's Place	34	163
McCourt	Thomas	Wellington Street	25	164
McCourt	Edward	Wellington Street	49	164
McCourt	Patrick	Wellington Street	53	164
McCourt	Thomas junior	Wellington Street	69	164
McCourt	Thomas senior	Wellington Street	73	164
McCourt	Mrs	Wellington Street	58	164
McCowan	Mary	Howard Street	3	147
McCoy	John	Nicholson Terrace	6	154
McCracken	Joseph	Alma Place	16	126
McCracken	Mrs M.	Grove Place	13	145
McCrea	David	Bennett Street Lower	57	129
McCrea	J. H.	Great James Street	31	144
McCrea	James	Ivy Terrace	32	147
McCrea	Alex	Cuthbert Street	21	171
McCrea	Mrs	Mountain View		176
McCrea & McFarland		Foyle Street		141
McCrea & McFarland		Queen's Quay		157
McCrea & McFarland		Mill Street		176
McCready	Thomas	Chamberlain Street	2	134
McCready	Mary A.	Foster's Terrace	173	148
McCready	Peter	Long Tower	33	150
McCready	Daniel	Distillery Lane Lower	7	171
McCready	Denis	Mill Street	36	176
McCready	Mrs	Meehan's Row	2	176
McCrossan	Eliza	Bennett Street Upper	23	129
McCrossan	William	Fahan Street	138	139

Surname	First Name	Street	House Number	Page Number
McCrossan	Harry	Marlborough Terrace	26	152
McCrudden	Mary	Nailor's Row	41	153
McCrudden	Patrick	Walker's Place	1	163
McCrystal	Patrick	Lecky Road	45	148
McCrystal	Mark	North Street	11	168
McCrystall	Michael	Alfred Street	20	168
McCrystall	John	Cross Street	36	171
McCullagh	Mrs	Alma Place	12	126
McCullagh	Miss	Bishop Street	120	130
McCullagh	W. J.	Demesne Terrace	14	137
McCullagh	Mrs	Foyleview Terrace	2	160
McCullagh	W. J.	Waterloo Place		164
McCullagh	Mrs	Glendermott Road	3	174
McCullagh	James	Violet Street Lower	33	178
McCulley	John	Dunfield Terrace	5	172
McCulloch	James	Ebrington Terrace	5	173
McCullough	S. G. & Co.	Waterloo Place		164
McCully	Mrs	Abercorn Road	33A	125
McCully	Mrs	Argyle Street	41	127
McCully	Patrick	Tyrconnell Street	2	163
McCully	Thomas	Limavady Road	Beech Grove	175
McCully	Thomas	Spencer Road	2	177
McCully	Thomas	Tamneymore		178
McCully	Thomas	Victoria Road	1	178
McCurdy	Samuel	Beechwood Avenue	51	128
McCurdy	Dr. D. A.	Pump Street	5	156
McCurdy	William	Westland Terrace	12	165
McCurry	Patrick	Bellevue Avenue	35	129
McCurry	Joseph	Marlborough Street	46	151
McCurry	Joseph	Strand Road		161
McCutcheon	Andrew	Bishop Street	25	129
McCutcheon	William	Bishop Street	220	131
McCutcheon	Misses	Butcher Street	11	132
McCutcheon	Misses	Carlisle Terrace	1	133
McDaid	Bernard	Argyle Street	65	127
McDaid	William	Brandywell Avenue	3	131
McDaid	Denis	Brandywell Avenue	11	131
McDaid	Michael	Brook Street Avenue	14	132
McDaid	Bernard	Creggan Street	15	135
McDaid	William	Elmwood Terrace	13	138
McDaid	John	Fahan Street	17	139
McDaid	John	Fahan Street	84	139
McDaid	Patrick	Foyle Road	112	142
McDaid	Anthony	Francis Street	11	143
McDaid	Miss	Francis Street	19	143
McDaid	Michael	Hamilton Street	15A	145
McDaid	James	Hamilton Street	15	145
McDaid	James	Hamilton Street	21	145
McDaid	Miss	John Street	7	147
McDaid	William	Lecky Road	261	149

Surname	First Name	Street	House Number	Page Number
McDaid	James	Lecky Road	28	149
McDaid	William	Lecky Road	58	149
McDaid	Miss	Lecky Road	62	149
McDaid	James	Bluebellhill Terrace	170	149
McDaid	Mrs	Bluebellhill Terrace	218	149
McDaid	Madge	Little James Street	2	150
McDaid	James	Long Tower	53	150
McDaid	James	Long Tower	83	150
McDaid	Mary	Nailor's Row	14	153
McDaid	Mrs	Northland Avenue	19	155
McDaid	Mrs	Northland Terrace	2	155
McDaid	James	Orchard Street	8	155
McDaid	Mrs	Rossville Street	38	158
McDaid	Mrs	Strand Road		161
McDaid	Fred	Wellington Street	15	164
McDaid	Michael	Windsor Terrace	8	166
McDaid	Dominick	Ashfield Terrace	41	166
McDaid	William	Creggan Road	67	166
McDaid	John	Creggan Road	109	166
McDaid	James	Mount Street	19	167
McDaid	Annie	Wesley Street	21	168
McDaid	Michael	Wesley Street	22	168
McDaid	Patrick	Alfred Street	8	168
McDaid	Anthony	Strabane Old Road	86	178
McDaid	Charles	Violet Street Upper	21	179
McDermid	John	Argyle Street	20	127
McDermott	Robert	Albert Street	14	126
McDermott	Daniel	Ann Street	19	127
McDermott	Daniel	Ann Street	18	127
McDermott	James	Argyle Street	10	127
McDermott	Mrs	Asylum Road	1	127
McDermott	Edward	Beechwood Avenue	3	128
McDermott	Ellen J.	Millar's Close		132
McDermott	E. J.	Bridge Street	50	132
McDermott	Mrs	Carlisle Road	32	133
McDermott	Edward	Creggan Street	21	135
McDermott	Michael	Fahan Street	89	139
McDermott	Stephen	Gordon Place	10	144
McDermott	Miss	Henrietta Street	6	146
McDermott	James	Howard Street	24	147
McDermott	Mary	Howard Place	8	147
McDermott	Michael	Ivy Terrace	1	147
McDermott	Hugh	Ivy Terrace	33	147
McDermott	Charles	Lecky Road	15	148
McDermott	Charles	Lecky Road		149
McDermott	Charles	Lecky Road	14	149
McDermott	Margaret	Lecky Road	124	149
McDermott	Ann J.	Stanley's Terrace	1	150
McDermott	Henry	Marlborough Avenue	9	151
McDermott	Charles	Pitt Street	8	156

Surname	First Name	Street	House Number	Page Number
McDermott	Daniel	Stanley's Walk	27	160
McDermott	Robert	Stanley's Walk	35	160
McDermott	Patrick	Rock Buildings		160
McDermott	R. & Co.	Strand Road		161
McDermott	Daniel	St. Columb's Wells	87	162
McDermott	John	St. Columb's Wells	91	162
McDermott	Charles	Wellington Street	41	164
McDermott	Charles	Wellington Street	38	164
McDermott	Mrs	William Street	19	165
McDermott	Neil	Creggan Road	6	167
McDermott	Mrs	North Street	23	168
McDermott	Mrs	Bond's Hill	25	169
McDermott	William	Irish Street	18	174
McDermott	Patrick	Margaret Street	16	175
McDermott	Samuel	Moore Street	22	176
McDermott	John	Spencer Road	8	177
McDermott & Starrett		Castle Street	5	133
McDevette	Michael	West-End Park	11	165
McDevitt	William	Bishop Street	126	130
McDevitt	William	Brandywell Road	4	131
McDevitt	John	Francis Street	55	143
McDevitt	Miss	Patrick Street	16	156
McDevitt	James	Rossville Street	82	158
McDevitt	J.	Shipquay Street	4	159
McDevitt	James	St. Columb's Wells	45	161
McDevitt	Miss	Victoria Place	4	163
McDevitt	Denis	Waterloo Street	11, 13	163
McDevitt	Michael	Columba Terrace	2	171
McDevitt	M. & Co.	Duke Street	38, 40	172
McDevitt	William	Bishop Street	71	129
McDevitte	Hugh	Beechwood Avenue	53	128
McDevitte	Edward	Fahan Street	69	139
McDevitte & Donnell		Princes Quay		157
McDonagh	Mrs	Asylum Road	3	127
McDonagh	Michael	Bennett Street Lower	18	129
McDonagh	Charles	Brook Street Avenue	15	132
McDonagh	James	Deanery Street	44	136
McDonagh	Mrs	Edenmore Street	17	138
McDonagh	Michael	Foyle Road	100	142
McDonagh	James	Great James Street		145
McDonagh	Edward	Nelson Street	29	153
McDonagh	Thomas	Kerr's Terrace	15	166
McDonagh	Miss	Bond's Place	2	170
McDonald	Miss	Argyle Street	19	127
McDonald	John	Carrigans Lane	27	133
McDonald	Patrick	Joseph Street	4	147
McDonald	Mrs	Park Avenue	3	156
McDonald	Frank	Philips Street	42	156

Surname	First Name	Street	House Number	Page Number
McDonnell	Mrs	Clarendon Street	69	134
McDonnell	James	Collon Terrace	12	135
McDonnell	Mrs	Harvey Street	17	146
McDowell	Miss L	Barry Street	35	128
McDowell	Thomas	Great James Street	38	145
McDowell	James	Laburnum Terrace	18	148
McDowell	Charles	Thomas Street	17	162
McDowell	William	Epworth Street	15	167
McDowell	John	Fountain Hill	59	173
McDowell	George	St. Columb's Wells	63	161
McDowell & Co.		Strand Road	38	161
McEldowny	William	Grafton Street	23	144
McElhinney	R A	Beechwood Avenue	20	128
McElhinney	Franck	Brandywell Avenue	1	131
McElhinney	Thomas	De Burgh Square	8	136
McElhinney	Robert	Sydney Terrace	1	145
McElhinney	Mrs	Henrietta Street	15	146
McElhinney	Frank	Bluebellhill Terrace	224	149
McElhinney	Miss	Magazine Street Upper		151
McElhinney	Thomas	Marlborough Street	6	151
McElhinney	Robert	Northland Road		154
McElhinney	Mark	Philips Street	24	156
McElhinney	James	Philips Street	26	156
McElhinney	T.	Queen's Quay		157
McElhinney	Edward	Aberfoyle Terrace	1	160
McElhinney	T.	Strand Road	38	161
McElhinney	Thomas	Boating Club Road		161
McElhinney	Mrs	Donegal Street	38	167
McElhinney	Thomas	Florence Street	5	173
McElroy	Andrew	Albert Street	36	126
McElroy	Thomas	Asylum Road	8	127
McElroy	Samuel	Bishop Street	45	129
McElroy	William	Barnewall Place	10	169
McElroy & Morris		Bishop Street	45	129
McElvenny	Miss M.	Foyle Road		142
McElwee	Archibald	Albert Street	5	126
McElwee	Alexander	Argyle Terrace	15	127
McElwee	William	Bellevue Avenue	15	129
McElwee	William	Bluebellhill Terrace	190	149
McElwee	George	Moore Street	6	176
McEnaney	Mrs	Bishop Street	185	130
McEnroe	B.	Duke Street	27	172
McEvoy	Denis	Pine Street	11	176
McFadden	William	Argyle Street	63	127
McFadden	Joseph	Bishop Street	110	130
McFadden	Charles	Bishop Street	212	131
McFadden	Miss Mary	Bishop Street	252	131

Surname	First Name	Street	House Number	Page Number
McFadden	William	Brandywell Road	28	131
McFadden	Bernard	Elmwood Terrace	33	138
McFadden	Michael	Fahan Street	51	139
McFadden	Joseph	Hollywell Street	15	147
McFadden	Patrick	Lecky Road	3	148
McFadden	John	Long Tower	45	150
McFadden	John	Moore Street	14	152
McFadden	John	Nelson Street	18	154
McFadden	William	Quarry Street	1	157
McFadden	Arthur	Quarry Street	5	157
McFadden	Bernard	Stanley's Walk	29	160
McFadden	Daniel	St. Columb's Wells	83	162
McFadden	Patrick	Union Street	7	178
McFarland	John	Bennett Street Lower	39	129
McFarland	Daniel	Alma Terrace	39	142
McFarland	Moore	Governor Road	8	144
McFarland	Alexander	Hawkin Street	16	146
McFarland	G. & Co.	Princes Quay		157
McFarland	Sir John	Strand Road	Aberfoyle	160
McFarland	Thomas	Cuthbert Street	19	171
McFarland	R.	Duke Street	88	172
McFarland	Edward	Moore Street	8	176
McFaul	James	New Street	3	133
McFaul	David	Dunfield Terrace	9	172
McFaul	William	Fountain Hill	60	174
McFaul	James	Glendermott Road	96	174
McFaul	John	Meehan's Row	4	176
McFeely	John	Bennett Street Lower	16	129
McFeely	Mary A.	Bridge Street	68	132
McFeely	James	Butcher Street	20	132
McFeely	Daniel	Elmwood Street	4	138
McFeely	Hugh	Fahan Street	27	139
McFeely	Patrick J.	Francis Street	59	143
McFeely	James E.	Great James Street	70	145
McFeely	Denis E.	Lawrence Hill		148
McFeely	D. F. & Co.	Patrick Street	3, 4, 5	156
McFeely	James E.	Strand Road	45	160
McFeely	James E.	Strand Road	49	160
McFeely	James E.	Strand Road	Hilden	160
McFeely	James	Benvarden Avenue	10	169
McFeely	Mrs	Chapel Road	19	170
McFeeters	Thomas	Bishop Street	146	131
McFeeters	George	Blee's Lane		131
McFeeters	Mrs	Blee's Lane		131
McFeeters	Samuel	Fountain Street	106	141
McFeeters	James	Ivy Terrace	15	147
McFeeters	James	Ivy Terrace	10	147
McFrederick	Mrs	Hamilton Street	4	145
McGaffigan	John	Nassau Street Upper	23	153
McGahey	James	Millar's Close		132

Surname	First Name	Street	House Number	Page Number
McGahey	William	Fountain Street	43	140
McGahey	John	Fountain Street	54	141
McGahey	Robert	Fountain Street	74	141
McGahey	Charles	Wapping Lane	14	163
McGahey	James	Chapel Road		170
McGahey	Miss	Strabane Old Road	70	178
McGandy	Daniel	Bond's Hill	7	169
McGarrigle	William	Alma Place	11	126
McGarrigle	Mrs	Barry Street	27	128
McGarrigle	Joseph	Ivy Terrace	14	147
McGarrigle	Thomas	Stanley's Walk	18	160
McGarrigle	Charles	Moore Street	20	176
McGarrigle	Mrs	Spencer Road	96	177
McGarry	John	Bellevue Avenue	25	129
McGarvey	Fanny	Argyle Terrace	18	127
McGarvey	J G	Bishop Street	87	129
McGarvey	John	Chamberlain Street	6	134
McGarvey	Mary	Church Wall	5	134
McGarvey	James	Foyle Road	120	142
McGarvey	James	Long Tower	51	150
McGarvey	Mary	Long Tower	12	150
McGarvey	David	Chapel Road	65	170
McGarvey	Thomas	Violet Street Upper	7	179
McGavigan	Patrick	Eglinton Place	3	138
McGavigan	James	Ferguson Street	40	140
McGaw	James	Carlisle Road	40	133
McGeady	James	Argyle Street	45	127
McGeady	John	Argyle Terrace	6	127
McGeady	James	Argyle Terrace	22	127
McGeady	John	Chamberlain Street	1	134
McGeady	Francis	High Street	8	146
McGeady	Catherine	Lecky Road	12	149
McGeady	James	William Street	23	165
McGeady	John	William Street	22	165
McGee	John	Glendermott Road	20	174
McGeehan	Charles	Grafton Avenue	53	127
McGeehan	William	Grafton Avenue	55	127
McGeehan	Neil	Beechwood Street	25	129
McGeehan	Miss	Cottage Row	2	131
McGeehan	Minnie	Bishop Street	184	131
McGeehan	Michael	Deanery Place	1	136
McGeehan	Bernard	Henrietta Street	3	146
McGeehan	Patrick	Nassau Street Upper	17	153
McGeoghagan	Mrs	Dungiven Road	97	173
McGeoghegan	Patrick	Fahan Street	146	139
McGeoghegan	Patrick	Rossville Street	9	158
McGeown	John	Rossville Street	24	158
McGettigan	Daniel	Argyle Street	3	127
McGettigan	Michael	Chamberlain Street	15	134
McGettigan	Francis	Chamberlain Street	17	134

Surname	First Name	Street	House Number	Page Number
McGettigan	Rev J	Creggan Street	Parochial H	135
McGettigan	Andrew	Dungiven Road	57	172
McGhee	William J.	Park Avenue	8	156
McGiddecon	Mrs	Moore Street	2	176
McGildowny	Rosetta	Ivy Terrace	11	147
McGill	Patrick	Great James Street		145
McGill	William	Walker's Place	29	163
McGill	Mrs	Fountain Hill	26	174
McGill	John	Fountain Hill	28	174
McGill	Charles	Fountain Hill	38	174
McGill	Mrs	Herbert Street	1	174
McGill	James	The Rock	13	160
McGill	Edward	Strabane Old Road	17	177
McGill	Patrick	Lower Road		151
McGillan	Henry	Stable Lane	1	159
McGillen	Hugh	Union Street	13	163
McGilligan	John	Orchard Row	18	155
McGilloway	Charles	Brandywell Road	14	131
McGilloway	James	Maybrook Terrace	3	135
McGilloway	Joseph	Hollywell Street	1	147
McGilloway	Mary J.	Foster's Terrace	161	148
McGilloway	John	Lecky Road	207	149
McGilloway	Thomas	Nassau Street Lower	17	153
McGilloway	Frank	Thomas Street	30	162
McGilloway	Mrs	Windsor Terrace	3	166
McGilloway	Dan	Gortfoyle Place	13	174
McGilloway	James	Gortfoyle Place	2	174
McGilloway	Patrick	Meehan's Row	9	176
McGilloway	John	Pine Street	19	176
McGilton	John	Foyleview Terrace	4	160
McGinlay	John	Stanley's Walk	2	159
McGinley	Bernard	Abbey Street	63	125
McGinley	Cassie	Bridge Street	60	132
McGinley	John	Donegal Place	8	137
McGinley	Michael	Fahan Street	126	139
McGinley	Patrick	Foyle Street	103	141
McGinley	Hugh	Rossville Street	17	158
McGinley	Hugh	Sloan's Terrace	9	159
McGinley	Patrick	Stanley's Walk	24	160
McGinley	Grace	Sugarhouse Lane	18	162
McGinley	Patrick	Townsend Street	4	162
McGinley	Miss	Victoria Place	2	163
McGinley	Mrs	Waterloo Street	33	163
McGinley	Patrick	William Street	97	165
McGinley	Annie	William Street	20	165
McGinley	John	Bond's Street	1	169
McGinley	Charles	Cross Street	18	171
McGinley	Mrs	Emerson Street	12	173
McGinley	Ellen	Union Street	33	178
McGinn	Michael	Sloan's Terrace	12	159

Surname	First Name	Street	House Number	Page Number
McGinn	George	St. Patrick Street	2	162
McGinn	Mrs A.	William Street	27	165
McGinn	Mrs A.	William Street		165
McGinness	Miss	Ferguson Street	57	140
McGinness	William	Duke Street	18	172
McGinnis	Edward	Bishop Street	97	129
McGinnis	Miss	Hollywell Row	77	148
McGinnis	Edward	Benvarden Avenue	11	169
McGinnis	William	Benvarden Avenue	13	169
McGinnis	Joseph	Clifton Street	3	170
McGinnis	John	Clifton Street	6	170
McGinnis	William	Derry View Terrace	1	171
McGinnis	Edward	Duke Street	3	172
McGinnis	Reps. James	Dungiven Road	11	172
McGinnis	David	Robert Street	6	176
McGinnis	James	Creggan Street	35	135
McGinnis	Mrs	William Street	113	165
McGinniss	James	Chamberlain Street	4	134
McGinniss	Thomas	Elmwood Street	5	138
McGinniss	John	Meadowbank Avenue	19	152
McGinniss	Abraham	Nelson Street	52	154
McGinniss	Patrick	Orchard Street	7	155
McGinniss	John	Wellington Street	71	164
McGinniss	Charles	Duke Street	47	172
McGinniss	William	Spencer Road	stables	177
McGinty	Michael	Great James Street	20	145
McGinty	James	High Street	9	146
McGinty	Mary	Long Tower	70	150
McGinty	Bernard	Long Tower	72	150
McGirr	James	Bishop Street	57	129
McGirr	Mrs	Carrigans Lane	23	133
McGirr	James	Mitchelburne Terrace	92	142
McGirr	Peter	Orchard Street	18	155
McGlinchey	Miss	Bishop Street	286	131
McGlinchey	Thomas	Brook Street Avenue	2	132
McGlinchey	Michael	Carrigans Lane	19	133
McGlinchey	Edward	New Street	7	133
McGlinchey	Mrs	Deanery Street	22	136
McGlinchey	Catherine	Deanery Street	34	136
McGlinchey	Andrew	Donaghy's Row	3	145
McGlinchey	Myles	Long Tower	34	150
McGlinchey	Andrew	Nailor's Row	30	153
McGlinchey	James	Nelson Street	1	153
McGlinchey	Charles jun	Nelson Street	39	154
McGlinchey	Thomas	Sloan's Terrace	10	159
McGlinchey	Charles	Spencer Road	138	177
McGlynn	Rev Hugh	Creggan Street	Parochial H	135
McGlynn	Mary	Quarry Street	14	157
McGlynn	Charles	Gortfoyle Place	11	174
McGoldrick	James	Strabane Old Road	6	177

Surname	First Name	Street	House Number	Page Number
McGonagle	Robert	Bellevue Avenue	39	129
McGonagle	Mrs	Bishop Street	196	131
McGonagle	John	Edenmore Street	1	137
McGonagle	James	Kildarra Terrace	11	146
McGonagle	Michael	Lecky Road	1	148
McGonagle	Catherine	Lecky Road	47	148
McGonagle	Hugh	Bluebellhill Terrace	168	149
McGonagle	Joseph	Bluebellhill Terrace	228	149
McGonagle	John	Northland Avenue		155
McGonagle	Miss	Stanley's Walk	31	160
McGonagle	Mrs	West-End Park	18	165
McGonagle	Thomas	Artisan Street	9	166
McGonagle	Hugh	Bond's Street	14	170
McGonigal	Hugh	Miller Street	9	152
McGonigal	Michael	Stanley's Walk	14	160
McGonigal	Daniel	Waterloo Street	8	164
McGonigle	William	Ann Street	14	127
McGonigle	W. J.	Infirmary Road		147
McGonigle	Daniel	William Street	34	165
McGonigle	James	Windmill Terrace	7	166
McGonigle	Mrs	Epworth Street	3	167
McGonigle	William	Chapel Road	9	170
McGonigle	John	Clifton Street	4	170
McGonigle	Thomas	Glendermott Road	40	174
McGonigle	Thomas	Glendermott Road	52	174
McGonigle	David	Simpson's Brae	13	177
McGonigle	Hugh	Violet Street Lower	6	178
McGowan	Charles	Abbey Street	12	125
McGowan	Patrick	Caroline Place	5	133
McGowan	Mrs	Eden Place	20	138
McGowan	Thomas	Ewing Street	26	139
McGowan	Mrs	Fountain Street	55	140
McGowan	Michael	Lecky Road	131	148
McGowan	Mrs	Lecky Road	120	149
McGowan	James	Long Tower	31	150
McGowan	Mrs	Moore Street	7	152
McGowan	Lawrence	Nelson Street	26	154
McGowan	Samuel	St. Columb's Wells	93	162
McGowan	Mrs	Walker's Place	19	163
McGowan	James	Wellington Street	30	164
McGowan	Patrick	Wellington Street	64	164
McGowan	Mrs	Wells Street Terrace	4	164
McGowan	Edward	Creggan Road	113	166
McGowan	Allan	Ashcroft Place	3	169
McGowan	Charles	Barnewall Place	25	169
McGowan	Joseph	Bond's Place	5	170
McGowan	John	Cuthbert Street	25	171
McGowan	John	Fountain Hill	73	174
McGowan	John	Moore Street	27	176
McGowan	Thomas	Spencer Road	122	177

Surname	First Name	Street	House Number	Page Number
McGowan	Joseph	Strabane Old Road	16	178
McGranaghan	John	Fitters Row	259	130
McGranaghan	William	Bishop Street	248	131
McGranaghan	Susan	Gresham's Row	3	145
McGranaghan	John	Bluebellhill Terrace	210	149
McGranaghan	John	Rossville Street	85	158
McGranaghan	William	Gortfoyle Place	1	174
McGranahan	Rev. J.	Crawford Square	22	135
McGranery	Daniel	Chamberlain Street	26	134
McGrath	J. P.	Castle Street		133
McGrath	Mrs	Cunningham Row	1	136
McGrath	J. P.	Marlborough Street	29	151
McGrath	Mrs	Waterloo Street	27	163
McGreavey	John	Argyle Street	37	127
McGreenery	James	Riverview Terrace	3	176
McGregor	Thomas	Barrack Street	5	128
McGregor	Alex	London Street	9	150
McGrellis	Mrs	Moore Street	12	152
McGrellis	Charles	Orchard Row	10	155
McGrellis	Hugh	Orchard Street	3	155
McGroarty	Hugh	Blucher Street	11	131
McGroarty	Patrick	Foyle Road	32	142
McGrorty	Patrick	Creggan Road	107	166
McGrory	Joseph	Bishop Street	83	129
McGrory	James	Castle Street		133
McGrory	Patrick junior	Donegal Place	12	137
McGrory	Mrs	Donegal Place	16	137
McGrory	James	Eden Place	3	138
McGrory	Mary A	Edward Street	8	138
McGrory	Hugh	Fahan Street	34	139
McGrory	W. J.	Lundy's Lane	2	150
McGrory	Bridget	Mary Street	2	152
McGrory	John	Palace Street	2	155
McGrory	Neil	St. Columb's Wells	95	162
McGrory	Edward	Kerr's Terrace	27	166
McGrory	Mrs	Marlborough Park	63	166
McGrory	Mrs	Creggan Road	8	167
McGrory	James	Lewis Street	35	167
McGrory	John	Barnewall Place	18	169
McGrory	Margaret	York Street	6	179
McGrotty	James	Fahan Street	76	139
McGrotty	E.	William Street	105	165
McGrotty	Edward	Mount Street	6	167
McGuiggan	Charles	Fulton Place	4	143
McGuiggan	Felix	Fulton Place	8	143
McGuiggan	Thomas	Violet Street Lower	51	178
McGuinness	Mrs	Abercorn Road	20	125
McGuinness	Samuel	Abercorn Road	20	125
McGuinness	Archibald	Bellevue Avenue	10	129
McGuinness	James	Bishop Street	16	130

Surname	First Name	Street	House Number	Page Number
McGuinness	Catherine	Bridge Street	66	132
McGuinness	Robert	Maybrook Terrace	2	135
McGuinness	Mrs	Eden Place	12	138
McGuinness	Mrs	Lawrence Hill		148
McGuinness	W. N.	Lawrence Hill	Clifton Holme	148
McGuinness	James	Osborne Street	3	168
McGuinness	William	Bond's Hill	2	169
McGuire	Thomas	Hamilton Street	20	145
McGuire	Annie	Lecky Road	262	149
McGuire	Mrs	Thomas Street	25	162
McGuire	Mrs	Windmill Terrace	23	166
McGuire	Thomas	Windmill Terrace	8	166
McGuire	John	Creggan Road	36	167
McGuire	Patrick	Spencer Road	48	177
McGurk	Peter	Donegal Place	4	137
McGurk	James	Glendermott Road	92	174
McGurnaghan	Mrs	Foyleview Terrace	17	161
McHugh	John	Millar's Close		132
McHugh	Miss	Chamberlain Street	11	134
McHugh	Most Rev Dr	Creggan Street	Parochial H	135
McHugh	Patrick	St. Columb's Terrace	89	148
McHugh	James	Creggan Road	87	166
McHugh	Henry	Donegal Street	1	167
McHugh	Joseph	Lewis Street	10	167
McIlhargey	J.	Waterloo Street	29	163
McIlhargey	Mrs C.	Duke Street	86	172
McIlroy	Robert	Westland Avenue	17	165
McIlroy	William	Dungiven Road	Rossdowney	173
McIlwaine	Samuel	Meadowbank Avenue	33	152
McIlwaine	Bella	Irish Street	22, 23	174
McIntosh	Alexander	Garden City	7	136
McIntosh	William R.	Queen Street	2	157
McIntyre	Hugh	Abbey Street	39	125
McIntyre	David	Abbey Street	43	125
McIntyre	Miss	Artillery Street	2	127
McIntyre	Robert	Bishop Street	132	130
McIntyre	Bernard	Bridge Street	29	132
McIntyre	William	Chamberlain Street	18	134
McIntyre	Patrick	Donegal Place	10	137
McIntyre	Edward	Fahan Street	158	139
McIntyre	Bernard	Ferguson Street	56	140
McIntyre	Mrs	Fountain Street	23	140
McIntyre	Mrs	George Street	2	143
McIntyre	Robert	George Street	16	143
McIntyre	Mrs	Glasgow Terrace	19	144
McIntyre	Hugh	Gordon Terrace	4	144
McIntyre	Hugh	Hamilton Street	7	145
McIntyre	Mrs	Nailor's Row		153
McIntyre	Joseph	Nailor's Row	48	153

116

Surname	First Name	Street	House Number	Page Number
McIntyre	Bernard	Orchard Row	1	155
McIntyre	Mrs	Quarry Street	9	157
McIntyre	John	St. Columb's Wells	29	161
McIntyre	Denis	St. Columb's Wells	74	162
McIntyre	Patrick	St. Columb's Wells	84	162
McIntyre	Denis	St. Patrick Street	12	162
McIntyre	Charles	Wells Street Terrace	1	164
McIntyre	Thomas J.	William Street	38	165
McIntyre	Charles	Artisan Street	2	166
McIntyre	John	Creggan Road	167	167
McIntyre	William	Creggan Road	50	167
McIntyre	William	Donegal Street	6	167
McIntyre	Philip	Alfred Street	42	168
McIntyre	John	Barnewall Place	4	169
McIntyre	William	Emerson Street	30	173
McIntyre	Mrs	King Street	13	175
McIntyre	Eliza	Limavady Road		175
McIntyre	William	Moore Street	17	176
McIntyre	Joseph	Spencer Road	34	177
McIntyre	John	Spencer Road	38	177
McIntyre, Hogg & Marsh		Queen Street		157
McIvor	Edward & Co.	Clarendon Street		134
McIvor	John	Hogg's Folly	8	146
McIvor	John	Duke Street	94	172
McIvor	Miss	Glendermott Road	30	174
McKane	John	Abbey Street	31	125
McKane	Joseph	Thomas Street	44	162
McKane	Thomas	Osborne Street	1	168
McKane	William	Clooney Terrace	40	170
McKane	Robert	Glendermott Road	102	174
McKane	W. J.	Pine Street	21	176
McKane	William	Violet Street Lower	4	178
McKane	Margaret	York Street	28	179
McKay	Marshall	Termonbacca		143
McKeague	James	Mount Street	13	167
McKeague	Patrick	Duke Street	3	172
McKee	Robert	Abercorn Road	22	125
McKee	William J.	De Burgh Square	2	136
McKee	John	Hawkin Street	39	146
McKeegan	Mrs	Orchard Row	17	155
McKeegan	Thomas	Stewart's Terrace	3	160
McKeegan	Joseph	Walker's Street	1	179
McKeever	Joseph	Creggan Street	7	135
McKeever	Maggie	Deanery Street	48	136
McKeever	Mrs	Elmwood Terrace	17	138
McKeever	Charles	Governor Road	27	144
McKeever	Mrs	Cranagh Terrace	1	148
McKeever	Henry	Bluebellhill Terrace	200	149
McKeever	Mrs	Little Diamond	4	150

Surname	First Name	Street	House Number	Page Number
McKeever	Michael	Strand Road Lower		161
McKeever	Miss	Dungiven Road	5	172
McKeever	John	Glendermott Road	66	174
McKelvie	M. A.	Rossville Street	54	158
McKenna	Mrs	Bishop Street	101	129
McKenna	Patrick	William Street	105	165
McKenna	Philip	Carlin Street	5	170
McKeown	Michael	Beechwood Street	20	129
McKeown	William	Brook Street Avenue	4	132
McKeown	Henry	Castle Gate		133
McKeown	Michael	Richmond Street	15	158
McKeown	James	Rossville Street	48	158
McKeown	Samuel	Spencer Road	117	177
McKeown & Co		Ferryquay Street		140
McKeown & Co.		Waterloo Street	24	164
McKernan	John	Fahan Street	11	139
McKernan	Joseph	Long Tower	58	150
McKillip	J.	Shipquay Street		159
McKimm	John	Long Tower	64	150
McKimm	Robert	Orchard Street	9	155
McKimm	Joseph	Windmill Terrace	26	166
McKinlay	Gabriel	Garden City	5	136
McKinlay	H. & Co.	Diamond		137
McKinlay	James	Ferguson Street	59	140
McKinlay	Robert	Wapping Lane	12	163
McKinlay	Mrs	Moore Street	19	176
McKinlay	John	Moore Street	25	176
McKinley	Catherine	Moore Street	1	176
McKinney	William	Bishop Street	153	130
McKinney	Alex	Bishop Street	234	131
McKinney	John	Bishop Street	236	131
McKinney	Mrs	Dark Lane	14	136
McKinney	Charles	Eden Place	18	138
McKinney	Moses	Foyle View	1	143
McKinney	John	Fulton Place	21	143
McKinney	John	Governor Road	19	144
McKinney	Mrs	Governor Road	21	144
McKinney	Lizzie	Ann Street	13	149
McKinney	William	Nassau Street Lower	42	153
McKinney	William	Orchard Lane	6	155
McKinney	P & Co.	Patrick Street	6, 7	156
McKinney	Robert	New Row	4	160
McKinney	Charles	Osborne Street	9	168
McKinney	James	Cross Street	7	171
McKinney	William	Cross Street	23	171
McKinney	Mrs	Duke Street	5	172
McKinney	Patrick	Union Street	2	178
McKinney	John	Violet Street Lower	42	178
McKnight	Thomas	Argyle Street	75	127

Surname	First Name	Street	House Number	Page Number
McKnight	John	Cross Street	35	171
McLaren	William	Marlborough Terrace	18	152
McLaren	William & Co.	Strand Road	57	160
McLaughglin	James	Baronet Street	1A	128
McLaughlin	Daniel	Abbey Street	33	125
McLaughlin	Mrs	Ann Street	9	126
McLaughlin	Mary Jane	Ann Street	4	127
McLaughlin	Patrick	Argyle Street	24	127
McLaughlin	Patrick	Beechwood Street	1	128
McLaughlin	Joseph	Beechwood Street	28	129
McLaughlin	John	Bennett Street Upper	5	129
McLaughlin	Michael	Bishop Street	55	129
McLaughlin	Samuel	Bishop Street	91	129
McLaughlin	William	Bishop Street	99	129
McLaughlin	William	Bishop Street	109	129
McLaughlin	John	Bishop Street	227	130
McLaughlin	John	Bishop Street	243	130
McLaughlin	Miss	Bishop Street	76	130
McLaughlin	James	Bishop Street	124	130
McLaughlin	Hugh	Bishop Street	200	131
McLaughlin	William	Bishop Street	248	131
McLaughlin	Miss	Bishop Street	256	131
McLaughlin	George	Bishop Street	280	131
McLaughlin	Joseph	Brandywell Road	24	131
McLaughlin	William	Brook Street	5	132
McLaughlin	Edward	Cable Street	13	132
McLaughlin	Catherine	Carrigans Lane	15	133
McLaughlin	Mrs	Clarendon Street Lower	3	135
McLaughlin	Thomas	Collon Terrace		135
McLaughlin	John	Corbett Street	15	135
McLaughlin	Bridget	Corbett Street	6	135
McLaughlin	John	Corbett Street	12	135
McLaughlin	Patrick	Creggan Street	19	135
McLaughlin	William	Creggan Street	29	135
McLaughlin	Joseph	Creggan Street	31	135
McLaughlin	Edward	Creggan Terrace	12	135
McLaughlin	Patrick	Dark Lane	10	136
McLaughlin	William	Deanery Place	2	136
McLaughlin	William	Eden Place	5	138
McLaughlin	Alexander	Eglinton Place	17	138
McLaughlin	Philip	Eglinton Place	19	138
McLaughlin	Pat	Eglinton Place	4	138
McLaughlin	John	Eglinton Terrace	3	138
McLaughlin	Edward	Elmwood Terrace	44	138
McLaughlin	Thomas	Elmwood Street	9	138
McLaughlin	John	Elmwood Street	10	138
McLaughlin	Margaret	Fahan Street	27	139
McLaughlin	Patrick	Fahan Street	8	139
McLaughlin	Charles	Fahan Street	70	139

Surname	First Name	Street	House Number	Page Number
McLaughlin	Miss	Fahan Street	140	139
McLaughlin	Mrs	Fountain Street	84	141
McLaughlin	Andrew	Fountain Place	19	141
McLaughlin	Mrs S.	Foyle Street	1	141
McLaughlin	Alex. H	Foyle Road	49	142
McLaughlin	John	Mitchelburne Terrace	99	142
McLaughlin	James	Fox's Lane	2	143
McLaughlin	Mrs	Fox's Lane	5	143
McLaughlin	Mary Ann	Frederick Street	1	143
McLaughlin	Thomas	Frederick Street	4	143
McLaughlin	Catherine	Fulton Place	20	143
McLaughlin	Philip	Glenbrook Terrace	9	143
McLaughlin	William	Glenbrook Terrace	21	143
McLaughlin	James	Grafton Street	21	144
McLaughlin	Mrs	Great James Street	67	145
McLaughlin	Michael A.	Great James Street	69	145
McLaughlin	Mrs	Gresham's Row	5	145
McLaughlin	James	Hamilton Street	17	145
McLaughlin	Andrew	Hamilton Street	18	145
McLaughlin	John	Harding Street	7	145
McLaughlin	Charles	Harvey Street	7	146
McLaughlin	Hugh	High Street	7	146
McLaughlin	Bernard	High Street	4	146
McLaughlin	Thomas	Howard Street	1	147
McLaughlin	William	Hollywell Street	10	147
McLaughlin	John	John Street		147
McLaughlin	John	Joseph Street	1	147
McLaughlin	John	Lecky Road	117	148
McLaughlin	Hugh	Lecky Road		148
McLaughlin	William	Lecky Road	2	149
McLaughlin	Patrick	Lecky Road	114	149
McLaughlin	William	Bluebellhill Terrace	158	149
McLaughlin	Patrick	Bluebellhill Terrace	212	149
McLaughlin	Patrick	Long Tower	63	150
McLaughlin	James	Long Tower	69	150
McLaughlin	William	Dixon's Close	4	151
McLaughlin	Eugene	Moore Street	6	152
McLaughlin	James	Mountjoy Street	21	152
McLaughlin	Annie	Nailor's Row	28	153
McLaughlin	Patrick	Nassau Street Lower	15	153
McLaughlin	John	Nassau Street Lower	10	153
McLaughlin	W. J.	Nassau Street Lower	26	153
McLaughlin	William	Nassau Street Lower	50	153
McLaughlin	Hugh	Nassau Street Upper	3	153
McLaughlin	Hugh	Nelson Street	71	154
McLaughlin	Mrs	Nelson Street	2	154
McLaughlin	Mrs Bridget	Nelson Street	34	154
McLaughlin	James	Northland Avenue	23	155
McLaughlin	Mrs Rose	Park Avenue	1	156
McLaughlin	Patrick	Philips Street	17	156

Surname	First Name	Street	House Number	Page Number
McLaughlin	William	Quarry Street	22	157
McLaughlin	Dr. J. N.	Queen Street	13	157
McLaughlin	Patrick H.	Richmond Street	10	158
McLaughlin	John	Rossville Street	69	158
McLaughlin	John	Rossville Street	81	158
McLaughlin	Mrs S.	Shipquay Place		159
McLaughlin	Patrick	Sloan's Terrace	8	159
McLaughlin	William	Strand Road		160
McLaughlin	James	The Rock	15, 17	160
McLaughlin	James	The Rock	25	160
McLaughlin	James	Strand Road	86	161
McLaughlin	John	St. Columb's Wells	103	162
McLaughlin	Mrs	St. Columb's Wells	109	162
McLaughlin	Miss	St. Columb's Wells	108	162
McLaughlin	Patrick	Sugarhouse Lane	1	162
McLaughlin	Mrs	Sugarhouse Lane	7	162
McLaughlin	William	Thomas Street	7	162
McLaughlin	James	Thomas Street	15	162
McLaughlin	Ellen	Union Street	2	163
McLaughlin	John	Waterloo Street	57	164
McLaughlin	John	Waterloo Street	34	164
McLaughlin	Patrick	Wellington Street	67	164
McLaughlin	J. C.	Westland Avenue	9	164
McLaughlin	Michael	Westland Terrace	10	165
McLaughlin	Michael	West-End Terrace	4	165
McLaughlin	Charles	William Street	79	165
McLaughlin	Eliza	William Street	90	166
McLaughlin	William	William Street	92	166
McLaughlin	William	Ashfield Terrace	33	166
McLaughlin	David	Creggan Road	60	167
McLaughlin	William	Mount Street	15	167
McLaughlin	Daniel	Cottage Row	12	168
McLaughlin	John	Alfred Street	14	168
McLaughlin	Mrs	Carlin Street	7	170
McLaughlin	Robert	Cross Street	25	171
McLaughlin	James	Cuthbert Street	23	171
McLaughlin	Lewis	Derry View Terrace	7	171
McLaughlin	William	Duddy's Row	3	171
McLaughlin	William	Duke Street	11	172
McLaughlin	Joseph	Dungiven Road	95	173
McLaughlin	Mrs	Fountain Hill	15	173
McLaughlin	Mrs	Fountain Hill	62	174
McLaughlin	John	Fountain Hill	90	174
McLaughlin	Robert	Gortfoyle Place	5	174
McLaughlin	Robert	Glendermott Road	62	174
McLaughlin	Miss	Margaret Street	7	175
McLaughlin	John	Mountain View		176
McLaughlin	Bernard	Primrose Street	21	176
McLaughlin	Francis	Riverview Terrace	7	176
McLaughlin	Ann	Strabane Old Road	56	178

Surname	First Name	Street	House Number	Page Number
McLaughlin	James	Victoria Park		178
McLaughlin	William	Violet Street Lower	34	178
McLaughlin	Thomas	Walker's Street	2	179
McLaughlin	Thomas	Walker's Street	4	179
McLaughlin	Mrs	Ann Street	12	127
McLaughlin & Leonard		William Street	42, 44	165
McLaughlin & O'Donnell		William Street	75	165
McLenaghan	Robert	Lecky Road	53	148
McLoone	Neil	De Burgh Terrace	3	136
McLoone	Neil & Co.	Linenhall Street		149
McLoone	N. & Co.	Linenhall Street		149
McLoone	Joseph	Foyleview Terrace	10	160
McLoone	Peter	Union Street	23	163
McLoughlin	Miss	Little James Street	10	150
McLucas	Andrew	Foyle View	5	143
McLucas	Joseph	Foyle View	11	143
McLucas	Joseph	Governor Road	34	144
McLucas	John	Orchard Row	24	155
McLucas	Archibald	Wesley Street	7	168
McMackin	James	Bennett Street Upper	19	129
McMahon	Michael	Creggan Terrace	13	135
McMahon	Hugh	Bluebellhill Terrace	206	149
McMahon	Hugh	London Street	12	150
McMahon	James	Long Tower	77	150
McMahon	Mrs	North Street	3	168
McManus	John	Bridge Street	11	131
McManus	Thomas	Bridge Street	15	131
McManus	Mrs	Hogg's Folly	14	146
McManus	Philip	Lecky Road	96	149
McManus	Henry	Wellington Street	59	164
McManus	Miss	Marlborough Park	59	166
McManus	Rose	Violet Street Lower	11	178
McMaster	Professor J.	College Avenue		155
McMenamin	Andrew	Alexandra Place	21	126
McMenamin	Hugh	Donegal Place	14	137
McMenamin	Michael	Ewing Street	5	139
McMenamin	William	Hamilton Street	14	145
McMenamin	Lizzie	Foster's Terrace	167	148
McMenamin	James	Miller Street	17	152
McMenamin	John	Nailor's Row	36	153
McMenamin	Catherine	St. Columb's Wells	21	161
McMenamin	John	Bond's Street	7	169
McMenamin	James	Dungiven Road	15	172
McMenamin	John	Dungiven Road	17	172
McMenamin	Edward	Dungiven Road	23	172
McMenamin	John	Dungiven Road	18	173
McMenamin	Robert	Margaret Street	12	175
McMenamin	John	Union Street	5	178

Surname	First Name	Street	House Number	Page Number
McMichael	James	De Burgh Square	6	136
McMichael	Mrs	Kerr's Terrace	19	166
McMichael	Mrs	Glendermott Road	22	174
McMichael Bros		Sackville Street	8	158
McMillan	William J	Albert Place	5	126
McMillan	David	New Street	4	133
McMillan	Charles	Creggan Road	83	166
McMonagle	Miss	Abercorn Road	25	125
McMonagle	Sarah	Blucher Street	9	131
McMonagle	Patrick	Butcher Street	15	132
McMonagle	John	Butcher Street	cellar	132
McMonagle	Dr J. F.	Clarendon Street	21	134
McMonagle	Daniel	Corbett Street	9	135
McMonagle	John	Eden Place	7	138
McMonagle	Mrs	Eglinton Place	14	138
McMonagle	Robert	Foyle Road	77	142
McMonagle	Charles	Joseph Street	7	147
McMonagle	Miss	Kennedy Place	3	147
McMonagle	P.	Magazine Street	1	151
McMonagle	James	Nelson Street	53	154
McMonagle	Miss	Philips Street	32	156
McMonagle	Pat	Waterloo Street	14	164
McMonagle	Joseph	Dungiven Road	67	173
McMorris	Edward	Argyle Street	50	127
McMorris	Robert	Governor Road	29	144
McMorris	Mrs	Wesley Street	4	168
McMorris	Robert J.	Bond's Street	18	170
McMorris	James	Fountain Hill	waterman's house	173
McMorris	Samuel	Primrose Street	9	176
McMoyle	Miss	Elmwood Terrace	6	138
McMullan	Hugh	Bishop Street	25	129
McMullan	Herbert	Sunnyside Terrace	2	131
McMullan	James	Bond's Street	49	169
McMullan	James	Clooney Terrace	30	171
McMullan	Joseph	Violet Street Lower	19	178
McMurray	R. J.	Castle Street	3	133
McMurray	Joseph	Ferguson Street	51A	140
McMurray	Mrs	Foyle Road	104	142
McMurray	T.	Shipquay Place		159
McMurray	R. J.	Westland Terrace	14	165
McNair	William	Kildarra Terrace	8	146
McNally	C T	Argyle Street	32	127
McNally	John	Infirmary Road	1	147
McNally	Patrick	Bluebellhill Terrace	176	149
McNamara	John	West-End Park	8	165
McNamee	John	Alexandra Place	24	126
McNamee	James	Shipquay Street	21	159
McNaught	Mrs	Strabane Old Road	76	178
McNaught	Michael	Sloan's Terrace	37	159

Surname	First Name	Street	House Number	Page Number
McNaughton	Thomas	Princes Street	11	156
McNaul	Robert	Fountain Hill	42	174
McNaul	Robert	Victoria Road		178
McNeary	Matthew	De Burgh Terrace	17	137
McNeary	Mark	Fairman Place	10	140
McNeary	Ellen J.	Foster's Terrace	185	148
McNeary	W. A.	Nicholson Square	15	154
McNeary & Burnside		Strand Road		160
McNeary & Wiley		Bishop Street	20	129
McNee	Mrs	Barry Street	20	128
McNeill	Mrs	Beechwood Avenue	18	128
McNeill	Henry	Henry Street	17	146
McNeill	Frederick	Wesley Street	24	168
McNeill	William	Distillery Lane Lower	9	171
McNeill	Miss	Limavady Road		175
McNeill	William	Spencer Road	Victoria Hall	177
McNelis	Mounted-Constable	Laburnum Terrace	20	148
McNerney	Sergeant	Strand Road Lower		161
McNulty	David	Alexandra Place	1	126
McNulty	Ernest	Alexandra Place	4	126
McNulty	Miss A.	Carlisle Road	14	133
McNulty	Edward	Deanery Street	5	136
McNulty	William	Donegal Place	15	137
McNulty	James	Fahan Street	98	139
McNulty	Thomas	Morrison's Close	2	139
McNulty	John	Fountain Street	65	140
McNulty	Mrs	Fulton Place	16	143
McNulty	George	Henrietta Street	1	146
McNulty	James	Linenhall Street	12	150
McNulty	John	Long Tower	71	150
McNulty	Ellen	Long Tower	24	150
McNulty	William J.	Long Tower	74	150
McNulty	Edward	The Rock	21	160
McNulty	James	St. Columb's Wells	101	162
McNulty	William	West-End Terrace	7	165
McNulty	Mrs	Duddy's Row	6	172
McNulty	John	Fountain Hill	31	173
McNulty	Ernest	Fountain Hill	50	174
McNulty	Mrs	Glendermott Road	32	174
McNulty	John	Spencer Road	66	177
McNutt	Miss	Culmore Road	Grian-Lagh	136
McNutt	John	Elmwood Terrace	37	138
McNutt	R. J. & Son	Ferryquay Street		140
McNutt	Miss	Fountain Place	8	141
McNutt	Henry	London Street	5	150
McNutt	Michael	Nelson Street	43	154
McNutt	Alex	Pennyburn		156

Surname	First Name	Street	House Number	Page Number
McNutt	David	Lewis Street	12	167
McNutt	Mrs	Strabane Old Road	94	178
McNutt	Samuel	Union Street	25	178
McPaul	Dominick	Bishop Street	120	130
McPheak	Mrs	Dark Lane	21	136
McPherson	Samuel	Alfred Street	34	168
McPherson	T.	Bond's Street	32	170
McPherson	Mrs	Clooney Terrace	17	170
McPherson	Joseph	Ebrington Street	1	173
McPherson	Miss	Glendermott Road	72	174
McPhilemy	John	Bishop Street	203	130
McQuade	Charles	Elmwood Terrace	40	138
McQuaid	John	Lecky Road	98	149
McQuaide	Mrs	Brook Street Avenue	1	132
McQuaide	Richard	Henrietta Street	7	146
McQuigg	George	Carlisle Pass		132
McQuigg	Daniel	Wellington Street	21	164
McQuigg	John	Wellington Street	54	164
McQuilken	Mrs	Adair Street	2	126
McReynolds	Daniel	Duke Street	58	172
McRitchie	Stanley	Clarendon Street	27	134
McRory	Edward	Governor Road	37	144
McShane	Patrick	Ann Street	6	127
McShane	Francis	Dungiven Road	26	173
McShane	Mrs	Fountain Hill	65	173
McShane	Patrick	Spencer Road	11	177
McShane	John	Spencer Road	43	177
McShane	William J.	Spencer Road		177
McShane	Very Rev John	Sunbeam Terrace	19	130
McShane	Kate	Bridge Street	19	132
McSheffrey	Edward	Fahan Street	28	139
McSherry	Thomas	Bridge Street	21	132
McSherry	Thomas	Bridge Street	25	132
McSherry	Mrs	Marlborough Park	53	166
McSorley	Mrs	Foster's Terrace	177	148
McSweeney	Bridget	Deanery Street	27	136
McSweenie	Nurse	Victoria Place		163
McSwine	Daniel	Bridge Street	16	132
McSwine	Alex	Fahan Street	65	139
McSwine	Mrs	Matty's Lane	34	162
McTaggart	James	Creggan Terrace	11	135
McVeigh	J	Beechwood Park	71	128
McVeigh	Andrew	Great James Street	51	144
McVeigh	Daniel	Magazine Street Upper		151
McVeigh	James	Nelson Street	9	153
McVeigh	J. & Co.	Market Buildings		161
McVeigh	James	Walker's Place	27	163
McVicer	Duncan	Barry Street	12	128
McVicker	John G.	Crawford Square	9	135

Surname	First Name	Street	House Number	Page Number
McVicker	R. & A.	Shipquay Street	25	158
McVicker	Thomas	St. Patrick Street	7	162
McWilliams	Michael	Strabane Old Road	74	178
Meehan	Timothy	Abbey Street	14	125
Meehan	Felix	Bishop Street	Governor	130
Meehan	Patrick	Brandywell Road	21	131
Meehan	John	Brook Street Avenue	3	132
Meehan	Mary	Francis Street	9	143
Meehan	Peter	Pump Street	17	156
Meehan	Miss	Sloan's Terrace	39	159
Meehan	Thomas	St. Columb's Wells	32	162
Meehan	Joseph	Chapel Road	2	170
Meehan	Charles	Riverview Terrace	14	176
Meenan	Daniel	Brandywell Road	3	131
Meenan	Patrick	Chamberlain Street	13	134
Meenan	Catherine	Lecky Road	9	148
Meenan	John	Mountjoy Street	8	153
Meenan	William	Northland Terrace	7	155
Meenan	Jeremiah	Wellington Street	65	164
Mehaffey	C. A. & Son	Commercial Buildings		141
Mehaffy	C A	Eden Terrace		137
Meharg	William	Clooney Terrace	22	171
Melaugh	John	Bishop Street	151	130
Melaugh	John	Bishop Street	224	131
Melaugh	William J.	Fahan Street	50	139
Melaugh	Charles	Hamilton Street	23	145
Melaugh	Charles	Lecky Road	263	149
Melaugh	John	St. Columb's Wells	23	161
Mellon	James	Artillery Street	3	127
Mellon	James	Bishop Street	139	130
Mellon	John	Governor Road	41	144
Mellon	James	Hogg's Folly	10	146
Mellon	Thomas	Hogg's Folly	15	146
Mellon	William	Orchard Lane	4	155
Mellon	Francis	Ashfield Terrace	43	166
Melville	John	Hawkin Street	19	146
Melville Hotel		Foyle Street		141
Menmuir	Mrs	Hawkin Street	44	146
Mercer	Thomas	Nassau Street Upper	15	153
Merchant	Ernest	Meadowbank Avenue		152
Mercier	Alphonse	Clarendon Street	44	135
Mernor	Edward	Pine Street	3	176
Merrick	John	St. Columb's Wells	86	162
Merrigan	John	Bishop Street	254	131
Mervyn	Miss	Spencer Road	92	177
Michael	Mrs	Nassau Street Lower	1	153
Millar	David	Henry Street	3	146
Millar	William	Ivy Terrace	30	147
Millar	Frederick	Kennedy Street	21	148

Surname	First Name	Street	House Number	Page Number
Millar	John	Strand Road Lower		161
Millar	Kate	Sugarhouse Lane	14	162
Millar	William	Nassau Street Lower	37	153
Millar	Rev. D. G.	Alexandra Terrace	7	154
Millar & Beatty		Bishop Street	7, 9	129
Millar & Beatty		Magazine Street Upper		151
Miller	Robert	Argyle Street	51	127
Miller	David	Asylum Road	4	127
Miller	John	Asylum Road	11	127
Miller	James	Bridge Street	38	132
Miller	Miss	Carlisle Road	69	133
Miller	Andrew	Dark Lane	16	136
Miller	Daniel	Deanery Street	16	136
Miller	Andrew	De Burgh Square	12	136
Miller	Andrew	Ferguson Street	22	140
Miller	John	Fountain Street	73	140
Miller	James	Fountain Street	80	141
Miller	Thomas	Foyle Street		142
Miller	Joseph	Howard Street	14	147
Miller	Mrs	Linenhall Street	15	149
Miller	John	Lower Road	3	151
Miller	George	Nicholson Square	1	154
Miller	David	Park Avenue	6	156
Miller	Dr. Joseph E.	Pump Street	18	157
Miller	David	Richmond Street	17	158
Miller	J. & F.	Richmond Street	19	158
Miller	Sir F. H.	Shipquay Place		159
Miller	J. & F.	Strand Road		161
Miller	John	Victoria Street	5	163
Miller	John	Windmill Terrace	21	166
Miller	William	Windmill Terrace	6	166
Miller	Robert	Ashfield Terrace	35	166
Miller	Richard	Dunfield Terrace	17	172
Miller	David	Fountain Hill	37	173
Miller	Mrs	Herbert Street	15	174
Miller	James	King Street	43	175
Miller	Joseph	Spencer Road	63	177
Miller	John	Spencer Road	69	177
Miller	Mrs	Spencer Road	20	177
Miller	J. & F.	Linenhall Street		149
Miller & Babington		Shipquay Street	33	158
Milligan	R. H.	Gordon Place	1	144
Milligan	George	Long Tower	39	150
Milligan	Charles	Mary Street	20	152
Milligan	Cecil D.	Meadowbank Avenue	5	152
MIlligan	Mrs	Mountjoy Street	25	152
Mills	Robert	Carlisle Road	49	132
Mills	Miss	College Terrace	9	135

Surname	First Name	Street	House Number	Page Number
Mills	Thomas	Edenmore Street	27	138
Mills	John	Great James Street	50	145
Mills	Mrs	Ivy Terrace	27	147
Mills	John	Northland Road	22	155
Mills	Alex	Orchard Row	6	155
Mills	A. & Co.	Strand Road		161
Mills	William	Benvarden Avenue	35	169
Mills	J. J.	Fountain Hill	36	174
Mills	Mrs	Fountain Hill	76	174
Mills	David	Pine Street	15	176
Mills	Mrs	Primrose Street	3	176
Mills	Thomas	Tamneymore		178
Milne	G. G.	Commercial Buildings		141
Milne	George G.	Rosemount Terrace	1	168
Ming	Henry	Collon Terrace	8	135
Minniece	T.	Pump Street	24	157
Mitchell	Joseph	Abercorn Road	58	125
Mitchell	Robert	Abercorn Place	11	126
Mitchell	Miss L	Abercorn Place		126
Mitchell	James	Abercorn Place	8	126
Mitchell	Miss	Argyle Street	11	127
Mitchell	Samuel	Aubrey Street	8	128
Mitchell	Robert	Aubrey Street	30	128
Mitchell	John	Bellevue Avenue	18	129
Mitchell	Joseph	Carlisle Road	9	132
Mitchell	William	Dark Lane	9	136
Mitchell	Robert	Dark Lane	15	136
Mitchell	William	Fahan Street	21	139
Mitchell	Mrs	Fairman Place	24	140
Mitchell	Robert	Ferguson Street	41	140
Mitchell	William Ltd	Commercial Buildings		141
Mitchell	James Ltd	Foyle Road		142
Mitchell	John	Governor Road	24	144
Mitchell	James Ltd	John Street	4	147
Mitchell	Joseph	Kennedy Street	9	148
Mitchell	William J.	Laburnum Terrace	16	148
Mitchell	R. Charles	Lawrence Hill	Kona Vista	148
Mitchell	James	Lecky Road	253	149
Mitchell	Stewart jun	Major's Row	2	151
Mitchell	Stewart sen	Major's Row	4	151
Mitchell	James	Meadowbank Avenue	7	152
Mitchell	Joseph	Nassau Street Lower	9	153
Mitchell	William	Nassau Street Lower	13	153
Mitchell	William	Orchard Row	16	155
Mitchell	W. G.	Princes Street	9	156
Mitchell	James	Quarry Street	shed	157
Mitchell	W. J.	Sackville Street	5	158
Mitchell	W. G.	William Street	36	165

128

Surname	First Name	Street	House Number	Page Number
Mitchell	David	Wesley Street	23	168
Mitchell	James	Bentley Street	5	169
Mitchell	William	Benvarden Avenue	19	169
Mitchell	John	Bond's Street	12	170
Mitchell	Joseph	Chapel Road	59	170
Mitchell	Alexander	Clooney Terrace	25	170
Mitchell	Joseph	Glendermott Road	76	174
Mitchell	John	Glendermott Road	80	174
Mitchell	David	Tamneymore		178
Mitchell	William	Strabane Old Road	3	177
Mitchell & Co.		Spencer Road	5	177
Molloy	Bernard	Adam Street	1	126
Molloy	James	Aubrey Street	24	128
Molloy	Miss	Bennett Street Upper	15	129
Molloy	John	Fountain Place	18	141
Molloy	Mrs	Fountain Place	30	141
Molloy	Hugh	Glasgow Street	4	143
Molloy	Daniel	Governor Road	1C	144
Molloy	Mrs	Linenhall Street	7	149
Molloy	Con.	Foyleview Terrace	13	161
Molloy	Michael	Townsend Street	2	162
Molloy	Edward	Walker's Place	28	163
Monaghan	Hugh	Barnewall Place	28	169
Moncrieff & Co.		Carlisle Chambers		172
Montague	Burton & Co.	Ferryquay Street	18	140
Montague	John	Lecky Road	104	149
Montague	Daniel	Nailor's Row	29	153
Montague	Daniel	Nailor's Row	49	153
Monteith	Marcus	Abercorn Road	63	125
Monteith	John	Ferguson Street	26	140
Monteith	John	Princes Street	15	156
Monteith	Mrs	Dungiven Road	32	173
Monteith	Mrs	Spencer Road	90	177
Montgomery	Joseph	Sunnyside Terrace	1	131
Montgomery	Margaret	Cedar Street	3	133
Montgomery	John	Creggan Terrace	5	135
Montgomery	J. R. Ltd	Foyle Street		142
Montgomery	J. R. Ltd	Foyle Road		142
Montgomery	Maitland	Grafton Terrace	2	144
Montgomery	Charlotte	Major's Row	3	151
Montgomery	Alexander	Major's Row	9	151
Montgomery	M.	Orchard Street		155
Montgomery	Miss	Palace Street	4	155
Montgomery	Alex. Ltd	Strand Road	76	161
Montgomery	Robert	Limavady Road	St. Claire Villa	175
Montgomery	J. R.	Foyle Road		142
Montgomery	J. R. Ltd	Queen's Quay		157
Moon	Henry	Marlborough Street	25	151
Mooney	Robert	Dacre Terrace		133

Surname	First Name	Street	House Number	Page Number
Mooney	Miss	Diamond		137
Mooney	William	Fountain Place	29	141
Mooney	D. A. & Co.	Foyle Street		141
Mooney	Misses	Great James Street	18	145
Mooney	Patrick	Nassau Street Lower	34	153
Mooney	David A.	Florence Terrace	5	154
Mooney	James	Orchard Row	26	155
Mooney	Mrs	Strand Road	Auburn	160
Mooney	William C. & Co.	Strand Road	22B	161
Mooney	James	Donegal Street	17	167
Mooney	Patrick	Osborne Street	18	168
Mooney	Mrs	Violet Street Lower	12	178
Moore	J B (V.S)	Bayview Terrace	7	128
Moore	James	Bishop Street	105	129
Moore	Miss	Carrigans Lane	25	133
Moore	Rebecca J.	Alexander Cottages	1	133
Moore	Edward	Clarence Place	5	134
Moore	Austin	Clarendon Street	51	134
Moore	Robert	Maybrook Terrace	1	135
Moore	Thomas	De Burgh Terrace	15	137
Moore	Stewart	Edenballymore	3	137
Moore	John	Ewing Street	30	139
Moore	J. & Co.	Ferryquay Street		140
Moore	John	Fountain Street	29	140
Moore	George	Harding Street	31	145
Moore	John	High Street	15	146
Moore	George	Long Tower	15	150
Moore	Daniel	Long Tower	47	150
Moore	John	Lower Road	10	151
Moore	William	Miller Street	16	152
Moore	Daniel	Nailor's Row	27	153
Moore	James	Nassau Street Lower	19	153
Moore	Ambrose	Nelson Street	19	153
Moore	Mrs	Nelson Street	37	154
Moore	Andrew	North Edward Street	5	154
Moore	Joseph	North Edward Street	6	154
Moore	John	Orchard Street		155
Moore	Samuel	Park Avenue	20	156
Moore	Rebecca	Pitt Street	5	156
Moore	Mrs	Rossville Street	60	158
Moore	Patrick	Stanley's Walk	4	159
Moore	Alex	St. Columb's Wells	35	161
Moore	Maggie	St. Columb's Wells	2	162
Moore	Edward	Thomas Street	20	162
Moore	Edward	Thomas Street	24	162
Moore	Patrick	Walker's Place	24	163
Moore	Ben	West-End Terrace	10	165
Moore	Richard	William Street	55	165
Moore	Mrs	Creggan Road	141	166

Surname	First Name	Street	House Number	Page Number
Moore	Mrs	Donegal Street	3	167
Moore	William	Mount Street	8	168
Moore	Thomas	Bond's Hill	29	169
Moore	Leslie	Derry View Terrace	5	171
Moore	Alexander	Dungiven Road	61	173
Moore	Samuel	Irish Street		174
Moore	Joseph	Pine Street	20	176
Moore	John	Strabane Old Road	29	177
Moore	John	Union Street	3	178
Moore & Anderson		Bishop Street	66	130
Moorehead	James	Limavady Road		175
Moorehead	John	Limavady Road		175
Moore's (Derry) Ltd		Bishop Street	10	130
Moore's Ltd		Bishop Street	25	129
Moran	Joseph	Brandywell Road	12	131
Moran	John	Eglinton Place	21	138
Moran	William	Eglinton Terrace	7	138
Moran	Robert	Bluebellhill Terrace	144	149
Moran	Richard	Lower Road	25	151
Moran	James	Nassau Street Lower	6	153
Moran	Mrs	Strand Road		160
Moran	James	Carlin Street	11	170
Morgan	James	Lecky Road		149
Moriarty	Rev. T. A. H.	Limavady Road	The Rectory	175
Morrell	James T	Duncreggan Road	Meadowbank	137
Morris	Mrs	Strand Road	34	161
Morris	John	Rossville Street	35	158
Morris	Mrs	Bridge Street	58	132
Morris	Mrs	Clarendon Street Lower	1	135
Morris	Annie	Wellington Street	13	164
Morrison	Hugh	Bishop Street	46	130
Morrison	James	Dacre Terrace		133
Morrison	Matthew	Deanery Street	50	136
Morrison	R. G.	De Burgh Terrace	9	136
Morrison	Henry	Fountain Street	41	140
Morrison	William	Fountain Street	61	140
Morrison	David	Fountain Street	56	141
Morrison	James	Foyle Street		141
Morrison	Matthew	Hawthorn Terrace	1	146
Morrison	Patrick	Hollywell Row	65	148
Morrison	Edward	Lecky Road	30	149
Morrison	Mrs	Marlborough Terrace	11	152
Morrison	S. & Co.	Abercorn Quay		157
Morrison	Samuel & Co.	Princes Quay		157
Morrison	S. & Co.	Queen's Quay		157
Morrison	Samuel & Co.	Strand Road	38	161
Morrison	James	Waterloo Street	46	164

Surname	First Name	Street	House Number	Page Number
Morrison	Charles	Creggan Road	79	166
Morrison	Samuel	Creggan Road	117	166
Morrison	Andrew	Lewis Street	25	167
Morrison	William	Cross Street	37	171
Morrison	Samuel & Co.	Duke Street	19	172
Morrison	Samuel & Co.	Duke Street		172
Morrison	James	Duke Street	39	172
Morrison	Robert	Alexander Terrace	1	176
Morrow	William	Abercorn Road	3	125
Morrow	John	Rossville Street	55	158
Morrow	James	Cuthbert Street	16	171
Morrow	William	Fountain Hill	17	173
Morrow & Co.		Fountain Street	85	140
Mortimer	John & Co.	Foyle Street		142
Mortimer	Mrs	Marlborough Street	1	151
Mortimer	John & Co.	Water Street		164
Mortland	William	Bond's Street	30	170
Morton	Sergeant	Dunfield Terrace	15	172
Moss	Ellen	Elmwood Terrace	22	138
Motherwell	Mrs	Francis Street	33	143
Mott	Mrs	West-End Park	17	165
Mount	Rosa	Creggan Street	3	135
Mount	William	Edenballymore	5	137
Mowat	Alexander	Argyle Street	64	127
Mowbray	John	Fountain Place	16	141
Mowbray	Robert	Hawthorn Terrace	6	146
Mowbray	William	Glendermott Road	14	174
Moyne	Mrs	Brook Street Avenue	11	132
Moyne	M.	Magazine Street	22	151
Muir	Alex	Bellevue Avenue	33	129
Muirhead	James C.	Orchard Street	17	155
Muldoon	William	Irish Street	3	174
Muldoon	John	Irish Street	19	174
Muldoon	Pat	Mill Street	32	176
Mulhearn	Mrs	Fahan Street	32	139
Mulhearn	Matthew	Union Street	31	178
Mulhern	Ellen	Miller Street	14	152
Mulhern	John	Cross Street	22	171
Mulhern	Mrs	Emerson Street	3	173
Mulholland	George	Baronet Street	4	128
Mulholland	Thomas	Stanley's Walk	49	160
Mulholland	Thomas	Wapping Lane	19	163
Mulholland	Samuel	Violet Street Upper	13	179
Mulholland	Mrs	Brandywell Avenue	19	131
Mulholland & Co		Bishop Street	4, 6, 8	130
Mullally	Alexander H.	Fairman Place	1	139
Mullan	James	Argyle Terrace	31	127
Mullan	John	Argyle Terrace	16	127
Mullan	Bernard	Bishop Street	31	129

Surname	First Name	Street	House Number	Page Number
Mullan	Michael	Bishop Street	222	131
Mullan	John	Brook Street Avenue	7	132
Mullan	Dr Joseph E.	Carlisle Road	41	132
Mullan	George	Dark Lane	19	136
Mullan	John	Donegal Place	stables	137
Mullan	John	Donegal Place	24	137
Mullan	James	Fahan Street	114	139
Mullan	John	Foyle Street		141
Mullan	Charles	Frederick Street	14	143
Mullan	John	Laburnum Terrace	6	148
Mullan	Bernard	Long Tower		150
Mullan	Patrick	St. Columb's Wells	102	162
Mullan	Miss M.	Wellington Street	51	164
Mullan	Mrs	Wesley Street	19	168
Mullan	John	Ebrington Street	2	173
Mullan	Mary	Fountain Hill	69	174
Mullan	Mrs	Strabane Old Road	62	178
Mullan	Edward	Union Street	19	178
Mullen	Miss	East Wall		137
Mulligan	William B.	Elmwood Terrace	38	138
Mullin	John	Donegal Place	18	137
Mullin	Frank J.	St. Columb's Wells	49	161
Mullin	Philip	St. Columb's Wells	56	162
Mullin	James	Derry View	6	171
Mullin	John	Meehan's Row	3	176
Mullin	Edward	Union Street	14	178
Mulrine	Patrick	Cross Street	5	171
Munn	William	Bishop Street	61	129
Munn	A.M.	Bishop Street	Registrar	130
Munn	Alfred Moore	Bishop Street		130
Munn	A. M.	Culmore Road	Lisleen	136
Murdock	Thomas	Hawkin Street	20	146
Murphy	James	Argyle Terrace	10	127
Murphy	Michael	Argyle Terrace	24	127
Murphy	E.	Bishop Street	26	130
Murphy	John M.	Demesne Terrace	11	137
Murphy	Patrick	Edenmore Street	11	138
Murphy	Elizabeth	Morrison's Close	4	139
Murphy	Thomas	Grove Place	11	145
Murphy	Patrick	Kildarra Terrace	12	146
Murphy	Mrs	Lecky Road	108	149
Murphy	James	Nicholson Terrace	8	154
Murphy	James	Sloan's Terrace	23	159
Murphy	Sarah	Ernest Street		167
Murphy	Edward	Alfred Street	26	168
Murphy	Denis	Margaret Street	15	175
Murphy	Samuel	Union Street	17	178
Murphy	W.	Commercial Buildings		141
Murphy	Thomas & Co	Foyle Street		142

Surname	First Name	Street	House Number	Page Number
Murray	James	Abbey Street	55	125
Murray	John	Alexandra Place	6	126
Murray	Henry	Argyle Street	21	127
Murray	William	Argyle Street	38	127
Murray	Charles	Bishop Street	231	130
Murray	Thomas	Blee's Lane		131
Murray	Charles	Brandywell Road	2	131
Murray	James	Brandywell Avenue	12	131
Murray	Neal	Bridge Street	45	132
Murray	Neil	Cable Street	1	132
Murray	Mrs	Deanery Street	9	136
Murray	Andrew	Deanery Street	31	136
Murray	Thomas	Deanery Street	37	136
Murray	Mrs	Fahan Street	7	139
Murray	Patrick	Foyle Road	55	142
Murray	David	Grove Place	20	145
Murray	Robert	Henrietta Street	14	146
Murray	Mrs	Henry Street	1	146
Murray	Michael	Hogg's Folly	6	146
Murray	John	Hollywell Street	8	147
Murray	Thomas	Ivy Terrace	20	147
Murray	Miss Norah	Laburnum Terrace	8	148
Murray	Owen	Meave's Row	197	149
Murray	Charles	Bluebellhill Terrace	208	149
Murray	Patrick	Market Street		152
Murray	Charles	Moore Street	1, 3	152
Murray	Alex	Nassau Street Lower	36	153
Murray	James	Nassau Street Upper	37	153
Murray	F. A.	New Market Street	6	154
Murray	Hugh	Rossville Street	28	158
Murray	William	Sackville Street	4	158
Murray	William	Waterloo Street	59	164
Murray	John	Wellington Street	1	164
Murray	Mrs	Windsor Terrace	10	166
Murray	Mrs	Alfred Street	2	168
Murray	John	Cuthbert Street	1	171
Murray	Margaret	Dungiven Road	89	173
Murray	Mrs	Fountain Hill	25	173
Murray	Mary	Mill Street	33	176
Murray	John	Meehan's Row	15	176
Murray	John	Strabane Old Road	38	177
Murray	John	Strabane Old Road	84	178
Murray	Miss	Violet Street Lower	31	178
Murray	Miss	Violet Street Lower	43	178
Murrin	James	Bond's Hill	22	169
Musselwhite	George	Wapping Lane	5	163
Mutch	James A	Argyle Terrace	5	127
Myers	Miss	John Street	23	147
Myers	Miss	Dungiven Road	73	173
Nash	Laurence	Argyle Terrace	2	127

Surname	First Name	Street	House Number	Page Number
Nash	Mrs	Bishop Street	144	131
Nash	John	Fahan Street	53	139
Nash	John	Gallagher's Square	8	143
Nash	Patrick	Glenbrook Terrace	5	143
Nash	James	Nelson Street	14	154
Nash	Lawrence	Northland Terrace	6	155
Nash	Laurence	Union Street	24	163
Naylor	Sydney	Bennett Street Lower	47	129
Neely	John	Bishop Street	213	130
Neely	Mrs	Dacre Terrace		133
Neely	Robert	Clarendon Street	9	134
Neely	Robert	Fountain Place	23	141
Neely	Adam	Gordon Place	7	144
Neely	R. jun	Magazine Street	12, 13	151
Neely	R & Co.	North Edward Street		154
Neely	Robert	Stewart's Terrace	13	160
Neely	Adam F.	The Rock	31	160
Neely	S. J.	Wesley Street	5	168
Neely	Robert	Bond's Street	6	169
Neely	Joseph	Distillery Brae Upper	2	171
Neely	Robert	Glendermott Road	18	174
Neill	Robert	Clarendon Street	41	134
Neill	Archibald	Grove Place	2	145
Neill	Robert	Shipquay Street	11	158
Nelis	Mrs	Bellevue Avenue	8	129
Nelis	John	Bishop Street	276	131
Nelis	John & Co.	Ferryquay Street		140
Nelis	Andrew	Kennedy Street	6	148
Nelis	George	Foster's Terrace	153	148
Nelis	Patrick	Foster's Terrace	153	148
Nelis	Francis	Foster's Terrace	175	148
Nelis	William	Lecky Road	126	149
Nelis	James	Mountjoy Street	9	152
Nelis	Thomas	Nassau Street Lower	48	153
Nelis	Mrs	Benvarden Avenue	55	169
Nelis & Sherrard		Duke Street	61	172
Nelson	Howard A	Bishop Street	13	129
Nelson	Thomas	Glasgow Terrace	35	144
Nelson	William	Great James Street	59	145
Nelson	Thomas E.	Strand Road	78	161
Nelson	Maurice	Ebrington Terrace	9	173
Nelson	William	Emerson Street	26	173
Nesbitt	Hannah	Harding Street	13	145
Nevin	Francis T	Eden Terrace		137
Nevin	Robert	Kennedy Place	8	147
Nevin	Mrs	Glendermott Road	8A	174
Newell	Robert B.	Aberfoyle Terrace	11	160
Newton	Robert	Edenmore Street	15	138
Nicell	Thomas	Park Avenue	10	156

Surname	First Name	Street	House Number	Page Number
Nicell	Patrick	Creggan Road	38, 40	167
Nicell	Michael	Cottage Row	8	168
Nichol	Walter	De Burgh Terrace	6	136
Nicholl	Andrew	Aubrey Street	15	128
Nicholl	Mrs	Bennett Street Upper	13	129
Nicholl	George	Brandywell Road	23	131
Nicholl	John	Ewing Street	11	139
Nicholl	Joseph	Nelson Street	63	154
Nicholl	Allan	Waterloo Street	23	163
Nicholl	Robert	Fountain Hill	54	174
Nicholl	Patrick	Margaret Street	1	175
Nicholl	Thomas	Mill Street	37	176
Nicholl	Robert	Union Street	20	178
Nicholson	James	Alfred Street	28	168
Nicholson	William	Bond's Hill	3	169
Nickle	John	Hamilton Street	25	145
Nimmon	R. & Co.	Strand Road	2, 4, 6	161
Ninon	Sarah	Quarry Street	7	157
Nixon	Robert	Charlotte Street	1	134
Nixon	John	Ferryquay Street		140
Nixon	James	Commercial Buildings		141
Nixon	Mrs	Windsor Terrace	2	166
Nixon	Matthew	Ernest Street		167
Nixon	George	Mount Street	5	167
Noble	Samuel	Brandywell Road	2	131
Noble	John	Carlisle Road	17	132
Noble	John	Chamberlain Street	19, 21	134
Noble	Thomas	Chamberlain Street	30	134
Noble	William	Fahan Street	16	139
Noble	Alex	Templemore Park		162
Noble	Alex	Alfred Street	16	168
Noble	John	Grafton Street	9	144
Nolan	R. H.	Carlisle Road	9	132
Nolan	R. H.	Myrtle Terrace		154
Nolan	James	Cross Street	28	171
Noonan	Miss	Shipquay Street		159
Norrby	Oscar	Creggan Road	101	166
Norrie	D. H.	Magazine Street Upper		151
Norrie	Mrs	Kerr's Terrace	23	166
Norris	William	Bellevue Avenue	21	129
Norris	Miss	Clarence Place	4	134
Norris	John	Corbett Street	5	135
Norris	Oliver	Fountain Street	114	141
Norris	John	Grafton Street	33	144
Norris	Mrs	Nassau Street Lower	39	153
Norris	James	Orchard Row	41	155
Norris	Mrs	Shipquay Street	4	159
Norris	Mrs	Glendermott Road	68	174

Surname	First Name	Street	House Number	Page Number
Norris	Miss	York Street	17	179
Nutt	Andrew	Fountain Street	36	140
Nutter	Samuel	Fountain Street	25	140
Nutter	Thomas	Fountain Street	37	140
O'Breslin	Joseph	William Street	60	165
O'Brien	Henry	Alexandra Place	2	126
O'Brien	Joseph	Marlborough Street	10	151
O'Brien	James	Marlborough Street	26	151
O'Brien	C. G.	Marlborough Street		151
O'Brien	Andrew S.	Bond's Hill	26	169
O'Brien	James	Florence Street	9	173
O'Bryan	John	Barrack Street	2	128
O'Bryan	George	Alexander Cottages	3	133
O'Bryan	James	George Street		143
O'Bryan	Minnie	Gordon Terrace	6	144
O'Bryan	James	Henry Street	6	146
O'Callaghan	Mrs	Butcher Street	15	132
O'Callaghan	John J.	Fahan Street	88	139
O'Callaghan	Constable	Dunfield Terrace	21	172
O'Carroll	Mrs	Beechwood Street	4	129
O'Connell	Mrs	Elmwood Terrace	9	138
O'Connell	Daniel	Howard Street	13	147
O'Connell	John	Rossville Street	18	158
O'Connell	Daniel	Walker's Place	17	163
O'Connell	Mrs	Herbert Street	3	174
O'Connor	Mrs	Charlotte Street	14	134
O'Connor	James	Creggan Street	45, 47	135
O'Connor	Miss	Ferryquay Street		140
O'Connor	James	Lone Moor		150
O'Connor	Matthew	Dixon's Close	1	151
O'Connor	John	Rossville Street	58	158
O'Connor	James	Creggan Road	14	167
O'Connor	John	Cottage Row	6	168
O'Connor	Thomas	Osborne Street	12	168
O'Connor	Bernard	Fountain Hill	116	174
O'Connor & Co.		Creggan Road	18	167
O'Doherty	H C	Bayview Terrace	5	128
O'Doherty	Joseph	Bishop Street	140	131
O'Doherty	H. C. & Son	Castle Street		133
O'Doherty	Joseph	Clarendon Street	65	134
O'Doherty	Dr Margaret	Clarendon Street	65	134
O'Doherty	Michael	Creggan Street	23	135
O'Doherty	William G.	Demesne Terrace	1	137
O'Doherty	James E & Co	East Wall	6	137
O'Doherty	Philip	East Wall	11	137
O'Doherty	James	Eglinton Place	15	138
O'Doherty	John	Fahan Street	110	139
O'Doherty	J	Ferguson Street		140
O'Doherty	Philip (M.P.)	Great James Street		145
O'Doherty	John K.	Great James Street	42	145

Surname	First Name	Street	House Number	Page Number
O'Doherty	Mrs	Great James Street	44	145
O'Doherty	Mr	Henrietta Street	8	146
O'Doherty	Edward H.	Magazine Street Upper	2	151
O'Doherty	Philip	Marlborough Avenue	31	152
O'Doherty	Cassie	Miller Street	8	152
O'Doherty	J.	New Market Street		154
O'Doherty	Mrs B.	Richmond Street	11	158
O'Doherty	James	Shipquay Street		158
O'Doherty	W. G. S.	Society Street		159
O'Doherty	W. G. Ltd	Strand Road		160
O'Doherty	Con	Waterloo Street	22	164
O'Doherty	Mrs	Park Villas	4	168
O'Doherty	Miss	Clooney Terrace	9½	170
O'Doherty	Miss	Dungiven Road	30	173
O'Doherty	William	Fountain Hill	80	174
O'Doherty	John	Fountain Hill	92	174
O'Doherty	Thomas	Glendermott Road	8	174
O'Doherty	Patrick	Spencer Road	142	177
O'Doherty W G Ltd		Bishop Street	15	129
O'Donnell	Thomas	Abbey Street	65	125
O'Donnell	Mary	Adam Street	8	126
O'Donnell	John	Argyle Street	47	127
O'Donnell	John	Bishop Street	251	130
O'Donnell	Patrick	Bishop Street	148	131
O'Donnell	Miss	Cottage Row	6	131
O'Donnell	John	Creggan Terrace	20	135
O'Donnell	Joseph	Demesne Terrace	12	137
O'Donnell	J. F.	Diamond		137
O'Donnell	James E	East Wall	6	137
O'Donnell	Joseph	Elmwood Terrace	8	138
O'Donnell	John	Elmwood Terrace	26	138
O'Donnell	James	Elmwood Street	2	138
O'Donnell	Thomas	Fahan Street	115, 117	139
O'Donnell	John	Fahan Street	137	139
O'Donnell	Neal	Fahan Street	40	139
O'Donnell	Mary	Fahan Street	40	139
O'Donnell	Bridget	Fahan Street	106	139
O'Donnell	John	Francis Street	61	143
O'Donnell	Charles	Glasgow Terrace	7	144
O'Donnell	Neal	Hamilton Street	8	145
O'Donnell	James	Hollywell Street	3	147
O'Donnell	John	Laburnum Terrace	19	148
O'Donnell	Joseph	Bluebellhill Terrace	214	149
O'Donnell	Joseph	Linenhall Street		150
O'Donnell	Catherine	Nelson Street	30	154
O'Donnell	Daniel	Park Avenue	12	156
O'Donnell	Dominick	Pennyburn Terrace	15	156
O'Donnell	George	Philips Street	35	156

Surname	First Name	Street	House Number	Page Number
O'Donnell	Michael	Rossville Street	40	158
O'Donnell	Joseph	Stanley's Walk	28	160
O'Donnell	Joseph	St. Columb's Street	9	161
O'Donnell	Hugh	St. Columb's Wells	70	162
O'Donnell	John	St. Patrick Street	9	162
O'Donnell	David	St. Patrick Street	13	162
O'Donnell	Charles	Tyrconnell Street	8	163
O'Donnell	Daniel	Tyrconnell Street	14	163
O'Donnell	James	Wellington Street	44	164
O'Donnell	Daniel	William Street	forge	165
O'Donnell	Joseph	William Street	91	165
O'Donnell	John	William Street	125	165
O'Donnell	Joseph	William Street	72	166
O'Donnell	William	Creggan Road	34	167
O'Donnell	Hugh	Creggan Road	52	167
O'Donnell	Constable Hugh	Benvarden Avenue	38	169
O'Donnell	Patrick	Fountain Hill	110	174
O'Donnell	William	Gortfoyle Place	8	174
O'Donnell	Edward	Glendermott Road	100	174
O'Donnell	Patrick	Strabane Old Road	4	177
O'Donohoe	Mrs	Waterloo Street	16	164
O'Flaherty	Mrs	Stanley's Walk	41	160
O'Hagan	Mrs	Argyle Street	67	127
O'Hagan	Patrick	Collon Terrace	17	135
O'Hagan	Philip	Duncreggan Road	Meadowbank	137
O'Hagan	John	Gallagher's Square	5	143
O'Hagan	Philip	Sackville Street	15	158
O'Hagan	Bernard	St. Columb's Wells	89	162
O'Hagan	John	Wellington Street	35	164
O'Hagan	Miss	Creggan Road	151	166
O'Hanlon	Thomas	Robert Street	8	176
O'Hara	Thomas	Mitchelburne Terrace	95	142
O'Hara	Francis	Sugarhouse Lane	17	162
O'Hara	Daniel	Walker's Place	9	163
O'Hara	Thomas	West-End Terrace	6	165
O'Hare	Michael	Creggan Street	37	135
O'Hare	Michael	Creggan Road	1	166
O'Hea	Albert	Bishop Street	249	130
O'Heney	John	New Market Street	4	154
O'Kane	Francis	Argyle Terrace	13	127
O'Kane	Bernard	Bishop Street	207	130
O'Kane	Patrick	Bishop Street	178	131
O'Kane	Bernard	Bridge Street	36	132
O'Kane	Michael	Cedar Street	4	133
O'Kane	Mrs	Chamberlain Street	20	134
O'Kane	Jos. G.	Commercial Buildings		141
O'Kane	P. & Co	Foyle Street		141
O'Kane	James	Frederick Street	9	143
O'Kane	James	Fulton Place	23	143

Surname	First Name	Street	House Number	Page Number
O'Kane	Michael	Glasgow Terrace	36	144
O'Kane	Patrick J.	Harvey Street	11	146
O'Kane	Roger	High Street	11	146
O'Kane	Michael	Hogg's Folly	1	146
O'Kane	John	John Street	3	147
O'Kane	Mary	Foster's Terrace	157	148
O'Kane	Frank	Meave's Row	201	149
O'Kane	Michael	Lundy's Lane	4	150
O'Kane	Frank	Long Tower	41	150
O'Kane	Patrick	North Edward Street	1	154
O'Kane	Joseph G.	Florence Terrace	1	154
O'Kane	John	Waterloo Street	10	164
O'Kane	P. & Co.	William Street	51	165
O'Kane	P. & Co.	Lewis Street	2, 4	167
O'Kane	Patrick	King Street	37	175
O'Kane	Mrs	Spencer Road	131	177
O'Kane	Michael	Argyle Terrace	41	127
O'Kelly	P J	Bellevue Avenue	17	129
Olphert	James	Edenmore Street	35	138
Olphert	Thomas	Ashcroft Place	6	169
Olphert	Mrs	Barnewall Place	13	169
Olphert	George	Ebrington Terrace	3	173
O'May	William	Clarendon Street	57	134
O'Neil	Corneilus	Grafton Terrace	6	144
O'Neill	Mrs	Sydney Terrace	4	145
O'Neill	Hugh	Hogg's Folly	2	146
O'Neill	C.	Northland Road	Ard-Owen	154
O'Neill	Patrick	Stanley's Walk	17	160
O'Neill	Mrs	St. Columb's Street	5	161
O'Neill	John	St. Columb's Wells	114	162
O'Neill	Rev.	Victoria Place	Parochial House	163
O'Neill	Charles	Ashfield Terrace	39	166
O'Neill	James	Cross Street	4	167
O'Neill	Mrs	Donegal Street	29	167
O'Neill	Patrick	Chapel Road	7	170
O'Neill	James	Chapel Road	25	170
O'Neill	Thomas	Chapel Road	29	170
O'Neill	John	Eglinton Place	27	138
O'Neill	Francis	Fahan Street	6	139
O'Neill	Mrs	Fairman Place	17	139
O'Neill & McHenry		Custom House Street		136
O'Neill & McHenry		Guildhall Street		145
O'Reilly	J. M.	Clarendon Street	19	134
O'Reilly	Mrs M	Elmwood Terrace	12	138
O'Reilly	John	Fahan Street	55	139
O'Reilly	Denis	Mitchelburne Terrace	84	142
O'Reilly	Miss	Francis Street	23	143

Surname	First Name	Street	House Number	Page Number
O'Reilly	Bernard	Great James Street	71	145
O'Reilly	Mrs	Laburnum Terrace	7	148
O'Reilly	Patrick	Marlborough Terrace	12	152
O'Reilly	Miss	Chapel Road	64	170
Orr	William A	Albert Street	10	126
Orr	Mrs	Bennett Street Upper	8	129
Orr	Henry	Charlotte Street	6	134
Orr	J. C.	Clarence Avenue	11	134
Orr	Andrew	Fountain Street	89	140
Orr	Robert	Fountain Street	88	141
Orr	John	Governor Road	30	144
Orr	Samuel	Great James Street	52	145
Orr	Robert	Harding Street	25	145
Orr	William	Linenhall Street	25	149
Orr	George	Mountjoy Street	14	153
Orr	Robinson	Mountjoy Street	28	153
Orr	Samuel	Nicholson Square	8	154
Orr	Mrs Sarah	Montrose Villas	1	154
Orr	James	Pitt Street	7	156
Orr	William	The Rock	14	160
Orr	Patrick	Epworth Street	7	167
Orr	James	Mount Street	11	167
Orr	John	North Street	29	168
Orr	Thomas	Cottage Row	36	168
Orr	Thomas	Cottage Row	44	168
Orr	William	Alfred Street	40	168
Orr	Mrs	Bond's Street	37	169
Orr	Patrick	Duke Street	55	172
Orr	Joseph	King Street	26	175
Orr	Mrs	Limavady Road	St. Columb's	175
Orr	Miss	Moore Street	33	176
Orr	Samuel	Pine Street	2	176
Orr	Joseph	Pine Street	10	176
Orr	James	Primrose Street	13	176
Orr	George	York Street	16	179
Osborne	Harry	Argyle Terrace	19	127
Osborne	John	Foyle Street		141
Osborne	William	Glendermott Road	84	174
Osborne	Miss	Iona Terrace		174
Osborne	Miss	Limavady Road	Ashlea	175
Osborne	D. C.	Limavady Road	St. Moiras	175
Osborne & Patton		Bank Place		128
Osborne & Patton		Shipquay Street		158
O'Sullivan	Florence	Butcher Street	1	132
O'Sullivan	Florence	Diamond		137
O'Sullivan	A. & Co.	Strand Road	19	160
Owen	Daniel	Union Street	16	178
Owens	William	Carlisle Road	35	132

Surname	First Name	Street	House Number	Page Number
Owens	Henry	Fahan Street	133, 135	139
Owens	Edward	Harvey Street	3	146
Owens	Charles	Foster's Terrace	181	148
Owens	Henry	Lecky Road	72	149
Owens	Michael	Stanley's Walk	7	159
Owens	George	Foyleview Terrace	11	161
Owens	Mrs	Mill Street	31	176
Oxford	Richard	Ferguson Street	45	140
Oxford	Christopher	Northland Avenue	3	155
Page	William	Quarry Street	11	157
Palmer	Mrs	High Street	17	146
Palmer	Mrs	Mary Street	16	152
Parke	Mrs	Abercorn Road	23	125
Parke	George	Abercorn Road	12	125
Parke	Alex	John Street	5	147
Parke	Matthew	Pump Street	9	156
Parke	Mrs	Cross Street	27	171
Parke	R. H.	Dunfield Terrace	41	172
Parke	John	Dungiven Road	49	172
Parke	Thomas	Meehan's Row	18	176
Parke	William	Tamneymore		178
Parker	John	Millar's Close		132
Parkhill	Thomas	Ferguson Street	44	140
Parkhill & Co.		Ewing Street		139
Parkinson	Mrs	Barry Street	7	128
Parvin	Mrs	Collon Terrace	11	135
Patrick	Robert	Grove Place	6	145
Pattenden	George	Strand Road	lodge	160
Patteron	Mrs	Meehan's Row	1	176
Patterson	Andrew	Barry Street	21	128
Patterson	James	Fountain Street	101	140
Patterson	Robert	Hempton's Close		141
Patterson	John	Gallagher's Square	3	143
Patterson	William	Great James Street	16	145
Patterson	Joseph	John Street		147
Patterson	William	Kennedy Street	22	148
Patterson	Joseph	Lawrence Hill		148
Patterson	Joseph	North Edward Street	4	154
Patterson	Mrs	Queen Street	7	157
Patterson	Joseph	Strand Road	55	160
Patterson	James	Florence Street	3	173
Patterson	Joseph	Spencer Road	22	177
Patterson Bros.		John Street	9	147
Patton	Mary Ann	Cable Street	9	132
Patton	David	Glasgow Street	6	144
Patton	Arthur	Lecky Road	118	149
Paul	Professor F. J.	College Avenue		155
Payne	Robert H	Barry Street	22	128
Payne	William	London Street	5	150
Payne	Joseph	Nassau Street Lower	24	153

Surname	First Name	Street	House Number	Page Number
Payne	Joseph	Mount Street	18	168
Peacock	Walter	Carlisle Road	16	133
Peacock	Walter	Spencer Road	134	177
Peacocke	Right Rev Joseph	Bishop Street	25	129
Pentland	William	Moat Street	4	152
Peoples	Hugh	Albert Street	13	126
Peoples	James	Lower Road	20	151
Peoples	William	Moore Street	26	176
Percy Hoare & Co		John Street	10	147
Perry	David	Beechwood Avenue	57	128
Perry	James W.	Fairman Place	14	140
Perry	Mrs	Fountain Place	24	141
Perry	David	Great James Street	4	144
Perry	Miss	Linenhall Street	31	149
Perry	Mrs	Linenhall Street		150
Perry	Alexander W.	Bond's Hill	Old Manse	169
Perry	The Misses	Bond's Hill	18	169
Perry	Mrs W. L.	Limavady Road	Sunnymede	175
Pettipice	Miss	Carlisle Road	44	133
Pews	William	Meehan's Row	5	176
Phillips	Benjamin	De Burgh Terrace	7	136
Phillips	J. S.	Demesne Terrace	9	137
Phillips	H. B.	Shipquay Street		159
Phillips	William	Limavady Road	Lanowlee Hall	175
Phillips	W. L.	May Street	4	175
Phillips	Mrs	Strabane Old Road	82	178
Phillips	Robert	Strabane Old Road	88	178
Phillips	Arthur	Victoria Park		178
Philson	Mrs	Fountain Hill	72	174
Philson	John	Fountain Hill	78	174
Pickens	James	Violet Street Lower	7	178
Pickett	Mrs	Edenmore Street	8	138
Pickett & Co		Diamond		137
Pierce	William	Northland Terrace	5	155
Piggot	James	Ferenize cottage		128
Pigott	Robert	Albert Street	30	126
Pine	Hugh	Rossville Street	66	158
Pinkerton	Mrs	Grafton Street	11	144
Pinkerton & Co.		Queen's Quay		157
Pitt	William	Bridge Street	20	132
Pitts	E. A.	Commercial Buildings		141
Platt	Richard	Albert Street	40	126
Platt	Charles	Carlisle Road	43	132
Platt	Mrs	Carlisle Road	45, 47	132
Platt	W. H.	Governor Road	10	144
Platt	Mrs	High Street	18	146

Surname	First Name	Street	House Number	Page Number
Platt	Miss	Princes Street	23	156
Platt	William	Stewart's Terrace	5	160
Platt	Mrs	West-End Park	15	165
Plews	Miss	Culmore Road	Shantallow	136
Plews	Robert	Windmill Terrace	10	166
Plews	William	Alfred Street	36	168
Plews	Alex	Mill Street	gasworks	176
Plews	Fred	Moore Street	31	176
Plews	William	Pine Street	29	176
Plummer	Thomas	Adair Street	4	126
Plummer	James	Bridge Street	15	131
Plummer	Miss	Columba Terrace	3	171
Pollock	Mrs	Abercorn Road	17	125
Pollock	William	Bennett Street Upper	12	129
Pollock	William	Bennett Street Lower	26	129
Pollock	J. A.	Carlisle Road	9	132
Pollock	William	Fairman Place	2	139
Pollock	Miss	Fountain Street	91	140
Pollock	John A.	Fountain Street		140
Pollock	James S.	William Street	93	165
Pollock	Samuel	Windmill Terrace	29	166
Pollock	Mrs	Creggan Road	36	167
Pollock	Miss	Rosemount Terrace	13	168
Pollock	J. H.	Deanfield	Ard-na-Hone	171
Pollock	John A. & Co.	Carlisle Road	8	133
Pollock	J. A. & Co.	Strand Road	1A	160
Pollock & Given		Sackville Street	13	158
Pomeroy	Thomas	King Street	11	175
Pomeroy	John	Margaret Street	5	175
Pooley	H. & Son	Foyle Street		142
Porter	Patrick	Alma Place	5	126
Porter	Mrs	Alma Place	6	126
Porter	Garnett	Barry Street	2	128
Porter	Mrs	Bennett Street Lower	32	129
Porter	Thomas	Cottage Row	1	131
Porter	David	Clarence Avenue	14	134
Porter	James	Deanery Place	5	136
Porter	Hazlett	Eden Terrace		137
Porter	Joseph	Elmwood Terrace	15	138
Porter	William	McLaughlin's Close	4	140
Porter	Robert	Foyle Road	53	142
Porter	Thomas	Governor Road	9	144
Porter	Robert	Lawrence Hill		148
Porter	Andrew T.	Marlborough Street	44	151
Porter	Denis	Patrick Street	10	156
Porter	James	Pennyburn		156
Porter	Thomas	Princes Street	1	156
Porter	Patrick	Rossville Street	51	158
Porter	Alex	Wapping Lane	11	163

Surname	First Name	Street	House Number	Page Number
Porter	Thomas	Wapping Lane	13	163
Porter	Hugh	West-End Park	3	165
Porter	Robert	Bond's Hill	30	169
Porter	George	Carlin Street	2	170
Porter	Mrs A.	Caw	Caw Villa	170
Porter	David	Dungiven Road	22	173
Porter	James	Fountain Hill	35	173
Porter	Alexander	Strabane Old Road	90	178
Porter	Thomas	Strabane Old Road	100	178
Porter & Co.		Victoria Chambers		132
Porter & Nelson		Abercorn Road		125
Porter & Porter		Carlisle Road	1	132
Porter & Roulston		William Street	4, 6	165
Porter Bros		Sackville Street	3	158
Porter Brothers		Abercorn Road	31	125
Pounds	Fred	Sloan's Terrace	33	159
Power	William	Fahan Street	10	139
Power	Thomas	Westland Avenue	29	165
Power	Mrs	Westland Terrace	1	165
Powers	William	Gallagher's Square	6	143
Poyntz	George	Argyle Street	15	127
Poyntz	James	Northland Villas	3	127
Price	Miss	Northland Villas	4	127
Price	A.	Shipquay Street	23	158
Price	H. & Co.	Shipquay Place		159
Prior	Thomas	Primrose Street	6	176
Prior & Co.		Ferryquay Street		140
Purcell	Patrick	Irish Street	20	174
Purcell	James	Strabane Old Road	12	178
Purdie	Thomas	Bridge Street	62	132
Quigg	Mary Ann	Abbey Street	59	125
Quigg	Robert	Emerson Street	1	173
Quigg	Mrs	Emerson Street	9	173
Quigley	Mrs	Alexandra Place	15	126
Quigley	James	Alma Place	8	126
Quigley	Miss	Bishop Street	77	129
Quigley	Mrs	Bishop Street	135	130
Quigley	John	Brandywell Road	8	131
Quigley	John	Brandywell Avenue	16	131
Quigley	John	Chamberlain Street	12A	134
Quigley	John	Chamberlain Street	24	134
Quigley	William	Dark Lane	11	136
Quigley	Patrick	Elmwood Terrace	11	138
Quigley	Joseph	Ewing Street	13	139
Quigley	Thomas	Ferguson Street	18	140
Quigley	Maggie	Kildarra Terrace	4	146
Quigley	Mary	Nelson Street	59	154
Quigley	James	Nelson Street	22	154
Quigley	Hugh	Northland Terrace	3	155

Surname	First Name	Street	House Number	Page Number
Quigley	John	Pitt Street	9	156
Quigley	Michael	Rossville Street	33	158
Quigley	Andrew	St. Columb's Wells	66	162
Quigley	Mrs	St. Columb's Wells	78	162
Quigley	Michael	St. Columb's Wells	96	162
Quigley	James	William Street	58	165
Quigley	William	Creggan Road	5	166
Quigley	Hugh	Creggan Road	95	166
Quigley	William	Creggan Road	129	166
Quigley	Hugh	Creggan Road	161	167
Quigley	Mrs	Creggan Road	54	167
Quigley	Hugh	Epworth Street	25	167
Quigley	John	Cottage Row	32	168
Quigley	John	Cottage Row	40	168
Quigley	John	Benvarden Avenue	1	169
Quigley	Hugh	Carlin Street	13	170
Quigley	Francis	Carlin Street	15	170
Quigley	William	Duke Street	71	172
Quigley	Hugh	Margaret Street	2	175
Quigley	Sarah	Spencer Road	24	177
Quigley	William	Spencer Road	132	177
Quigley	William	Victoria Road		178
Quinlan	Mrs	Ebrington Street	17	173
Quinn	John	Bishop Street	233	130
Quinn	Sergeant, R.I.C.	Foyle Street		141
Quinn	William	Hogg's Folly	18	146
Quinn	Joseph	Long Tower	32	150
Quinn	Mrs	Orchard Row	28	155
Quinn	Patrick	Sloan's Terrace	35	159
Quinn	Ellen	St. Columb's Wells	118	162
Quinn	Michael	Walker's Place	22	163
Quinn	Susan	Wellington Street	42	164
Quinn	Michael	Spencer Road	125	177
Quinn	James	Union Street	9	178
Quinn	James	York Street	30	179
Rabbitt	William	Maybrook Terrace	4	135
Rafferty	Thomas	Clarence Place	8	134
Rafferty	John	Violet Street Lower	47	178
Rainbird	Mrs	Cottage Row	28	168
Ramsay	Margaret	Fountain Place	5	141
Ramsay	William	Long Tower	65	150
Ramsay	Samuel	Long Tower	14	150
Ramsay	James	Long Tower	22	150
Ramsay	Michael	Long Tower	66	150
Ramsay	Charles	Marlborough Terrace	3	152
Ramsay	J.	Marlborough Terrace	6	152
Ramsay	David	Nelson Street	69	154
Ramsay	James	Clyde Street	2	157
Ramsay	Charles	Rossville Street	2	158
Ramsay	Mrs	Walker's Place	13	163

Surname	First Name	Street	House Number	Page Number
Ramsay	Sam	Walker's Place	26	163
Ramsay	William	Walker's Place	30	163
Ramsay	James	Artisan Street	7	166
Ramsay	John	Creggan Road	26	167
Ramsay	William	Creggan Road	28	167
Ramsay	John J.	Primrose Street	1	176
Ramsay	Mrs	Violet Street Lower	2	178
Rankin	Mrs	Albert Place	19	126
Rankin	Robert	Bishop Street	155	130
Rankin	James	Millar's Close		132
Rankin	George	Edenmore Street	3	137
Rankin	James	Edenmore Street	12	138
Rankin	John	Francis Street	39	143
Rankin	Andrew	Nassau Street Lower	29	153
Rankin	George	Palace Street	St. Augustine's Chruch	155
Rankin	Alex	Rosemount Avenue	3	168
Rankin	Mrs	Bentley Street	1	169
Rankin	Alex	Clooney Terrace	8	171
Rankin	William	Cross Street	1	171
Rankin	Rev. L.	Limavady Road	Duniris Manse	175
Rankin	John	Foyle Road	54	142
Rankin & Knox		Foyle Street		142
Ree	Robert J.	Marlborough Street	27	151
Reed	Mrs	Northland Road	Red Roof	155
Rees	Claud	Marlborough Street	9	151
Reeves	William	Dark Lane	5	136
Reeves	Joseph	Fountain Street	64, 66	141
Reid	Andrew	Albert Street	3	126
Reid	Joseph	Brandywell Road	32	131
Reid	J. K.	Culmore Road	The Elms	136
Reid	John	Fahan Street	126	139
Reid	Robert	Fountain Street	38	140
Reid	James	Fountain Street	104	141
Reid	James	Governor Road	4	144
Reid	Andrew	Grafton Street	19	144
Reid	James	Great James Street		144
Reid	J. Kelso	Linenhall Street		149
Reid	Vincent	Nassau Street Lower	2	153
Reid	Mrs	Princes Street	15	156
Reid	Miss	St. Joseph's Avenue	1	162
Reid	John	Benvarden Avenue	14	169
Reid	Albert	Bond's Street	27	169
Reid	Mrs	Bond's Street	29	169
Reid	James	Bond's Place	13	170
Reid	Thomas	Chapel Road	8	170
Reid	James	Columba Terrace	7	171
Reid	Benjamin	Deanfield	Lesbury	171

Surname	First Name	Street	House Number	Page Number
Reid	W. I.	Duke Street	16	172
Reid	William	Spencer Road	9	177
Reid	Robert C.	Spencer Road	85	177
Reid	Miss	Spencer Road	42	177
Reid	Andrew	Spencer Road	84	177
Reid	Robert	Violet Street Upper	8	179
Reid & Co.		Bridge Street	10	132
Reid & Co.		Carlisle Road	12	133
Reid & Co.		Carlisle Road	1	132
Reilly	James	Alexandra Place	7	126
Reilly	Edward	Bridge Street	56	132
Reilly	John	New Street	1	133
Reilly	Jane	Ferguson Street	63	140
Reilly	Benjamin	Hawkin Street	1	146
Reilly	Mrs	William Street	39	165
Reilly	Mrs	Lewis Street	33	167
Reilly	Robert	Bond's Street	43	169
Reilly	Mrs	Spencer Road	78	177
Reuben	B.	Hawkin Street	14	146
Reynolds	Constable E.	Foyle Road	79	142
Reynolds	William	Market Street		152
Reynolds	Charles	Nicholson Terrace	12	154
Reynolds	James	Shipquay Street		159
Reynolds	Mrs	Bond's Hill	11	169
Rice	Miss	Edenmore Street	21	138
Richards	Evan	Mountroyal		155
Richards	Evan & Co.	William Street	73	165
Riddell	C. C.	Spencer Road	12	177
Riddles	Thomas	Charlotte Street	16	134
Ripsher	C. J.	Bond's Hill	15	169
Risk	Samuel	Spencer Road	115	177
Ritchie	Mrs	Mountjoy Street	12	153
Ritchie	Thomas	Bond's Place	7	170
Roache	James	Bishop Street	194	131
Robb	James	Bishop Street	94	130
Robb	Samuel	New Street	8	133
Robb	Andrew	East Wall	8, 9	137
Robb	Andrew	Marlborough Villas	4	151
Robb	John	Cuthbert Street	12	171
Robb	Samuel	Spencer Road	39	177
Roberts	Hugh	Florence Terrace	2	154
Roberts & Sons		Foyle Street		141
Robertson	William	Argyle Street	58	127
Robertson	Andrew	Park Avenue	Daisyville	156
Robertson	William	Dungiven Road	19	172
Robertson	Robert	Glendermott Road	5	174
Robinson	Constable A	Albert Street	22	126
Robinson	Mrs	Argyle Terrace	37	127
Robinson	Annie	Blucher Street	19	131
Robinson	Mrs	Alexander Cottages	6	133

Surname	First Name	Street	House Number	Page Number
Robinson	M. A.	Crawford Square	4	135
Robinson	James	Donegal Place	19	137
Robinson	James	Gordon Terrace	7	144
Robinson	Joseph	Gordon Terrace	11	144
Robinson	William	Howard Street	23	147
Robinson	Thomas	Orchard Street	12	155
Robinson	H. R.	Queen's Quay		157
Robinson	M. A.	Shipquay Place		159
Robinson	James	Strand Road Lower		161
Robinson	J. M.	Market Buildings		161
Robinson	H. S.	Templemore Park		162
Robinson	Samuel	Wapping Lane	47	163
Robinson	Mrs	West-End Park	6	165
Robinson	James	Windmill Terrace	4	166
Robinson	John	Barnewall Place	3	169
Robinson	Samuel	Barnewall Place	14	169
Robinson	Miss A.	Chapel Road	17	170
Robinson	H. W.	Chapel Road		170
Robinson	Mrs	Chapel Road	58	170
Robinson	James	Dervock Street	5	171
Robinson	James	Dungiven Road	39	172
Robinson	Joseph	Margaret Street	19	175
Robinson	Joseph	Primrose Street	23	176
Robinson	James	Victoria Road		178
Robinson	Andrew T.	Violet Street Upper	15	179
Robinson	Fisher	York Street	22	179
Robinson & Davidson		Richmond Street	3	158
Rochfort	Miss	Great James Street	61	145
Rock	Michael	The Rock	11	160
Rock	M. J.	Duke Street	102	172
Rodden	William	Deanery Street	36	136
Rodden	Mrs	St. Columb's Wells	79	162
Rodden	Elizabeth	Wesley Street	10	168
Roddy	Miss	Abercorn Road	18	125
Roddy	Daniel	Bishop Street	59	129
Roddy	Margaret	Caroline Place	13	133
Roddy	Rose	Eglinton Terrace	5	138
Roddy	William	Glasgow Street	3	143
Roddy	Sarah	Long Tower	11	150
Roddy	Rose	Long Tower	10	150
Roddy	Henry J.	Stanley's Walk	40	160
Roddy	James	Union Street	6	163
Roddy	Daniel	Wellington Street	55	164
Roddy	Daniel junior	Wellington Street	57	164
Roddy	Denis	William Street	57	165
Roddy	Thomas	Fountain Hill	82	174
Roddy	William	Strabane Old Road	66	178
Roddy	Mrs	Strabane Old Road	72	178
Roddy	Daniel	Violet Street Upper	9	179

149

Surname	First Name	Street	House Number	Page Number
Roden	James A.	Carlisle Terrace	3	133
Rodgers	William	Fahan Street	107	139
Rodgers	Anthony	Fahan Street	120	139
Rodgers	James	Ferguson Street	53	140
Rodgers	Rebecca	Mitchelburne Terrace	87	142
Rodgers	Henry	Great James Street	27	144
Rodgers	Margaret	Hogg's Folly	9	146
Rodgers	William	Marlborough Avenue	27	152
Rodgers	Sarah	Marlborough Avenue	29	152
Rogers	Thomas	Edenballymore	Creggan	137
Rooks	W. J.	Magazine Street	2	151
Rooks	W. O.	Victoria Street	11	163
Rooney	John	Brandywell Road	9	131
Rooney	Michael	Brook Street	4	132
Rooney	Edward	Chamberlain Street	25	134
Rooney	Jenny	Elmwood Road	1	138
Rooney	Patrick junior	Patrick Street	9	156
Rooney	Patrick senior	Patrick Street	12	156
Rooney	Miss	Patrick Street	13	156
Rooney	Rose	Rossville Street	67	158
Rooney	James	Waterloo Place		164
Rooney	James	Duke Street	65	172
Rosato	Charles	Fountain Street	6	140
Rosborough	Robert J.	Barnewall Place	8	169
Rosborough & Co.		Ferryquay Street		140
Rosborough & Co.		Magazine Street	6	151
Ross	Stuart C	Bishop Street	16	130
Ross	Alex	Collon Terrace	15	135
Ross	J.	Culmore Road	Shantallow	136
Ross	Thomas	Pennyburn		156
Ross	James	Pump Street	15	156
Ross	J.	Shipquay Street		158
Ross	William	Glendermott Road	17	174
Ross	Mrs	Glendermott Road	54	174
Ross	J.	Waterloo Street		164
Rossan	Ernest	Tyrconnell Street	20	163
Rossitter	Miss	Limavady Road	Soldiers' Home	175
Roulston	William	Crawford Square	14	135
Roulston	Christopher	Miller Street	20	152
Roulston	Miss	New Market Street		154
Roulston	Mrs	Northland Road	Maplemount	155
Roulston	Robert	Park Avenue	Laurel Villa	156
Roulston	William	Queen Street	5	157
Roulston	James	Sir E. Reid's Market	2, 3	159
Roulston	David	Westland Terrace	11	165
Roulston	Albert	Bond's Hill	24	169
Roulston	Samuel J.	Maybrook House		135

Surname	First Name	Street	House Number	Page Number
Roulston	Mark & McLaughlin	Foyle Street		142
Roulston & Smyth		Strand Road	25	160
Roulston & Smyth		William Street	47	165
Roulstone	William	Charlotte Place	1	134
Roulstone	J. & R.	Foyle Street		142
Rountree	F. T.	Shipquay Street		158
Routledge	Benjamin	Abercorn Road	44	125
Routledge & Co.		Carlisle Road	44	133
Rowan	Miss	Westland Avenue	1	164
Roycroft	Constable James	Stewart's Terrace	16	160
Ruddock	Josph A.	Bishop Street	54	130
Ruddock	Miss A. H.	Shipquay Street		159
Rundle	Harris Ltd	Shipquay Street		159
Rush	Ellen	Lecky Road	32	149
Russell	James	Albert Street	8	126
Russell	Mrs	Beechwood Avenue	35	128
Russell	Joseph	Bishop Street	40	130
Russell	James	Clarendon Street	31	134
Russell	James	Lorne Street		150
Russell	R. & Sons	Magazine Street		151
Russell	Robert	Miller Street	11	152
Russell	Mrs	Orchard Row	29	155
Russell	H.	Orchard Street	10	155
Russell	Mrs	Limavady Road	Glenard	175
Rutherford	Robert	Alexandra Place	3	126
Rutherford	Samuel	Alexandra Place	11	126
Rutherford	Robert	Aubrey Street	1	128
Rutherford	Mrs	Barrack Street	8	128
Rutherford	Mrs	William Street	36	165
Rutledge	William	Duke Street	82	172
Ruttle	Mrs	Beechwood Park	79	128
Ryan	George	Foyle Road	51	142
Ryan	Mrs	Marlborough Avenue	11	151
Ryan	Mrs	North Street	37	168
Ryans	Anthony	Glasgow Terrace	13	144
Ryans	Patrick	Nassau Street Upper	6	153
Ryans	Edward	Rossville Street	56	158
Sabary	James	Brandywell Avenue	21	131
Salmon	Patrick	Richmond Street	17	158
Salvo	Elizabeth	Duke Street	17	172
Saunderson	Daniel	St. Columb's Wells	68	162
Saunderson	Joseph	Walker's Place	44	163
Saville	R. W.	Melrose Terrace	20	175
Sawers & Co.		Strand Road	3	160
Sawyers	Constable	Laburnum Terrace	5	148
Sawyers	Andrew	Fountain Hill	52	174

Surname	First Name	Street	House Number	Page Number
Scarlett	John	Argyle Street	5	127
Scarlett	William	Florence Street	14	167
Schlindwein	Frank	Beechwood Avenue	37	128
Schlindwein	Frank	Long Tower		150
Scott	John	Abercorn Place	6	126
Scott	Robert	Adair Street		126
Scott	Mrs	Albert Place	3	126
Scott	James	Barrack Street	1	128
Scott	Harry E	Beechwood Avenue	33	128
Scott	Robert	Bishop Street	69	129
Scott	M. & M.	Diamond		137
Scott	James	Fountain Place	28	141
Scott	G. D.	Commercial Buildings		141
Scott	John	Mitchelburne Terrace	93	142
Scott	Robert	Foyle Road	115	142
Scott	John	Governor Road	3	144
Scott	Rev. F. R.	Great James Street		145
Scott	John	Lecky Road	151	148
Scott	William	Nassau Street Lower	25	153
Scott	Miss	Northland Road	Ard-na-Loc	155
Scott	John	Northland Avenue		155
Scott	Mrs	Philips Street	37	156
Scott	Joseph	Windmill Terrace	9	166
Scott	Edward	Benvarden Avenue	34	169
Scott	Samuel	Duke Street	52	172
Scott	Archibald	Fountain Hill	66	174
Scott	Matthew	Spencer Road	54	177
Scott	Samuel	Union Street	4	178
Scott	Francis	Violet Street Lower	48	179
Scott M & M		Bishop Street	1	129
Scott Motor Company		Foyle Road		142
Scully	Miss	Lawrence Hill		148
Searle	George	Ivy Terrace	9	147
Seaton	Mrs	Fountain Place	22	141
Selfridge	Rebecca	Bishop Street	102A	130
Selfridge	Alexander	Glasgow Street	5	144
Selfridge	William	Shipquay Street	6	159
Selfridge	Alex	Bond's Hill	12	169
Selfridge	Mrs	Ebrington Terrace	10	173
Selfridge	Francis	Simpson's Brae	7	177
Semple	Mrs	Carlisle Road	43	132
Semple	William	Edenballymore	Creggan	137
Semple	William & Co.	Ferryquay Street		140
Semple	J. J.	Foyle Street		141
Semple	Charles	Harding Street	2	145
Semple	Professor R. J.	College Avenue		155
Semple	William & Co.	Pump Street	1	156
Semple	Samuel	Clooney Terrace	33	'170

Surname	First Name	Street	House Number	Page Number
Semple	Mrs	Dungiven Road	Back-mountain	173
Semple	David	Strabane Old Road	48	178
Semple David		Foyle Street	20	142
Sexton	Charles E.	Glendermott Road	82	174
Shanaghan	Edward	Harding Street	3	145
Shanagher & McLaughlin		Butcher Street	13	132
Shannon	John	Grove Place	7	145
Shannon	William	Nelson Street	47	154
Shannon	J. & Co.	New Market Street	3	154
Shannon	William	Claremount Villas	North lodge	154
Shannon	Mrs	Pump Street	11	156
Shannon	William	Mount Street	16	168
Shannon	Charles	Bond's Hill	5	169
Shannon & Rutledge		Fountain Street	85	140
Sharkey	James	Beechwood Street	3	128
Sharkey	Patrick	Caroline Place	21	133
Sharkey	David	Cedar Street	9	133
Sharkey	David	Fahan Street	3	139
Sharkey	Patrick	Bluebellhill Terrace	194	149
Sharkey	Mrs	Rossville Street	27	158
Sharkey	Henry	St. Columb's Wells	111	162
Sharkey	Patrick	Chapel Road	11, 13	170
Sharkey	Hugh	Dungiven Road	6	173
Sharkey	William	Violet Street Lower	15	178
Sharp, Perrin & Co.		Queen Street	14	157
Sharpe	Lizzie	Lecky Road	125	148
Shea	Rev M	Edenballymore	Creggan	137
Sheath	Joseph	Orchard Row	13	155
Shee	Joseph	Hollywell Street	6	147
Sheehan	Daniel	Nailor's Row	39	153
Sheehy	Edward	Howard Place	9	147
Sheekey	James	Bond's Street	13	169
Sheerin	John	Elmwood Street	24	138
Sheerin	Andrew	Orchard Street	St. Columb's Hall	155
Sheerin	Mary	Quarry Street	8	157
Sheerin	Bernard	Union Street	29	163
Sheil	Ellen	Richmond Street	8	158
Sheil	Mrs	Foyle Street		141
Sheill	D.J.	Bishop Street	10	130
Sheils	Joseph	Eden Place	6	138
Sheils	Patrick	Fahan Street	85	139
Sheils	John	Fox's Lane	4	143
Sheils	John	Fulton Place	10	143
Sheils	Mrs	Governor Road	23	144
Sheils	Dominick	Great James Street	76	145

Surname	First Name	Street	House Number	Page Number
Sheils	Ross	Moat Street	6	152
Sheils	Bernard	Nailor's Row	10	153
Sheils	Hugh	Nelson Street	16	154
Sheils	Kate	Rossville Street	87	158
Sheils	John	Strand Road		161
Sheils	John	Strand Road	80	161
Sheils	Mrs	Thomas Street	1	162
Sheils	Mrs	Wapping Lane	25	163
Sheils	Dominick J.	Westland Avenue	37	165
Sheils	Andrew	Osborne Street	10	168
Sheils	Mrs	Benvarden Avenue	31	169
Sheils	Mrs	Chapel Road	5	170
Sheils	Sarah	Glendermott Road	48	174
Sheils	Mrs	Union Street	23	178
Sheldon	Samuel J	Beechwood Avenue	45	128
Shepherd	William	Albert Street	28	126
Shepherd	Hugh	Francis Street	51	143
Shepherd	W. J.	Orchard Street	23	155
Sheppard	Mrs M. A.	Park Villas	3	168
Sheran	Mary	Ann Street	11	149
Sheridan	Miss	Bishop Street	226	131
Sheridan	Hugh	Deanery Street	42	136
Sheridan	Robert	Patrick Street	14	156
Sherman	Richard	Ivy Terrace	2	147
Sherrard	Hugh	Elmwood Terrace	32	138
Sherrard	William J.	Fahan Street	103	139
Sherrard	Joseph	Great James Street	15	144
Sherrard	Samuel	William Street	85, 87	165
Sherrard	Rachel	Dungiven Road	93	173
Sherrard	Samuel	Glendermott Road	88	174
Sherry	James B.	Benvarden Avenue	2	169
Shields	Mrs	Abercorn Road	15	125
Shields	John	Edenballymore	Creggan	137
Shields	William	Glasgow Street	3	143
Shields	Robert	Henry Street		146
Shields	Irvine	Magazine Street	4	151
Shields	Irwin	Richmond Street	4	158
Shields	Francis	Wapping Lane	33	163
Shields Ltd		Society Street	6	159
Shiels	Bridget	Philips Street	21	156
Shiels	Helena	Wellington Street	27	164
Shiels	Patrick	Florence Street	12	167
Shier	Richard	Fahan Street		139
Shinwell	David	Union Street	25	163
Shirley	Robert	Abercorn Road	50	125
Sidebottom Bros.		Carlisle Road	15	132
Sidebottom Bros.	George	Carlisle Road	17	132
Silvester	A. E.	Clarence Avenue	13	134

Surname	First Name	Street	House Number	Page Number
Silvester	A. E.	Custom House Street		136
Simmons	R. P. & Co.	Carlisle Road	30	133
Simmons	A. E.	Richmond Street		158
Simmons	F. J.	Fountain Hill	41	173
Simms	John	Brook Street Avenue	5	132
Simms	Mrs	Fountain Street	71	140
Simms	William	Linenhall Street	10	150
Simms	John	Glendermott Road		174
Simpson	James	Baronet Street	1	128
Simpson	Miss	Deanery Street	40	136
Simpson	Charles	Ferguson Street	36	140
Simpson	James	Governor Road	36	144
Simpson	G. W.	Kennedy Place	5	147
Simpson	Robert	Bond's Street	53	169
Simpson	David	Clooney Terrace	54	171
Simpson	Sam	Cross Street	38	171
Simpson	William S.	Dunfield Terrace	31	172
Simpson	John	Dungiven Road	71	173
Simpson	Mrs	East Avenue	2	173
Simpson	Robert	East Avenue	4	173
Simpson	Joseph	Fountain Hill	120	174
Simpson	Mrs	King Street	9	175
Simpson	William	King Street	15	175
Simpson	Robert	King Street	45	175
Simpson	Thomas	Termon Street	1	178
Simpson	Mrs	Victoria Park		178
Sinclair	Archibald	Hawthorn Terrace	4	146
Sinnott	Thomas	Fountain Street	53	140
Skeat	Mrs	Duke Street	69	172
Skelly	Mrs	Rossville Street	62	158
Skinner	R. J.	Lecky Road		149
Skinner	R. J.	West-End Park	1	165
Slevin	Robert	Bishop Street	238	131
Slevin	Francis	Donegal Place	20	137
Slevin	Edward	Fahan Street	4	139
Slevin	Margaret	Nailor's Row	33	153
Sloan	David	Argyle Street	39	127
Sloan	George	Rosemount Avenue	4	168
Small	Edward	Beechwood Avenue	6	128
Smalls	John	Lecky Road		149
Smalls	John	Lecky Road	112	149
Smallwood	Robert	Ivy Terrace	5	147
Smallwoods	William	Dungiven Road	27	172
Smallwoods	Thomas	Dungiven Road	37	172
Smallwoods	William	St. Columb's Road		175
Smallwoods	Joseph	Limavady Road		175
Smallwoods	Samuel	Primrose Street	10	176
Smiley	Joseph	Clarendon Street	11	134
Smiley	T. & J.	Waterloo Place		164
Smith	Robert	Aubrey Street	7	128

Surname	First Name	Street	House Number	Page Number
Smith	John	Brook Street	1	132
Smith	Matthew	Carlisle Road	73	133
Smith	Mrs	Castle Street	3	133
Smith	David	Charlotte Place	4	134
Smith	Richard	Charlotte Street	22	134
Smith	Arthur	Claremont Street		134
Smith	Charles	Corbett Street	13	135
Smith	James	Dark Lane	2	136
Smith	William	Elmwood Terrace	29	138
Smith	Edward	Ferguson Street	16	140
Smith	Robert	Fountain Street	31	140
Smith	John	Fountain Street	98	141
Smith	Mar	Foyle View	6	143
Smith	William	Great James Street		144
Smith	Mrs	Harvey Street	10	146
Smith	Constable	Laburnum Terrace	21	148
Smith	Blair	Lawrence Hill		148
Smith	J. W. T.	Lawrence Hill	Breezemount	148
Smith	Andrew	Lecky Road	29	148
Smith	Henry	Lecky Road	39	148
Smith	Alexander	Little James Street	14	150
Smith	William	Long Tower	82	150
Smith	Charles	Nelson Street	10	154
Smith	Edward	Nelson Street	24	154
Smith	Herbert	Northland Road		155
Smith	Professor D.	College Avenue		155
Smith	William	Northland Avenue	2	155
Smith	Mrs	Orchard Street	15	155
Smith	Thomas	Society Street	7	159
Smith	Mark	Stewart's Terrace	8	160
Smith	John	Wellington Street	60	164
Smith	Edward	Artisan Street	18	166
Smith	Mrs	Creggan Road	22	167
Smith	William	Alfred Street	17	168
Smith	William	Barnewall Place	21	169
Smith	John	Benvarden Avenue	3	169
Smith	William	Bond's Hill	17	169
Smith	Mrs	Carlin Street	19	170
Smith	Mrs M. A.	Caw	Lisnagowan	170
Smith	Patrick	Chapel Road	47	170
Smith	John A.	Chapel Road	55	170
Smith	Charles	Chapel Road	62A	170
Smith	William	Cuthbert Street	5	171
Smith	David	Dunfield Terrace	11	172
Smith	William	Emerson Street	6	173
Smith	James	Emerson Street	32	173
Smith	Samuel	Glendermott Road	46	174
Smith	Samuel	Glendermott Road	86	174
Smith	Robert	Limavady Road	Clooney Park	175

Surname	First Name	Street	House Number	Page Number
Smith	John	Strabane Old Road	92	178
Smith	Charles	Tamneymore		178
Smith	Samuel	Violet Street Lower	27	178
Smith	William	Shipquay Street		159
Smith & Co.		Shipquay Street		159
Smy	William	Ewing Street	7	139
Smyth	Samuel	Argyle Terrace	4	127
Smyth	James	Bishop Street	35	129
Smyth	G. H.	Clarence Avenue	7	134
Smyth	Mrs	Ferryquay Street		140
Smyth	R.& Co.	Foyle Street	44	142
Smyth	Samuel	Foyle Street		142
Smyth	William	Glasgow Terrace	27	144
Smyth	Mrs	Governor Road	16	144
Smyth	James	Hogg's Folly	19	146
Smyth	William	Lecky Road		149
Smyth	James	Linenhall Street	5	149
Smyth	James	Long Tower		150
Smyth	Matthew	Nassau Street Upper	33	153
Smyth	Miss	Rockmount Villas	1	154
Smyth	Robert & Son	Princes Quay		157
Smyth	James	St. Columb's Wells	37	161
Smyth	Rev. Michael	Victoria Place	Parochial House	163
Smyth	Joseph	William Street	89	165
Smyth	G. H.	William Street	111	165
Smyth	Robert	Windmill Terrace	20	166
Smyth	William	Donegal Street	12	167
Smyth	John	Mount Street	17	167
Smyth	Mrs	Rosemount Terrace	7	168
Smyth	Hugh	Benvarden Avenue	24	169
Smyth	Charles	Chapel Road	3	170
Smyth	Miss	Deanfield	Dunavon	171
Smyth	John	Carlisle Chambers		172
Smyth	Thomas	Margaret Street	20	175
Smyth	John	Spencer Road	130	177
Smyth	Miss	York Street	5	179
Smyth	Robert	Fairbank		128
Snodgrass	Thomas	Spencer Road	21	177
Spain	David	Abercorn Road	58	125
Speers	Mrs	Abercorn Road	41	125
Speers	Miss	Abercorn Road	55	125
Speers	James	Fountain Street	44	141
Speers	David	Lewis Street	21	167
Spence	T. A.	Commercial Buildings		141
Spence	Mrs	Lawrence Hill		148
Spence	Mrs	Queen Street	4	157
Spence	Miss	Park Villas	5	168
Spencer	Arthur	Clarence Avenue	4	134

Surname	First Name	Street	House Number	Page Number
Spiller & Bakers		Princes Quay		157
Spillers & Bakers Ltd		East Wall		137
Spillers & Bakers Ltd		Newton Buildings		141
Spratt	William	Alfred Street	7	168
Spratt	Edward	Clooney Terrace	21	170
Sproule	Constable	Argyle Street	43	127
Stafford	Robert	Harding Street	11	145
Stafford	Mrs	Princes Terrace	5	156
Starrett	David	Ferguson Street	30	140
Starrett	Edward	Sloan's Terrace	34	159
Starrett	William	Creggan Road	77	166
Starrett	William	Cottage Row	16	168
Starrett	Miss	Bond's Place	1	170
Starrett	Patrick	Violet Street Lower	35	178
Starrett	William	York Street	12	179
Starritt	Mrs	Grafton Street	31	144
Starritt	Alex	Princes Street	27	156
Starritt	Miss	St. Columb's Court	3	161
Starritt	Samuel	Duke Street	25	172
Starrs	Mary	Moore Street	4	152
Steadman	James H.	Crawford Square	13	135
Steadman	J. H.	Foyle Street		141
Steele	Andrew	Academy Terrace	2	126
Steele	John	Charlotte Street	8	134
Steele	John	Ferguson Street	32	140
Steele	Andrew	Ivy Terrace	29	147
Steele	Mrs	Ivy Terrace	4	147
Steele	Daniel	Wellington Street	63	164
Steele	Mrs	Osborne Street	5	168
Steen	Thomas	Nicholson Square	12	154
Stephenson	Andrew	Artisan Street	20	166
Sterritt	Mrs	Marlborough Terrace	13	152
Stevenson	William	Abercorn Road	56	125
Stevenson	Samuel	Bishop Street	250	131
Stevenson	Isaac	Culmore Road	Hampstead	136
Stevenson	S. B.	Foyle Street		141
Stevenson	Robert	Sydney Terrace	2	145
Stevenson	Archibald	Grove Place	22	145
Stevenson	R. J.	Magazine Street	9	151
Stevenson	John	Marlborough Terrace	27	152
Stevenson	John	Orchard Row	20	155
Stevenson	S. B.	Strand Road		161
Stevenson	H & Co.	Waterloo Place		164
Stevenson	H. & Co.	William Street	95	165
Stevenson	Doctor	Bond's Hill	Bond's hill house	169
Stevenson	Hugh & Co.	Duke Street	36	172
Stevenson	John	Duke Street	100	172

Surname	First Name	Street	House Number	Page Number
Stevenson	Ellen	St. Columb's Road		175
Stevenson	John	May Street	6	175
Stewart	Mrs	Albert Street	21	126
Stewart	Richard	Albert Place	9	126
Stewart	David	Barry Street	29	128
Stewart	John	Beechwood Park	73	128
Stewart	William	Bennett Street Upper	1	129
Stewart	Samuel	Cedar Street	5	133
Stewart	Robert	Garden City	13	136
Stewart	George E.	Demesne Terrace	8	137
Stewart	Samuel	Edenmore Street	25	138
Stewart	Joseph	Edenmore Street	36	138
Stewart	Isaac	Fairman Place	16	140
Stewart	Mrs A. McC.	Waterloo Place		164
Stewart	R. K.	William Street	121	165
Stewart	William	Lewis Street	7	167
Stewart	Mary A.	North Street	9	168
Stewart	Mrs	Benvarden Avenue	29	169
Stewart	William	Benvarden Avenue	20	169
Stewart	Mrs	Duke Street	76	172
Stewart	Miss	Duke Street	92	172
Stewart	John	Dungiven Road	9	172
Stewart	William	Olive Terrace	1	176
Stewart	Samuel & Co	Foyle Street	22	142
Stewart	Miss	Francis Street	37	143
Stewart	John	Governor Road	31	144
Stewart	Robert	Governor Road	33	144
Stewart	Alex	Governor Road	39	144
Stewart	T. A.	Grafton Street	13	144
Stewart	James	Henry Street	21	146
Stewart	William	Ivy Terrace	13	147
Stewart	William	John Street		147
Stewart	William	Kennedy Street	16	148
Stewart	Michael	St. Columb's Terrace	95	148
Stewart	Edward	Lecky Road	80	149
Stewart	John	Lower Road	11	151
Stewart	Margaret	Mary Street	4	152
Stewart	Andrew	Nassau Street Lower	11	153
Stewart	Mrs	Nassau Street Lower	41	153
Stewart	William	Nelson Street	61	154
Stewart	William	Nelson Street	64	154
Stewart	Robert	Nicholson Square	4	154
Stewart	A. McC.	Northland Road	Hollylodge	154
Stewart	William	Princes Terrace	4	156
Stewart	S & Co.	Princes Quay		157
Stewart	James	Sackville Street	21	158
Stewart	G. E.	Shipquay Street	25	158
Stirling	Mrs	George Street	5	143
Stirling	William C.	Marlborough Street	8	151
Stone	Harry	Bentley Street	12	169

Surname	First Name	Street	House Number	Page Number
Storey	Mrs	Foyle Road	109	142
Storey	J. C.	Grove Place	12	145
Strahan	Professor James	College Avenue		155
Strain	Andrew	Princes Street	25	156
Strain	John	Walker's Place	23	163
Strange	Andrew	Kennedy Place	2	147
Strange & Co		Abercorn Road	42	125
Strawbridge	Patrick	Bluebellhill Terrace	198	149
Strawbridge	James	Ashfield Terrace	45	166
Strawbridge	David	Herbert Street	8	174
Strawbridge	Mrs	Margaret Street	17	175
Strawbridge	John	Violet Street Lower	20	178
Streams	Edward	Albert Street	34	126
Stringer	Thomas	De Burgh Terrace	8	136
Strunks	Joseph	Princes Street	2	156
Stuart	Miss	Edenbank	Willmount	154
Stuart	Rev. Dr.	Chapel Road		170
Stuart	R. & J.	Duke Street	3	172
Stubbs	Mrs	Mount Street	4	167
Swan	Robert	Glendermott Road	38	174
Swan	Mrs	Glendermott Road	42	174
Swann	W J	Beechwood Avenue	14	128
Swann	James Aitkin	Lone Moor		150
Swann	W. J. & Co.	Waterloo Street		164
Sweeney	Catherine	Ann Street	21	127
Sweeney	William	Barry Street	15	128
Sweeney	Margaret	Fitters Row	255	130
Sweeney	George	Fitters Row	257	130
Sweeney	Mrs	Dark Lane	7	136
Sweeney	P.	Newton Buildings		141
Sweeney	P.	Foyle Street	45	141
Sweeney	Alexander	Foyle Road	64	142
Sweeney	Catherine	Howard Street	5	147
Sweeney	Miss	Howard Street	7	147
Sweeney	Hugh	Howard Street	27	147
Sweeney	James	Lecky Road	57	148
Sweeney	Myles	Bluebellhill Terrace	162	149
Sweeney	Michael	Market Street		152
Sweeney	Mrs	Mountjoy Street	15	152
Sweeney	John	Mountjoy Street	10	153
Sweeney	Daniel	Nailor's Row	9	153
Sweeney	Sarah	Nailor's Row	34	153
Sweeney	John	Orchard Lane	7	155
Sweeney	Charles	Queen Street	1	157
Sweeney	Mrs	Strand Road Lower		161
Sweeney	Michael	Strand Road		161
Sweeney	George	St. Columb's Wells	107	162
Sweeney	Edward	St. Columb's Wells	112	162
Sweeney	Austin	Sugarhouse Lane	16	162
Sweeney	Frank	Thomas Street	14	162

Surname	First Name	Street	House Number	Page Number
Sweeney	Margaret	Waterloo Street	61	164
Sweeney	Patrick	William Street	40	165
Sweeney	Edward	Creggan Road	153	166
Sweeney	Hugh	Cottage Row	10	168
Sweeney	Edward	Carlin Street	8	170
Sweeney	John	Cross Street	33	171
Sweeney	Francis	Florence Street	25	173
Sweeney	John	Herbert Street	2	174
Sweeney	Frank	King Street	46	175
Sweeney	Mrs	Simpson's Brae	17	177
Sweeney	Michael	Elmwood Street	26	138
Sweeney & Co.		East Wall		137
Sweenie	Mrs	Florence Terrace	4	154
Sweeny	Mrs	Clarendon Street	10	134
Sweeny	John	Clarendon Street Lower	2	135
Sweeny	C.	Foyle Street		141
Sweeny	H.	Strand Road	20	161
Synnott	William	Victoria Street	19	163
Taggart	John	Albert Street	23	126
Taggart	James	Brandywell Road	16	131
Taggart	Samuel	Clarendon Street	43	134
Taggart	Mrs	Cunningham Row		136
Taggart	Samuel	Foyle Road		142
Taggart	Mrs	Grafton Street	27	144
Taggart	Samuel	John Street	16, 17	147
Taggart	Joseph	Nassau Street Upper	8	153
Taggart	Mrs	Mountain View		176
Taggart	Robert	Spencer Road	100	177
Tait	William	Brook Street Avenue	12	132
Tallon	Sergeant T.	Victoria Road	9	178
Talon	Miss A.	Walker's Place	32	163
Tate	Daniel	Park Terrace	2	144
Tate	Miss M.	Distillery Lane Lower	9	171
Tate	Stewart	Emerson Street	31	173
Taylor	James	Barry Street	26	128
Taylor	Edward	Collon Terrace	10	135
Taylor	John & Sons	Ferryquay Street		140
Taylor	John	Fountain Street	111	140
Taylor	Mary	Alma Terrace	41	142
Taylor	Cassie	Gallagher's Square	1	143
Taylor	Mrs	Great James Street	23	144
Taylor	Robert	Lecky Road	255	149
Taylor	William	Shipquay Street		159
Taylor	John	Sloan's Terrace	28	159
Taylor	William	West-End Park	9	165
Taylor	John	Creggan Road		167
Taylor	Alex	Ashcroft Place	4	169
Taylor	James	Barnewall Place	26	169
Taylor	Joseph	Fountain Hill	53	173

Surname	First Name	Street	House Number	Page Number
Taylor	Andrew	Fountain Hill	55	173
Taylor	Mrs	Fountain Hill	70	174
Taylor	Joseph	Herbert Street	4	174
Taylor	Samuel	Herbert Street	14	174
Taylor	M. & L.	Spencer Road	18	177
Teagan	Joseph	Riverview Terrace	5	176
Tearney	Joseph	Fahan Street	38	139
Tearney	Mrs	Fahan Street	42	139
Teasey	William	Bond's Place	8	170
Tedlie	Mrs	Dungiven Road	107	173
Tedlie	James	Glendermott Road	78	174
Tees	James	Aberfoyle Terrace	33	160
Temple	John	Fountain Street	68	141
Temple	William	George Street	1	143
Temple	John	George Street	3	143
Temple	Mrs	Victoria Street	6	163
Temple	William	Wapping Lane	49	163
Temple	Mrs	Glendermott Road	2	174
Templeton	Edward	Asylum Road	9	127
Thewayter	Captain J.	May Street	2	175
Thomas	Leonard	Barnewall Place	16	169
Thomas	Andrew	Argyle Street	52	127
Thompson	John	Abercorn Road	26	125
Thompson	David	Abercorn Place	14	126
Thompson	George A	Albert Street	16	126
Thompson	James	Argyle Street	46	127
Thompson	N R	Victoria Terrace	10	127
Thompson	Daniel	Aubrey Street	32	128
Thompson	John	Bellevue Avenue	12	129
Thompson	John	Bellevue Avenue	24	129
Thompson	John	Bridge Street	19	132
Thompson	N. R.	Carlisle Road	18, 20	133
Thompson	Samuel	Carrigans Lane	2	133
Thompson	J. P.	Castle Street		133
Thompson	Andrew	Charlotte Street	2	134
Thompson	John P.	Clarendon Street	13	134
Thompson	W. R.	Clarendon Street	13	134
Thompson	J. H.	College Terrace	12	135
Thompson	Rev James	Crawford Square	21	135
Thompson	D.	Culmore Road	Sorrento	136
Thompson	Robert	Duncreggan Road	Meadowbank	137
Thompson	Henry	Ferryquay Street		140
Thompson	John	Mitchelburne Terrace	88	142
Thompson	David	Glasgow Street	6	144
Thompson	William & Co.	Linenhall Street		149
Thompson	Mrs	Marlborough Street	3	151
Thompson	Robert M.	Marlborough Street	36	151
Thompson	James F.	Marlborough Street	38	151
Thompson	Mrs	Marlborough Street	40	151
Thompson	Stewart	Marlborough Avenue	3	151

Surname	First Name	Street	House Number	Page Number
Thompson	Robert	Meadowbank Avenue		152
Thompson	Mrs	Nassau Street Upper	5	153
Thompson	Alex	Northland Road		155
Thompson	George	Northland Avenue	21	155
Thompson	William & Co.	Prince Arthur Street		156
Thompson	William & Co.	Queen's Quay		157
Thompson	John	Queen Street	11	157
Thompson	William & Co.	Shipquay Street		158
Thompson	Miss	Shipquay Street	4	159
Thompson	Constable W. J.	Stewart's Terrace	20	160
Thompson	Mrs	The Rock	35	160
Thompson	Robert	Strand Road Lower		161
Thompson	M. A.	Market Buildings		161
Thompson	Dealtry P.	Westland Terrace	2	165
Thompson	Andrew	Creggan Road	105	166
Thompson	Sergeant H.	Florence Street	2	167
Thompson	Thomas	Wesley Street	12	168
Thompson	William	Duke Street	23	172
Thompson	Alex & Co.	Duke Street	74	172
Thompson	T. G.	Dungiven Road	105	173
Thompson	Malcolm	Ebrington Terrace	4	173
Thompson	T. H.	Melrose Terrace	9	175
Thompson	George	Strabane Old Road	27	177
Thompson	Henry	Victoria Park		178
Thompson Bros		Bishop Street	21	129
Thompson Edwards Co.		Strand Road		161
Thomson & Co.		Rosemount Avenue		168
Thornton	Mrs	Mountjoy Street	20	153
Thorpe	William	Glendermott Road	19	174
Tibbs	John H.	Northland Road	Dun Creich	155
Tiernan	Mrs	Westland Avenue	31	165
Tierney	James	Demesne		137
Tierney	Patrick	Nailor's Row	40	153
Tierney & Kelly		Foyle Street	22	142
Tighe	Mrs	Mitchelburne Terrace	86	142
Tillie	Mrs Marshall	Northland Road	Duncreggan House	155
Tillie	Mrs	Caw	Elslow	170
Tillie & Henderson		Abercorn Road		125
Tillie & Henderson		Foyle Road		142
Tillie, McDermott & Munn		Shipquay Street		159
Timoney	Edward	Bluebellhill Terrace	178	149
Tinney	Edward	Clarendon Street	7	134
Tinney	Hugh	Fahan Street	23	139
Tinney	Edward	Rock Buildings		160

Surname	First Name	Street	House Number	Page Number
Tinney	Edward	Strand Road	82	161
Todd	Finlay L	Beechwood Park	75	128
Todd	Lt. Col. W. G.	Custom House Street		136
Todd	M. F.	Rossville Street	32	158
Todd	Mrs	Union Street	1	163
Todd	William G.	Melrose Terrace	7	175
Todd & Mark		Shipquay Street	6	159
Toland	John	Adam Street	4	126
Toland	Robert	Bishop Street	262	131
Toland	Rose	Brandywell Avenue	15	131
Toland	Michael	Donegal Place	13	137
Toland	William	Eglinton Place	12	138
Toland	Michael	Eglinton Place	18	138
Toland	James	Howard Street	26	147
Toland	James	Sloan's Terrace	32	159
Toland	Michael	Stanley's Walk	46	160
Toland	James	Artisan Street	4	166
Toland	Henry	Artisan Street	6	166
Toland	George	Violet Street Lower	40	178
Tomb	James & Son	Waterloo Street		164
Tomkins	William	Kennedy Place	13	147
Toms	Stanley	De Burgh Terrace	5	136
Tonathy	John	Meadowbank Avenue		152
Toner	Constable D	Elmwood Terrace	46	138
Toner	Hugh	Fulton Place	15	143
Toner	James	Nelson Street	48	154
Toner	John	Sugarhouse Lane	20	162
Toner	Reps. John	Fahan Street	61, 63	139
Torrens	Samuel	Elmwood Terrace	28	138
Torrens	Mrs	Little James Street		150
Torrens	Thomas	Little James Street		150
Torrens	John	Wapping Lane	45	163
Torrens	James	Violet Street Lower	26	178
Torrens	Samuel	Violet Street Lower	52	179
Tosh	Mrs	Windmill Terrace	11	166
Tosh	Robert	Violet Street Lower	37	178
Towers	Mrs	Crawford Square	6	135
Townsley	David	Northland Avenue	5	155
Toye	Edward	Glasgow Street	2	143
Toye	Mrs	Glasgow Street	2	143
Toye	James	Lundy's Lane	1	150
Toye	Patrick	Stanley's Walk	36	160
Toye	E. J.	Market Buildings		161
Toye	James	Waterloo Street	15	163
Tracey	Thomas	Bridge Street	72, 74	132
Tracey	Jane	Eglinton Terrace	1	138
Tracey	Thomas	John Street	1	147
Tracey	Thomas	John Street		147
Tracey	Michael	Waterloo Street	67	164
Tracey	Michael	William Street	2	165

Surname	First Name	Street	House Number	Page Number
Tracey	Mrs	Meehan's Row	16	176
Tracy	John	Custom House Street		136
Tracy	John	Dervock Place	5	171
Tracy	Annie	Dungiven Road	12	173
Tracy	Mrs	Margaret Street	8	175
Tracy	Patrick	Union Street	18	178
Trainor	George	Nelson Street	4	154
Trainor	Thomas	Alfred Street	22	168
Travers	Mrs	Fahan Street	59	139
Travers	Bernard	Fahan Street	93	139
Travers	Margaret	Nelson Street	36	154
Travers	James	Nelson Street	46	154
Traynor	Mrs	Elmwood Street	18	138
Traynor	Patrick	Glasgow Street	1	143
Trimble	James	Hawkin Street		146
Trotter	Henry	Albert Street	12	126
Trotter	Alex	Kennedy Street	14	148
Tucker	Miss	Bishop Street	100	130
Tully	Francis	Glenbrook Terrace	19	143
Turner	R S	Beechwood Avenue	41	128
Turner	John	Mitchelburne Terrace	81	142
Turner	John	Henry Street	9	146
Turner	Robert	Meadowbank Avenue	27	152
Turner	John	Simpson's Brae	5	177
Tyler	John & Sons	Foyle Street		141
Underwood	William A.	Glenbrook Terrace	17	143
Ussher	James	King Street	2	175
Ussher	Alex	King Street	4	175
Vaughan	Alfred	Hawkin Street	10	146
Verscheur	William	Spencer Road	46	177
Villa	Denis	Creggan Terrace	9	135
Villa	Patrick	Elmwood Terrace	19	138
Villa	Laurence	Fulton Place	5	143
Vincent	George	Hawkin Street	31	146
Virtue	Mrs	Great James Street	58	145
Virtue	Miss D.	Victoria Street	13	163
Wade	John	Glasgow Street	1	143
Wade	James	Nassau Street Upper	7	153
Wade	Constable	Benvarden Avenue	8	169
Wade	William	Dungiven Road	45	172
Wadsworth	Mrs	Duke Street	13	172
Wafer	Lloyd	Dunfield Terrace	7	172
Waldren	Miss	Great James Street	62	145
Walker	Robert	Bellevue Avenue	16	129
Walker	Patrick	Blucher Street	13	131
Walker	Robert	Charlotte Place	2	134
Walker	James W.	De Burgh Square	1	136
Walker	Andrew	De Moleyn Park	1	137
Walker	Thomas	Diamond		137
Walker	James	Ewing Street	9	139

Surname	First Name	Street	House Number	Page Number
Walker	David	Fairman Place	22	140
Walker	William	Fountain Street	51	140
Walker	William	Fountain Street	93	140
Walker	David	Glasgow Street	3	143
Walker	Miss	Great James Street		145
Walker	Misses	Grove Place	15	145
Walker	William	Magazine Street		151
Walker	William	Meadowbank Avenue	15	152
Walker	John	Nassau Street Upper	1	153
Walker	Constable J. H.	Nicholson Square	17	154
Walker	William	Claremount Villas	1	154
Walker	Robert	Union Street	27	163
Walker	John	Windmill Terrace	12	166
Walker	Thomas	Wesley Street	9	169
Walker	William	Alfred Street	5	168
Walker	Henry	Alfred Street	9	168
Walker	Susan	Barnewall Place	7	169
Walker	James	Bond's Street		169
Walker	Samuel	Bond's Street	28	170
Walker	George	Strabane Old Road	7	177
Walker	Herbert	Strabane Old Road	9	177
Walker	Mrs	Strabane Old Road	19	177
Walker	Thomas	Victoria Park	gate lodge	178
Walker	John	Violet Street Lower	8	178
Walker	Robert	York Street	10	179
Walker	Andrew & Co.	Duke Street	32	172
Walker	James	Duke Street	100	172
Walker	Andrew	Florence Street	15	173
Walker	James	Glendermott Road	9	174
Walker	Andrew	Glendermott Road	15	174
Wallace	Robert	Abercorn Road	19	125
Wallace	Robert	Albert Street	11	126
Wallace	Thomas	Sunbeam Terrace	11	130
Wallace	Mrs	Bishop Street	70	130
Wallace	Miss	Clarendon Street	34	135
Wallace	Miss	Diamond		137
Wallace	William J.	Hawkin Street	33	146
Wallace	Robert	Henry Street	15	146
Wallace	William	Marlborough Street	19	151
Wallace	Miss	Meadowbank Avenue	11	152
Wallace	T.	Market Buildings		161
Wallace	James	Creggan Road	46	167
Wallace	Albert	Alfred Street	3	168
Wallace	Mrs	Irish Street	2	174
Wallace	R.	Spencer Road	120	177
Wallace	Thomas	Violet Street Lower	24	178
Wallace	Hugh	York Street	21	179
Waller	H. E. & Co.	Castle Street	9	133
Waller	H. E.	Culmore Road	Troy	136
Wallis	George	Nicholson Terrace	10	154

Surname	First Name	Street	House Number	Page Number
Walls	John J.	Foyle Street		141
Walls	Robert	Orchard Row	19	155
Walls	James	William Street	25	165
Walmsley	George	Bluebellhill Cottage		160
Walsh	Philip	Alexandra Place	10	126
Walsh	Hugh	Clarendon Street	8	134
Walsh	Hugh	Diamond		137
Walsh	Thomas	Foyle Road	63	142
Walsh	Miss	Kennedy Place	1	147
Walsh	John	Nelson Street	31	154
Walsh	John	Northland Avenue	20	155
Walsh	H.	Shipquay Street	2	159
Walsh	John	Stanley's Walk	8	160
Walsh	Mrs	Union Street	14	163
Walsh	James	Primrose Street	25	176
Wands	James	Ebrington Gardens		170
Ward	John	Sunnyside Terrace	3	131
Ward	G. R.	Clarence Avenue	10	134
Ward	Samuel	Dark Lane	23	136
Ward	William	Fahan Street	113	139
Ward	Vincent & Son	Foyle Road		142
Ward	Patrick	Gallagher's Square	10	143
Ward	Mrs Vincent	John Street	2	147
Ward	V. & Son	John Street		147
Ward	John	Marlborough Avenue	7	151
Ward	Joshua	Nassau Street Lower	5	153
Ward	Mrs	Waterloo Street	20	164
Ward	Patrick	William Street	101	165
Ward	John	Violet Street Lower	39	178
Ward & Co.		Sackville Street	15	158
Wardlaw	Miss	Mountjoy Terrace	7	153
Warke	John	Abercorn Road	52	125
Warke	Mrs	College Terrace	5	135
Warke	Miss	Alexandra Terrace	4	154
Warke	Matthew	Windmill Terrace	27	166
Warke	John	Emerson Street	7	173
Warke	Joseph	Emerson Street	34	173
Warke	Charles	Moore Street	35	176
Warnock	Thomas	Melrose Terrace	19	175
Warrell	Charles	Shipquay Street	21	159
Warren	Miss Ellen	Cottage Row	4	131
Wasson	Robert	Fountain Street	62	141
Wasson	John	Ivy Terrace	8	147
Wasson	John	Park Avenue	21	156
Wasson	Joseph	Creggan Road	97	166
Wasson	Joseph	Lewis Street	9	167
Wasson	James	Moore Street	9	176
Wasson	Joseph	Termon Street	2	178
Watchman	Louis	Victoria Terrace	12	127
Watchman	Tuck & Co	Fahan Street	35, 37	139

Surname	First Name	Street	House Number	Page Number
Waterstone	Arthur	Fountain Place	33	141
Waterstone	William	Bond's Street	31	169
Watkins	Robert	Benvarden Avenue	57	169
Watkins	Miss	Union Street	8	178
Watson	John J	Abercorn Road	33	125
Watson	John James	Bridge Street	5	131
Watson	Samuel	Carrigans Lane	3	133
Watson	Joe	Eden Place	13	138
Watson	Miss	Ferguson Street	65	140
Watson	Mrs	McLaughlin's Close	3	140
Watson	Miss	Foyle Road	58	142
Watson	Mrs	Harvey Street	14	146
Watson	Andrew	Mountjoy Terrace	10	153
Watson	Andrew	North Edward Street		154
Watson	Dr. J.	Northland Road		154
Watson	Mrs	Orchard Row	14	155
Watson	John James	Orchard Street	1	155
Watson	Mrs	Shipquay Place		159
Watson	William	St. Columb's Street	11	161
Watson	Albert	Westland Avenue	27	165
Watson	R. M. & Co.	William Street	41	165
Watson	Robert	Bond's Hill	27	169
Watson	Major James	Chapel Road		170
Watson	Miss	Clooney Terrace	32	171
Watson	R.	Dungiven Road		173
Watson	Andrew	Tamneymore		178
Watt	David & Co.	Abbey Street	17	125
Watt	Gerald A.	Culmore Road		136
Watt	A. A.	Culmore Road	Thornhill	136
Watt	A. A. & Co	Linenhall Street		149
Watt	David & Co.	Queen's Quay		157
Watt	A. A. & Co.	Rossville Street	4	158
Watt	G.	Shipquay Street	33	159
Watt	A. A. & Co.	Shipquay Street	33	159
Watt	David & Co.	William Street	94	166
Watt	James	Creggan Road	91	166
Watt	David & Co.	Duke Street		172
Watt	David & Co.	Duke Street		172
Watt	David & Co.	Simpson's Brae		177
Watt	D. & Co.	Spencer Road		177
Watt	D. & Co.	Clarendon Street Lower		135
Watt	D & Co	Fahan Street		139
Watt	David & Co.	Bond's Hill		169
Watt David & Co. store		Frederick Street		143
Watters	S. B.	Market Buildings		161
Watters	Constable George	Rosemount Terrace	10	168
Watterson	Joseph	Claremont Street		134

Surname	First Name	Street	House Number	Page Number
Webb	David	Eden Place	9	138
Webb	John	Thomas Street	19	162
Wedlock	James	St. Columb's Court	5	161
Weir	Patrick	Governor Road	2	144
Weir	William A.	Magazine Street	14	151
Weir	Willima A.	Shipquay Street		159
Weir	W. H.	Aberfoyle Terrace	35	160
Welch	J. H.	Culmore Road	Dunruadh	136
Welch, Margetson & Co.		Carlisle Road	18, 20	133
Welch, Margetson & Co.		Fountain Street		140
Welsh	W. J.	Simpson's Brae	15	177
West	William	Beechwood Avenue	10	128
West	Henry	Ebrington Street	13	173
West & McCay		Ferryquay Street		140
Whan & Co.		Sackville Street	21	158
White	James	Academy Terrace	3	126
White	William	Albert Street	26	126
White	Thomas	Castle Street	1	133
White	John	Chamberlain Street	8	134
White	Mrs	Chamberlain Street	22	134
White	Thomas	Clarence Avenue	22	134
White	William	Fountain Street	45	140
White	George	Fulton Place	17	143
White	Rev. D. S. H.	Great James Street		145
White	Joseph	Great James Street	32	145
White	William	Miller Street	15	152
White	Miss	Orchard Row	37	155
White	David	The Rock	19	160
White	Ellen	St. Columb's Wells	40	162
White	Joseph	Glendermott Road	27	174
White	Mrs	Ivy Terrace	39	147
White	Thomas	St. Columb's Terrace	103	148
Whiteside	Alex	Henrietta Street	5	146
Whiteside	John C.	Princes Street	3	156
Whiteside	George	Benvarden Avenue	6	169
Whiting	George J.	Kennedy Place	7	147
Whitten	Joseph	Demesne		137
Whittington	John	Beechwood Avenue	15	128
Whittington	James	Bellevue Avenue	9	129
Whittington	Miss J.	Mountjoy Terrace	3	153
Whittington	David	Westland Avenue	15	165
Whittington	Mrs	Florence Street	18	167
Whittington & Miller		Pump Street	1	156
Whoriskey	Hugh	Philips Street	25	156
Whoriskey	Miss	Union Street	12	163

Surname	First Name	Street	House Number	Page Number
Whyte	Jacob	Clarendon Street	18	134
Whyte	Joseph	Commercial Buildings		141
Whyte	Andrew	Gordon Place	5	144
Whyte	J. S.	Marlborough Street	14	151
Whyte	Frederick	Glendermott Road	12	174
Wightman	Alexander	Lawrence Hill		148
Wightman	A.	Shipquay Street	10	159
Wiley	Mrs	Albert Place	8	126
Wiley	James P	Argyle Terrace	30	127
Wiley	Rebecca	Nicholson Terrace	3	154
Wiley	James	Aberfoyle Terrace	7	160
Wilkin	George	Gordon Terrace	8	144
Wilkinson	Miss	Bellevue Avenue	41	129
Wilkinson	Samuel	Glenbrook Terrace	13	143
Wilkinson	Mrs	Great James Street	35	144
Wilkinson	William	Bluebellhill Terrace	186	149
Wilkinson	John	Orchard Row	33	155
Williams	Thomas	Beechwood Avenue	63	128
Williams	Mrs	Brandywell Road	19	131
Williams	Thomas	Fountain Street	7	140
Williams	James	Lower Road	35A	151
Williams	William	Marlborough Avenue	8	152
Williams	Mrs	Marlborough Avenue	22	152
Williams	J. A.	Northland Road	The Willows	155
Williams	John	Pump Street	20	157
Williams	H.	Shipquay Street	32	159
Williams	H.	Sir E. Reid's Market	1	159
Williams	John	William Street	18	165
Williams	Richard	Kennedy Street	4	148
Williamson	Thomas	Charlotte Street	13	134
Williamson	James	Horace Street	2	146
Williamson	Samuel	Princes Street	21	156
Williamson	James	Richmond Street	14	158
Williamson	Alex	Kerr's Terrace	11	166
Williamson	Joseph	Kerr's Terrace	13	166
Williamson	Mrs	Creggan Road	137	166
Williamson	David	Lewis Street	5	167
Williamson	Charles	Bond's Street	22	170
Williamson	John	Pine Street	8	176
Williamson Bros		Strand Road		161
Willmann	Romain	Aberfoyle Terrace	29	160
Willmann	Romain	Market Buildings		161
Willoughby	John	Emerson Street	27	173
Wills	James	Quarry Street	18	157
Wilson	Margaret	Abercorn Road	36	125
Wilson	John	Barry Street	13	128
Wilson	Walter W	Bishop Street	13	129
Wilson	John	Bishop Street	145	130

Surname	First Name	Street	House Number	Page Number
Wilson	Mrs	Bridge Street	20	132
Wilson	Rachel	Bridge Street	20	132
Wilson	John	Charlotte Street	10	134
Wilson	Alex	Edenmore Street	30	138
Wilson	Michael	Fahan Street	102	139
Wilson	David	Ferguson Street	3	140
Wilson	James	Fountain Street	79	140
Wilson	William	Fountain Place	13	141
Wilson	Henry	George Street	4	143
Wilson	William	Gordon Place	11	144
Wilson	William	Grove Place	14	145
Wilson	William	Henry Street	5	146
Wilson	Thomas	Henry Street	7	146
Wilson	Robert	Henry Street	22	146
Wilson	Samuel	John Street	8	147
Wilson	James	Cranagh Terrace	3	148
Wilson	A. & Co.	Lorne Street		150
Wilson	John	Northland Terrace	9	155
Wilson	Joseph	Princes Street	8	156
Wilson	A. & Co.	Abercorn Quay		157
Wilson	Edward	Rossville Street	31	158
Wilson	Samuel	Rock Villas	2	161
Wilson	Samuel	St. Joseph's Avenue	4	162
Wilson	Mrs	Wapping Lane	43	163
Wilson	William	Wellington Street	48	164
Wilson	William	Westland Avenue	21	165
Wilson	Mrs	Creggan Road	24	167
Wilson	John	Epworth Street	11	167
Wilson	Thomas	Lewis Street	22	167
Wilson	John	Mount Street	1	167
Wilson	Thomas	North Street	7	168
Wilson	Joseph	North Street	25	168
Wilson	William	Clooney Terrace	48	171
Wilson	Samuel	Clooney Terrace	6	171
Wilson	James	Duke Street		172
Wilson	Mrs	Dungiven Road	25	172
Wilson	Alex	Ebrington Terrace	14	173
Wilson	John	Emerson Street	23	173
Wilson	John	Fountain Hill	30	174
Wilson	R. A.	Limavady Road	Hinton	175
Wilson	Edward	Limavady Road		175
Wilson	James	May Street	1	175
Wilson	David	May Street	5	175
Wilson	William	Mill Street	forge	176
Wilson	Robert	Moore Street	18	176
Wilson	David	Violet Street Lower	59	178
Wilson	Joseph	York Street	26	179
Wilson	William J.	Strand Road	38	161
Wilson & Co.		Ferryquay Street		140
Wilson & Elliott		Shipquay Street	8	159

Surname	First Name	Street	House Number	Page Number
Wilson (factory)	Joseph	Bishop Street	89	129
Wilton	R M	Eden Terrace		137
Wilton	David	Fountain Street	47	140
Wilton	Captain J. M.	Marlborough Avenue	21	152
Winters	Miss	Lecky Road	115	148
Wiseman	Sergeant T. W.	Harding Street	4	145
Wolfe	William A	Abercorn Road	5	125
Wood	Mrs	Duke Street	84	172
Woodburn	Matthew	Beechwood Avenue	55	128
Woodburn	Professor G.	College Avenue		155
Woods	Patrick	Argyle Terrace	32	127
Woods	John	Bishop Street	217	130
Woods	Mrs	Bishop Street	60	130
Woods	John	Foyle Road	78	142
Woods	Matthew	Governor Road	25	144
Woods	Annie	North Edward Street	3	154
Woods	Mrs	Windmill Terrace	1	166
Woolsey	Frederick	Abercorn Road	61	125
Woolsey	Garnett	De Moleyn Park	2	137
Woolworth	F. W. & Co.	Ferryquay Street	14, 16	140
Woolworth	F. W.	Market Street		152
Wordie & Co.		Foyle Street		142
Wordie & Co.		Abercorn Quay		157
Workman	Robert	Beechwood Avenue	25	128
Wray	David	Academy Terrace	9	126
Wray	Henry	Albert Street	24	126
Wray	David	Bishop Street	50	130
Wray	Miss	Castle Street		133
Wray	James	Charlotte Place		134
Wray	Miss	Dark Lane	12	136
Wray	Mrs	Fairman Place	20	140
Wray	John	Alma Terrace	43	142
Wray	Mrs	Kennedy Place	11	147
Wray	David	Marlborough Street	7	151
Wray	Michael	Nailor's Row	37	153
Wray	R. J.	Wapping Lane	37	163
Wray	William	Wapping Lane	39	163
Wray	Mrs	Dunfield Terrace	25	172
Wray	Henry	Tamneymore		178
Wright	Thomas	Bishop Street	101½	130
Wright	Miss	College Terrace	8	135
Wright	Thomas B.	Fairman Place	9	139
Wright	Thomas	Ferguson Street	20	140
Wright	Frederick	Gordon Terrace	2	144
Wright	William	Mountjoy Terrace	11	153
Wright	Thomas	Orchard Row	30	155
Wright	Robert	Victoria Street	3	163
Wright	Albert	Victoria Street	7	163
Wright	John	Victoria Street	15	163
Wright	Alex	Cuthbert Street	13	171

Surname	First Name	Street	House Number	Page Number
Wright	Richard	Fountain Hill	88	174
Wright	Alexander	Spencer Road	72	177
Wylie	T. C.	Castle Street	7	133
Wylie	Thomas E.	Grafton Street	15	144
Wylie	Richard	Philips Street	22	156
Wylie	Mrs	St. Columb's Court	4	161
Yach	Maurice	Abercorn Road	42	125
Yach	Maurice	Harding Street	16	145
Yanarelli	A. & Co.	Strand Road		160
Yannarelli	A. & Co.	Strand Road	31	160
Young	Sergeant Philip	Abercorn Place	10	126
Young	Ernest	Academy Terrace	8	126
Young	James	Albert Place	12	126
Young	Alexander	Barrack Street	6	128
Young	George	Bellevue Avenue	20	129
Young	Henry	Bishop Street	198	131
Young	John	Eden Place	16	138
Young	Thomas	Fountain Street	103	140
Young	David	Hempton's Close		141
Young	Alexander	Fountain Place	34	141
Young	Alex	Foyle Road	71	142
Young	Elizabeth	Mitchelburne Terrace	90	142
Young	James	Fulton Place	3	143
Young	John	Henry Street	19	146
Young	Robert	Ivy Terrace	3	147
Young	John	Marlborough Street	12	151
Young	William	Moat Street	5	152
Young	James	Nailor's Row	38	153
Young	Mrs	Sloan's Terrace	30	159
Young	H. E.	Strand Road	13	161
Young	J. Ff.	St. Columb's Court		161
Young	Thomas	Donegal Street	24	167
Young	James	Osborne Street	6	168
Young	Gilbert	Caw	Broomhill	170
Young	Joseph	Dungiven Road	85	173
Young	David	King Street	10	175
Young & Ingram	John Ff.	Commercial Buildings		141
Young & Moore		Water Street		164
Young & Rochester		Ebrington Gardens		170
Zammitt	Charles	Artillery Street	3	127
Zammitt	Charles	John Street		147

www.ingramcontent.com/pod-product-compliance
Lightning Source LLC
Chambersburg PA
CBHW061741270326
41928CB00011B/2330

*9 7 8 0 8 0 6 3 5 8 0 0 0 *